THE HIGH IMPACT CHURCH

A fresh approach to reaching the unchurched

LINUS J. MORRIS

ISBN #1-880828-78-2

Published by:
TOUCH Publications, Inc.
PO Box 19888
Houston, Texas 77224-9888
(713) 497-7901
Fax (713) 497-0904

Printed in the United States of America

What Others Are Saying...

Linus and his colleagues have been working for years among some of the most pagan, post-Christian people in Europe, and have carved out lively Christian communities there. They have a great deal to teach us, and I trust that this book will be widely read and digested by those who dare to add an extra chapter, so to speak, to the Acts of the Apostles in our generation. It is certainly needed.

■ *Rev. Michael Green*
Canon of Coventry Cathedral and Adviser in Evangelism
to the Archbishops of Canterbury and York, England

The author has done a thorough and masterly job of assimilating an enormous amount of material gathered from lectures and extensive reading, and applying it to his chosen topic. The book is eminently readable. The work is a "block-buster" in the best sense of the term.

■ *Eddie Gibbs*
Professor, Fuller Theological Seminary, Author

One objective of Sports Outreach America is to encourage post-career athletes to begin new careers in church planting. They can play a major role. This book describes exactly the kind of church we want them to invest their lives in.

■ *Ralph K. Drollinger*
Executive Director, Sports Outreach America

Church planting is at the heart of God's plan for fulfilling the Great Commission as we race toward the year 2000. In *The High-Impact Church*, Linus Morris offers a thoroughly biblical and practical strategy for reaching the unchurched in Western culture. It's required reading for leaders who want helpful direction in developing a more dynamic ministry.

■ *Kevin Springer*
Pastor, Author

TABLE OF CONTENTS

ACKNOWLEDGMENTS

The list of people who have contributed directly or indirectly to this project is substantial.

First of all there are my mentors over the years who have inspired me with their commitment to Christ, compassion for lost people and dedication to go to the ends of the earth to carry out the high calling Christ has given us to fulfill the great commission: Jody Dillow who first shared the gospel with me, John Flack who led me to Christ, Ron Thurman who first discipled me, Pete Guillquist who trained me in my early days of ministry, Bud Hinkson who inflamed my heart with vision and died charging forward for the kingdom, Hal Lindsey who helped me look for His coming, Bill Counts who believed in me and taught me how to teach, Al Wollen and Ray Steadman, pastors with integrity who weren't bound by tradition, Francis Schaeffer who defended the gospel but never lost sight of loving people, James Houston whose emphasis on spirituality drew me to Regent College, Ian Rennie and Clark Pinnock—Regent professors who taught me about spiritual renewal, C. Peter Wagner who inspired me toward church planting and the growth of the church, Arthur Glasser who expanded my horizons for mission, Eddie Gibbs who has mentored me along the way, Larry DeWitt who provided the model from which we began, Carl George, Bob Logan and John Wimber who carry the vision for church planting and church growth and Ralph Neighbour who is the chief advocate of the cell-structured church. These and others have left lasting deposits in my life. I am a collage of their ideas and characteristics.

A second group I want to acknowledge is my co-laborers with whom I have interacted and experimented. The core of the Light and Power House gang of Mark Arrington, Tom and Naomi Brewer, Birdie Caldwell, Bill and Bev Counts, Hal and Jan Lindsey, Hud and Nancy McWilliams, Juanita Saunders, Steve and Nancy Snyder; the pioneer church planting team of Gary and Tricia Edmonds and Chris and Debbie Hall; the faithful Amsterdam team of Rick and Judy Grossman, Dan and Wendy McConnell and Marty and Carey Uhler who are moving the vision on out. Together we have hammered out strategies to reach the lost and mobilize them for fruitful ministry. More recently Steve and Linda Adams and Julie Thurman have put their shoulders to the plow.

A third group that has been instrumental in this work is the faithful support team who have stood with us over the years, prayed for us and partnered with us financially: of note are Carolyn, Nancy and Jack, Jack and Kay, Phil and Linda, Scott and Kathy, Bob and Carol, Dean and Lois, Dan and Jan, Mark and Lynn, Rocky, Ellen, Les and Tillie, Charlie and Nancy, Bruce and Gem, Michael, Steve, Jerry, Phil and Laina, Bob and Mardell, Jack, Ruth, Dan and Sue, Gerry and Betty, Florence and Grace, Ron, Maynard and Linda, Rich and Carol, Dandie and Mike, Kent and Joan, Chuck and Carolyn, Jack and Marjorie, Don and Jeanette, Ward and Carol, John and Paula, Jim and Kay, Boyd and Freita, Del and Marsha, Marshall and Kathy, Mark and Laura, Charles and Mary, Jack and Claire, Len and Dianne, Bill and Sue, Ralph and Karen, Vince and Paula, John and Kim, Warren and Joan, Vance and Nina, John and Carol and Roland and Chris. I am indebted to these stewards and trust that their return will exceed their investment.

A fourth group that is to be commended is those who have made specific contributions to this book. Rick and Judy Grossman gave significant input to the chapter on programming; Steve and Linda Adams, Brad Bailey, John Graham, Dan McConnell, Pat Stone, Warren Stratton and Mark Wickman served as readers and gave content suggestions; Joey Beckham and Randall Neighbour believed in the vision, Leslie Morris labored relentlessly and sacrificed significantly to edit the manuscript and Marjorie Lee Chandler added the badly needed finishing polish. May their faith and labor be rewarded.

Finally, my family is to be acknowledged for not only traversing the world in obedience to the call of God with me but for participating fully as co-laborers in the work of evangelism and church planting. To Sharon, Laina, Kristin, Stephanie, Leslie, Linus Jr. and Kathryn, thanks. To all of the above—and to those who will follow—I say:

> Fight the good fight,
> finish the race and
> keep the faith,
> knowing that there is
> a crown of righteousness
> to be awarded on that day.
> > *2 Timothy 4:7-8*

And,

> Do not put out the Spirit's fire!
> > *1 Thessalonians 5:19*

■ *Linus J. Morris*

FOREWORD

T hese are exciting and important days for the mission of Jesus Christ around the world. Christ's church is virtually exploding in many Third World countries. Literally tens of thousands of men, women, young people and children are being added to the church each day in Africa, Latin America and Asia. In stark contrast, most Christian churches in the Western World are either in decline or are stagnant at best.

Linus Morris has witnessed this decline and stagnation of the church in a most dramatic way as he has ministered in the United States and Western Europe for most of the past two decades. However, his experiences have not led him to despair. Quite to the contrary, while ministering in some of the most difficult environments imaginable in western society, Dr. Morris has allowed God to teach him some vital and important lessons about strategic ministry in today's world.

Many of those significant insights and practical suggestions are found in this book. Linus shares with us how we, under the guidance and empowering of the Holy Spirit, can establish "high-impact" churches which can be used powerfully by the Lord of the church. He contends that "breakthrough thinking" is needed if the church is to touch the lives of those who have been captured by secularism and if we are to reach people in modern western culture with the gospel.

I agree—and I believe that you will agree also as you read this very helpful and stimulating volume. This is a practical book. It goes far beyond theory. The message conveyed by Dr. Morris will communicate powerfully and practically to any pastor, church-planter, or Christian leader who is concerned with being used strategically to impact major urban centers, cities, towns and even rural areas with the kind of disciple making ministry to which our Lord has called all of us.

This book answers the vital question, "How can we establish new churches or revitalize existing churches so that those same churches can make a profound impact on our communities and the world?" Linus presents a wonderfully integrated model of spiritual leadership, group dynamics, body ministry, powerful worship and a deep reliance on the Holy Spirit which together can lead us and our churches to vital ministry and explosive growth.

As you read prayerfully these pages, you will be encouraged to cultivate a "kingdom heart" which will provide an authentic passion for the fruit, love, values and authority of the kingdom of God. As we look upon our communities, nation and world with "kingdom eyes," we will see more clearly the reality of the spiritual warfare we encounter as we storm the principalities of this world in the power of the Holy Spirit. In addition, we will be enabled to more effectively establish strongholds for Christ and His church in a secular world wherever our Lord has called us to minister.

All of us would do well to seriously consider the message of this book. I pray that you will be encouraged and strengthened in your ministry principles which are shared with us so simply and effectively.

By the grace of our Lord Jesus Christ and by the empowering of the Holy Spirit, may each of us become high-impact ministers of Christ's church and may the churches which he has entrusted to our care be authentically high-impact churches—to the glory of Christ and to the expansion of His kingdom!

■ *Paul A. Cedar*
Evangelical Free Church of America

INTRODUCTION

T he response to our survey shocked us. As Christian Associates went door to door in a small Dutch suburb we knew that the majority of people would probably be unchurched.

They were.

What we had not expected was the widespread enthusiasm for a new approach to the church.

What should the church be like? we asked. The answers were sometimes humorous—"fewer candles," "no statues," "snacks and food." But others named significant ingredients of a contemporary church:

"More exciting."

"Friendlier."

"More relevant."

"Not so sad."

"More attractive."

"Upbeat."

"More compatible with reality."

"A place to meet God."

"Celebrative."

The responses we received from our survey indicate that more than ever before the church has a wide open door to attract the millions of unchurched people in the West.

For the better part of the 20th century, the Western church has been losing ground—contemporary people have many negative perceptions about the church. But there is also a growing interest in innovative churches that offer hope and substance. Unchurched people say they are searching for a down-to-earth spiritual experience that meets their needs in modern society.

This book is about the untapped potential for churches willing to reach out to the unchurched. For the past fifteen years I have been on a search to discover the principles and dynamics of a practical, reproducible church that impacts both individuals and society. The result of this quest I call the "high-impact church" — one that is innovative in evangelism, worship, pastoral care, preaching and organizational structure.

The word "impact" implies the striking of one body against another.

"Impact" implies striking one body or object against another. The Western world desperately needs churches that strike against prevailing spiritual indifference and impact society with the gospel of Jesus Christ.

Though there are signs of promise for the church as we enter the coming millennium, for the past several decades the church (as a whole) has been static in the United States and in decline in Europe. The growth of Christianity is not even keeping up with the growth in population. Many churches are still too trapped in tradition to effectively reach the unchurched.

As we round the corner of the year 2000, only a flexible, tailored strategy of the local church will appeal to modern men and women. Churches can and *must* change if they expect to attract the unchurched and lift Christianity from being an irrelevant subculture within society.

THE BEGINNING

My first experience in trying to establish a high-impact church was in starting the Crossroads Evangelical Church in suburban Geneva, Switzerland. We earnestly desired to reach unchurched people and had a sketchy plan and a lot of faith in God with which we moved forward.

We found that the people we reached out to were open to Christ and it wasn't long before we packed a group of adults in the living room of a small home and squeezed the children's ministry into two bedrooms. We kept growing and when we reached 65 people we knew we had to move to a larger facility.

Growth brought changes in the dynamics of this new church. At first, most people who came had been invited by one of our three church-planting families. These newcomers then began inviting their own friends as evangelism became an every-member activity.

Our initial organization was informal and relational. Our family-like team planned, contacted people and held Bible studies and other ministry activities together. Most of our decisions were made by consensus. But, as we grew, this casual structure no longer worked.

We wisely began delegating responsibilities on the basis of gifts and specialized talents. One person organized and administrated, another taught, and I led worship and acted as a catalyst for recruiting and keeping people involved. Our roles as the pastors of the church shifted from doing all the ministry ourselves to enlisting others to help us.

A more formal organization emerged—not so much by design, but by necessity. Although we successfully "birthed" this church, touching many lives with the gospel, much more could have been accomplished if we had better understood the dynamics of church growth and development before we started. The proverbial tail wagged the dog.

Our small staff was not adequately prepared for dealing with change and the church reached a plateau. There was frequent frustration about what should be done, and who should do it. Eventually, two leaders resigned, leaving the third couple to pastor the church.

The bittersweet experience of founding the Crossroads Evangelical Church of Geneva led me on a search to discover the organizational dynamics of a rapidly growing church. My ministry experience in the U.S. and Europe and my studies at Regent College in Vancouver, Canada already convinced me that the Western world was in need of a fresh approach to the church if the Great Commission was going to be fulfilled. (Part I of this book defines the historical and present social and cultural situations which demand a new church model.)

I joined the pastoral staff of a church which had experienced dynamic growth over a ten year period and enrolled in the Doctor of Ministry program of Fuller Theological Seminary. I also researched dozens of churches which were having a high impact on their surrounding communities and then verified the resulting model, this time in Amsterdam. I now lead a mission organization, Christian Associates International, whose goal is to establish high-impact churches in the major cities of Europe.

HIGH-IMPACT CHURCH MODEL FOR TODAY

The best way to visualize the high-impact church is to picture an apple. The high-impact church, like an apple, has three parts: the core, the flesh and the surface. The core of the church is its spiritual life. This is what nourishes the rest of the apple. If the core is not healthy, the apple will not develop properly—it will rot from the inside out. (Part II of this book discusses the spiritual and theological core of the high-impact church.)

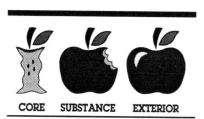

CORE   SUBSTANCE   EXTERIOR

Like the apple, the high-impact church has "flesh," or inner substance. The part that satisfies and is the substance of the church is the ministry of its members. (Part III of this book presents a workable strategy to mobilize and equip every member of the church for effective evangelism, edification and pastoral care.)

The third part of the apple is its exterior or skin. This part is the most visible and either attracts or repels prospective consumers. The high-impact church, like the apple, needs shape and eye appeal. The exterior of the apple corresponds to the church's visible evangelism, programming, organizational structure and leadership. (These characteristics, essential for the effectiveness of the high-impact church, are the subject of Part IV.)

JOHNNY APPLESEED

Within every healthy apple is the ability to reproduce, not only other apples—but orchards. As a young boy, one of my favorite stories was about a man called "Johnny Appleseed." His real name was John Chapman and he planted apple seeds wherever he found suitable soil. The result was the beginnings of many orchards throughout the United States.

The church, like an apple tree, is meant to reproduce itself. Churches big and small, existing and newly planted, are to reach the unchurched, grow and multiply. Men and women who have a passion to plant and develop orchards of high-impact churches can make a difference in their surrounding community and the world — and fulfill the Great Commission.

There is hope for the church! An increasing number of churches in Europe and North America are reformulating the way they carry out the mission of Christ. These churches are impacting their communities with the Good News of the gospel.

WHAT'S IN THIS FOR YOU?

This book is more than theory — it presents a practical model that will guide your church into the next century. Despite the decades of cynicism and apathy toward Christianity in Europe and her cultural offshoots, there is an emerging openness to the gospel in contemporary form.

The High-Impact Church is a resource for pastors, church planters and lay persons who long for the spiritually lost to find Christ, and for the church to grow. This model brings together the most effective and strategic principles of a church that is biblically based, spiritually vital, culturally sensitive and organizationally sound.

Just as there are many varieties of apples, there will be variations in applying the high-impact principles which I advocate. Every country, culture and city is different; activities initiated in one place might not be appropriate in another. The high-impact church, however, circumvents these differences because it is principle-centered, rather than program-centered. This book is about the high-impact model of ministry, applicable to any size congregation — anywhere around the globe.

It is my hope that *The High-Impact Church* will serve as a challenge to your church's vision and a guide to its future strategy.

Note:

Throughout this book, the pronouns "he," "him" and "his" are often used in the traditional sense, referring to both men and women. This usage is for simplicity and does not imply that only men can assume leadership roles in the high-impact church.

Also, to be sensitive, some of the names in the stories have been changed.

PART I

THE NEED FOR HIGH-IMPACT CHURCHES

Revitalizing the Church and Recapturing the West

1

VISION: TO EVANGELIZE THE WEST

*Modern Western culture "is the most widespread, powerful
and pervasive among all contemporary cultures....
It is this culture that, more than almost any other,
is proving resistant to the gospel."*

—Lesslie Newbigin[1]

WHAT'S GOD GOT TO DO WITH IT?

Anne, an M.D. in Holland, openly said she was a confirmed atheist. Her family had lived through the atrocities of World War II and saw neither God nor good in the world about them. They considered the church to be out of touch with reality.

Anne and her husband had no opportunities to get to know Christian believers, so we invited them to our home for dinner and to church picnics at a nearby park. As our friendship with them grew so did their curiosity about matters of faith.

One Sunday morning my message was "Facing Up to the Fear of Change," a topic chosen to fit our "visitor-sensitive" Sunday morning celebrations at the Crossroads International Church. I was pleased to catch a glimpse of Anne in the audience.

My sermon began by telling about the popular movie, *Back to the Future*, where the hero, Marty McFly, travels into the future and then back to the past to avert impending disasters in the present. I listed significant changes in the world — particularly the Western world — during the last 300 years and talked about greater changes coming in the next century. "One thing is certain — there will be changes!" I concluded.

I presented a strategy for coping with change, including a relationship with Jesus Christ. Although I was speaking to a cafeteria-size audience, I felt like I was speaking directly to Anne as I said, "God is the only One who can guide us because He transcends time and change. You can trust Him."

Typical of many Europeans who have pushed faith aside, the idea of God having any bearing on life was totally foreign to this young professional woman. Several days after my message, I asked Anne what she thought of the Sunday service. "I really liked what you said until you began talking about God. What has God got to do with anything?" she asked bluntly.

THE WAY THE WEST WAS LOST

Anne's response echoes the sentiment of millions of Westerners. Most Christian churches assume that people still hold Christian world-views, and are using the same methodologies that the church has used for centuries. In contrast, the high-impact church recognizes that the Western world has a drastically different perception of life than it did a few decades ago, let alone a century ago.

In order to reach the unchurched — folks like Anne — it is critical to understand the common way of perceiving, thinking and living called modern Western culture. Through university and technical networks, multi-national corporations and the media, this outlook is also saturating the former Soviet Bloc countries and the so-called "Two-Thirds World."

The predominant underlying influence of modern Western culture today is secularism. This philosophy seeks to relegate religion to the private sphere. It accepts only facts and influences derived from the here and now. Secularism maintains that the only real world is that which can be experienced by the five senses. The philosophical secularist is, therefore, a person who is anti-religious, negating God's significance in life.[2]

Humanism is the core of secular philosophy. Secularism is man-centered rather than God-centered. Instead of all things being created by and for God, secularists believe that man's will and purpose — individually or nationally — is defined by man's achievements and skill.[3] Human reason is the final court of appeal and the chief value of life is the right to life, liberty and the pursuit of happiness.

> # The high-impact church recognizes that the Western world has a drastically different perception of life than it did a few decades ago.

Few people consciously embrace the philosophy of secularism, but the influence of secularism has a tremendous impact on the Western world-view. Actually, most of us, whether we realize it or not, are caught up in the process of secularism. All about us, we are influenced by the pragmatic view of reality where meaning is found only within the universe itself.

SYMPTOMS OF SECULARISM

The average Westerner sees no spiritual significance to life beyond the material values of here and now. He or she does not turn to a supernatural power for direction, (except a small minority of Christians worldwide and others who are involved in Eastern-type spiritualist religions).

Consider the profile of secularism in the West:

- *Materialism:* Political and social decisions are not based on the will of God as revealed in the Bible, but on the basis of their economic effect and benefit. Things are measured monetarily.
- *Hedonism:* The Westerner spends his or her life and energy on maximizing personal pleasure and self-fulfillment. If it feels good, do it!
- *Skepticism:* A Westerner thinks that Christianity has been tried and it did not work. (The Westerner is seldom enthusias-

tic about anything, except, perhaps, sports.) For the European, the good news of the gospel is neither considered good — nor newsworthy!

- *Individualism:* "I stand or fall alone;" "I am the master of my fate;" "You have to look out for number one," are common expressions that reveal the premises of the Westerner.
- *Relativism:* The axiom of the indifferent pluralistic society — "It does not matter what you believe as long as you believe it sincerely."
- *Pessimism:* Most people neither see any hope for the future nor think their choices have meaning beyond the present.
- *Uncertainty:* Global realignment, political tension, ethnic strife, terrorism and economic recession cumulate in a growing anxiety about what the future holds.
- *Post-Christian:* The Westerner feels that Christianity does not belong to the present and the future, but to the past. The image of being a Christian means returning to the Middle Ages, becoming intellectually dishonest and saying "no" to a scientific world view.[4]

SECULAR JOHN

In Holland, my Dutch neighbor, John, was a 36-year-old business-man. About a week after we moved into our new home, John and I were chatting over our backyard fence. "What international company do you work for?" he asked. When I told him I led a contemporary international church, he looked bewildered. First of all, in his thinking, the terms contemporary and church did not fit together. And, I'm sure he was perplexed about having a contemporary religious neighbor!

Though cautious at first, John discovered that my working with a church didn't make me so strange after all. We developed a friendship as we went running and met for coffee. In one of our conversations, I mentioned that I often prayed while I ran. John just stared at me. *Being religious on Sunday was one thing, but why would anyone want to drag it into the week?* he thought.

John was not hostile toward the church. He appreciated the architecture of some of the cathedrals and respected traditional religion, but he felt no need for church personally. Forty years earlier his family – along with most people living in the Netherlands – had stopped going to church. It was just not something people did any more. The church (as they perceived it) did not interest them.

Apart from our friendship, John has no contact with a contemporary expression of Christianity. John's life is focused on spending time, energy and money on career, family, friendships, recreation and vacation. He does not conceive of how God could make a difference in his life and has no idea that he needs God's forgiveness and saving grace.

TWO CATEGORIES OF THINKING: FACT AND FAITH

Millions of people in the United States, Canada and Europe – just like John – have unwittingly chosen secularism: abortion-rights activists, politicians who feel that their extra-marital affairs should not be a campaign issue, and parents lobbying to remove prayer from the public schools. These and other secularists proclaim: Don't impose your moral convictions on me! Everywhere you look, the moral ties of our society are being severed.

Secularism defines two ways of thinking – fact and faith. Facts are based on anything that can be experienced through the five senses. Only facts are acceptable in the public realm. If something is categorized as faith it is considered a private matter and inappropriate for public domain.

The "real" world, according to secularism, encircles only those things which can be scientifically explained by cause and effect and expressed in scientific and mathematical terms. Secularists ask: Can you see it? Can you prove it? Science, technology and bureaucracy is grounded in this Western world view – governed by facts. Most business, politics, education, the military and mass media also embrace a secular view.[5]

In secularism, faith is considered "less real." Value systems deemed different for each individual, are kept out of the public sphere and are relegated to the private realm of marriage, family, leisure pursuits and, most of all, religious beliefs.

In the West, religion is a deeply private experience reflecting the preferences and personal beliefs of each individual. Scandals in current American politics demonstrate that an increasing number of voters do not believe that a candidate's moral behavior should have any bearing on their right to be elected. Europeans have long accepted the separation of morality and "electibility."

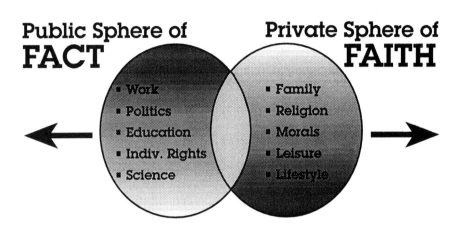

In the West, the public and private spheres are kept separate even though many religious people service the public sector. Religion and morals cross over into the public sector only when they further the purposes of the public sphere. In the United States, secularism is a deistic (a distant God who does not interfere) civil religion, and in Europe it is a ceremonial religion.

The consequence of a secularization, that excludes both morals and religion from the public sphere, is that increasing numbers of those in Western society have either left the church or assigned it to a minor status in their lives.[6] More and more people are becoming nominal or notional Christians who are influenced more by a secular mind-set than they are by values and beliefs.[7]

Western society has become increasingly de-Christianized, leading to the loss of the social significance of religious ideas and institutions.[8] Christian ideas and precepts have a decreasing influence in the public realm. Personal fulfillment has replaced public obligation. Secularism has created a moral and spiritual vacuum.

OPENING THE DOOR TO DARKNESS

Monica Hill, British editor of the Church Growth Digest, states, "When people cease to believe in God, they do not believe in nothing, [instead] they believe in anything!"[9] Although Western culture is secular it is not totally atheistic. Secularism has ushered in spiritual forces of darkness.

This darkness is evidenced by an increased belief in the transcendental. Horoscopes, the paranormal and an explosive interest in the occult reflect people's longings for a supernatural power to overcome evil and the limitations of life.[10] A TV program on CNN (Cable Network News) revealed how psychics, previously relegated to fairs and carnivals, are now hanging out their shingles in American shopping malls. They line one of the main streets of Barcelona.

There is a prevalent interest in the spiritual realm, but the evil of spiritism has captivated people's curiosity. Germany has only 30,000 Christian clergy compared to 90,000 witches and fortune-tellers;[11] France has fewer than 36,000 Roman Catholic clergy, yet more than 40,000 professional (licensed) astrologers. Many other astrologers, faith healers, mediums, necromancers and fortune tellers practice undercover.[12] Meanwhile 400 publishers fill French magazine racks with occult literature.[13]

FOREBODING FORCES

Non-Christian Religions

Non-Christian religions and cults have moved into the spiritual vacuum created by secularism. Muslims now comprise 3 percent of Germany and England and 7 percent of France. According to Peter Brierley, executive director of Christian Research Association in Europe, a new mosque is built in Britain every two weeks. And in Germany there is now one mosque for every twelve Evangelical Lutheran churches.[14]

In 1990 there were close to a half million Hindus in the United States and Hinduism is expected to maintain steady growth in the 21st century. Likewise, Buddhism and the eclectic Baha'i have made gains in attracting adherents in the West.[15] Immigration and guest workers account for the majority of the increase, but non-Christian religions are also making inroads among Westerners.

Cults

Cults (groups that base their beliefs on a single leader other than Christ and writings other than the Bible) are also penetrating the West. Non-orthodox groups such as Jehovah's Witnesses, Children of God, The Church of the Latter Day Saints (Mormons) and The Worldwide Unification Church (Moonies) actively proselytize, adding to the Western world's religious pluralism. These groups report significant gains in membership. In America, Mormons now hold a 2 percent share of the U.S. population.[16]

Cults and groups with cultic tendencies are infiltrating the world's burgeoning cities with their unorthodox teachings. Some of these groups claim to represent Christianity but do not honor the basic doctrines of the Christian faith — the Trinity, the deity of Christ, and the saving work of the death and resurrection of Christ.[17]

New Age

Many individuals and groups identify themselves as "New Age." Others who do not call themselves "New Age" are still influenced by New Age philosophy. Although there is no central organization, elements of the New Age Movement promote world domination through a one-world economy, a one-world government and a one-world religion.

New Age ideas reflect the relativism of Western culture, claiming that all religions have some of the truth.[18] This philosophy is ages old, rooted in ancient Buddhism and Hinduism. New Age edifies the release of the divine nature in each person.[19]

New Paganism

Neo-paganism, a primitive pantheistic spiritualism, rejects the Christian idea of salvation based on the revelation, death and resurrection of Jesus Christ.[20] Nazism, an example of Neo-paganism, attempted to return to the primitive or pagan sub-structure of life — blood, race, nation, soil. Adolph Hitler, the leader of Nazism in the 1930-40s, was outwardly religious. Hitler combined pantheism, rationalism, primitive superstitions (about blood, soil, and race) and a rejection of the Judeo-Christian heritage and the Christian church.[21]

Paganism is deeply rooted in European history. Psychologist Carl Jung said that Christianity in Europe is like a cathedral built on the foundations of a pagan temple—it has not really reached the deeper regions of the soul of European man.[22] Reason in modern technology, technocracy and capitalism suppressed paganism for a time, but now, according to professor W. A. Visser 't Hooft, there appears to be a new movement toward elevating the primitive elements of life—the new paganism.

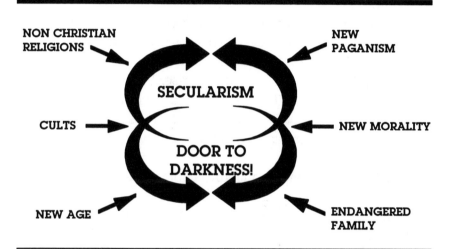

Christianity did not totally destroy paganism in Europe. European secularism has been a 19th-century seedbed for paganism's resurgence. Primitive pagan forces lie under the surface in every human society. This aberrant religion may be driven back, even forced into hiding, but it does not disappear. Wherever true Christianity is in decline, paganism resurfaces.

New Morality

Accompanying shifts in religious convictions lead to changes in society's moral values. Everywhere there is an abandonment of social standards based on Christian teaching. The exclusion of values and faith from the public sphere has resulted in a loss of morality in Western culture. Abortion, violent crimes, alcoholism, drug addiction, mental and physical abuse of children, AIDS and other socially contracted diseases are on the rise in both the U.S. and Europe.[23]

Children and adults watch more horror and pornographic films than ever in their homes, causing fragmentation and breakdown of wholesome family life. A popular song sung by Tina Turner asks, "What's love got to do, got to do with it?" and sadly concludes, "What's love but a secondhand emotion." The moral decline in modern secular Western society shows that love, values, religion and faith have increasingly less to do with "it" (value of life) than ever before.

Endangered Family

The most tragic victim of secularism has been the family. According to a recent British survey, marriage is in steep decline. In Great Britain, 28 percent of babies are born outside of marriage and lone parent households are on the rise. Single persons living alone now account for more than a quarter of all British households. The percentage of working husbands and stay-at home-wives is just a fraction over 7 percent, around 1.4 of 19.5 million British families.[24]

At a deeper level, more and more people are seeing a smaller and smaller connection between the gospel and their own lives. Throughout Western society, the privatization of values is an unseen battle waged against the family. Cohabitation has risen sharply,[25] and divorce rates increased rapidly.[26] Unmarried and single family households are increasingly common and the traditional family (husband, wife and children living under the same roof) is declining.

WHAT IS THE ANSWER?

Neither secularism nor the dark forces accompanying it have liberated people from meaninglessness, superstition and fear. Modern-day Westerners may be better off materially and technologically; spiritually and morally they are not.

A letter I received from a young French friend expressed life's desperation. "No one has ever said 'I love you' to me," Jean Paul wrote. "People tell me that God loves me. But I hear nothing and see nothing to prove it. I need to hear the words 'I love you' so I can believe in myself and feel like life is worth living. Linus, I'm lost and alone."

What can be done to reach sceptical Jean Paul, atheistic Anne or secular John—and millions more just like them—with the gospel? How can the church impact people infected with a modern secular world view?

The West needs to be re-evangelized! Only Christ can meet the need for human transcendence and meaning expressed by St. Augustine: "You have made us for yourself, O God, and our hearts are restless until they find their rest in You."

The high-impact church is a fresh approach to proclaim the gospel faithfully, make it visually attractive and provide the genuine missionary encounter so desperately needed between the gospel and modern Western culture.

2

A FRESH APPROACH TO THE CHURCH

Whatever happened to the dynamic Christianity that spread through Europe and spilled over to her cultural offshoots?

SPIRITUAL EPIDEMIC

Nominality is epidemic in all Western countries. In the United States, church attendance has dropped from a high of 49 percent in 1958 to about 40 percent in 1992.[1] Eighty-five percent of American Protestant churches are either stagnated or dying.[2]

In Australia and New Zealand, church attendance is at an all time low. A century ago Europe was the most Christian continent in the world; now it is the most secular. Throughout Europe church attendance is declining. Even in Catholic Ireland where church attendance is far higher than other Western countries, there has been a clear drop-off in the numbers of those who worship regularly.[3]

The reference to unreached in this book refers both to non-believers who do not attend church, and to church goers who have a nominal, façade of faith. More than ever before, the West needs a new model of the church to stem the tide of church dropouts and nominality.

WHAT IS A NOMINAL CHRISTIAN?

The nominal Christian maintains a formal relationship with a church but is not appreciably affected by the gospel. Nominality implies a gap between an associated identity (through church attendance) and an actual commitment (through faith). Nominal Christians—consciously or unconsciously—ignore or rationalize biblical imperatives. They usually do not consider God's direction in life decisions.[4]

There are at least five types of nominal Christians. Those who:

1. Attend church faithfully, but do not understand a personal relationship with Jesus Christ.
2. Attend church regularly, but for cultural reasons.
3. Attend church only for major church festivals (Christmas, Easter, etc.) and ceremonies (weddings, baptisms, funerals).
4. Hardly ever attend church, but maintain a church relationship for security, emotional family ties, or tradition.
5. Never attend a specific church, yet, in a traditional sense, consider themselves believers in God.[5]

The definitive factor in nominality is the absence of an abiding personal relationship with Jesus Christ evidenced by faith and obedience. The beliefs, values and behavior of nominal Christians cannot be distinguished from cultural norms.[6] In reality they are secularists with a veneer of Christianity. Their belief in God makes little difference in their day-to-day decisions. They perceive the world (and their lives) in terms of the here and now.

Even when secular Christians make decisions based on moral values, they do not comprehend morality as stemming from God or being empowered by God.[7] Nominal Christians bask in the notion of a loving, comforting God who helps them during difficult times. They may go to church occasionally, but the biblical principles of "repentance...turning away from an old life and spiritual rebirth to a new life...commitment and lifelong surrender" are not included in their concept of faith in God.[8]

Nominality is widespread in the West but particularly endemic in Europe where the greater portion of the population could be classified as secular or nominal Christians. European church members show a huge gap between affiliation and active attendance.[9] Also, the number of faithful, active Christians is a declining percentage of Europe's population.[10]

VENEER CHRISTIANITY

The large number of nominal Christians in the western world is a "good news"/"bad news" scenario:

The good news is that Western culture is still nominally Christian rather than non-Christian or anti-Christian. The majority of Westerners still associate with the church, creating a residual veneer of Christianity. In 1980, Religious Research Consultant Dr. David Barrett estimated that two-thirds of the European population fit this category.

The bad news is that the West in general, and Europe in particular, is becoming de-Christianized as increasing numbers of people defect from the church. Whereas in other regions of the world the proportion of Christians is increasing, in North America it's static; and in Europe it's declining. One finds a remnant of Christian influence, but in Western society this influence is mostly waning.

The picture of nominality is even darker if one differentiates between cultural Christianity and true-conversion Christianity. On the European continent, according to Kalevi Lehtinen of Finland:

> Less than 10 percent of the population can say that they know Jesus Christ as their Savior. Then, another 20-25 percent in European countries are just vaguely religiously inclined toward Christianity. In every European country the majority of the population, anywhere from 50 to 80 percent, are indifferent in their relationship to Jesus Christ and to Christianity.[11]

Unless these trends are reversed, the United Kingdom and much of Europe will move from being nominally Christian to being a non-Christian society. The bulk of the population will be totally outside the faith.[12] Current trends document increasing disengagement from the institutional church.

This drift is confirmed by the large numbers of Europeans and

Americans withdrawing church memberships. From 1972 to 1982 more than 1.5 million members of Germany's Protestant Church (EKD, acronym for the Evangelisch Kirk of Deutschland) officially severed their membership.[13] Church membership in the United Kingdom declined by about 100,000 annually during the 1980s.[14]

In the U.S., church attendance has hovered around 42 percent and more recently dipped to 40 percent, significantly lower than the high of 49 percent in 1958.[15] Mainline church bodies (Presbyterian, Episcopalian, Methodist, United Church of Christ, three Lutheran bodies and the Christian Church/Disciples of Christ) dropped from 76 percent of American Protestantism in 1920, to 56 percent in 1993.[16] From 1976 to 1986 the communicant membership of all Protestant denominations declined by 9.5 percent, while the national population increased by 11.4 percent.[17] What used to be considered "mainline" churches are now being called "sideline" churches by some church analysts.[18]

The people born in the United States during 1910 to 1930 have been described as "the most church-going generation in American history."[19] However, in 1988, according to Win Arn of the American Institute for Church Growth, 169 million out of America's 240-million population, either had no religious affiliation (96 million or 40 percent) or professed Christianity in name only (73 million or 31 percent).[20] The U.S. is now considered a "mission field" by Christians from other nations.

Along with the decline in mainline denominations and the plateau of church attendance nationwide, there is a growing sentiment that religion is losing its influence in the United States. While many Americans consider religion personally important, nearly two out of three (63 percent) believe that religion is losing its impact on social issues. By comparison, in 1957, only 14 percent saw a decline in religious influence, while 69 percent believed the influence of religion was then increasing. [21]

Research analyst George Barna foresees a "rough ride" for the future of the church. He concludes that by the year 2000, less than half the adult population will consider religion very important in their daily lives, and barely one out of three adults will attend church on Sunday.[22]

WHY SO MUCH NOMINALITY?

The underlying reason for so much nominality is that the church is permeated by secular culture. Many Westerners look to science and technology — not Christ and the church — as a guide for decisions and future hope. The world view that limits reality to those things that can be empirically verified has influenced theological premises.

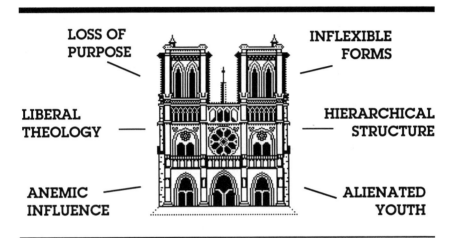

LOSS OF PURPOSE

INFLEXIBLE FORMS

LIBERAL THEOLOGY

HIERARCHICAL STRUCTURE

ANEMIC INFLUENCE

ALIENATED YOUTH

It is difficult to ascertain to what extent the countries of Europe — even those under the influence of the Reformation — were ever truly evangelized. The Reformation brought change, but how many of the Europeans who became Protestant really experienced conversion is an open question.

For many, belief was a matter of convenience and location, not conviction. The religious group that dominated a particular geographical location was declared to be the official religion of that area. Even if we allow that Europeans were evangelized, the tendency with the passing of generations, has been toward professing faith without an understanding of a personal relationship with Jesus Christ.

LIBERAL THEOLOGY

As secular thinking began to dominate the church in the 19th and 20th centuries, it opened the way for theological erosion called "liberalism." With the rise of rationalism and liberal theology, the Bible was undermined as the reliable revelation of God's truth. Instead, emphasis was placed on social, moral and political issues and complex theologies.

Luther, Calvin and the other reformers held fast to the principle that Scripture alone is the only foundation for preaching and teaching in the church. During the Reformation, the slogan *sola scriptura* with its message of *sola gratia* (grace alone) was the bedrock of Protestant faith and action. With the rise of liberalism, however, Protestant mainline churches in Europe and America lost their confidence in biblical authority. Subsequently, preaching, evangelism, church life and Christian ethics were eroded. The door was opened to secularism.

I realized firsthand the deadening effect of liberalism shortly after I became a Christian in 1963. I could hardly wait to tell a former schoolmate about my conversion to Christ. My friend had talked to me about Christ earlier and gone to seminary after finishing his university studies. I went to his campus and excitedly told him that I now believed in Christ as Savior and Lord! I was stunned when he wistfully responded, "I wish I could still believe that." Unfortunately, his seminary professors undermined his faith in the miracles of the Bible, the virgin birth and the Resurrection of Jesus.

LOSS OF PURPOSE

Somewhere in the journey the church lost its sense of purpose. The church was no longer driven by a sense of mission and conviction that each generation must be evangelized and discipled. Evangelism was directed primarily toward other continents.

The Western church suffers from blurred vision and loss of passion. Because of nominality, many churches are—in effect—dying. Author Dean Kelly makes this assessment of the major denominational churches of North America in his book, *Why Conservative Churches are Growing*, when he says:

> A final reason for using the word dying is that the process we see at work in the churches is probably not reversible. Having once succumbed to debility, a church

is unlikely to recover, not because measures leading to recovery could not be prescribed and instituted, but because the persons who now occupy positions of leadership and fellowship in the church will not find them congenial and will not want to institute them. They prefer a church which is not too strenuous or demanding—a church, in fact, which is dying.[23]

This assessment applies to nominal churches everywhere. Kelly captures the heart of the problem of secularization in the church: the church has forgotten its true spiritual nature and purpose.

Kelly goes on to say that the church can never be thought of simply as a religious institution. Churches as institutions die precisely because they only appear to be religious but have, in fact, turned away from the revelation of God in Christ and the reality of God in history. They have lost their grip on the gospel, or rather, allowed the gospel to lose its grip on them.[24]

> **The Western church is suffering from blurred vision and loss of passion.**

Providing meaning in life is a crucial place where the church has failed. Unfortunately, the church lost its evangelistic mission and accommodated itself to the cultural climate. It ceased enabling people to live with a purpose in a world without purpose. Secularism filled the void left by a traditional and purposeless church.

The average church member has little sense of mission. Even people who believe in God and actively support the institution of the church may not believe they are a chosen people—to be salt, light and leaven in the world. The fact that the typical local church has lost its mission is a judgment upon those leading the church.[25]

HIERARCHICAL STRUCTURE

Limited opportunities for Christians to express their faith contributed to nominalism. Historically, both Catholic and Protestant churches have maintained a medieval hierarchical structure dominated by professional clergy. Only a relatively small number of people were actually involved in "ministry."

Lay movements arose from time to time, but the average Christian was primarily a passive listener. Historically, there has been little understanding, training or opportunity for church members to minister using their individual spiritual gifts.

If an artist sketched the hierarchical model of the church using the Apostle Paul's imagery of the church as a body, I'm afraid the emerging figure would not be what Paul envisioned. It would rather be a deformed figure with a huge mouth (the clergy), a dwarfed torso and limbs (the laity) and an oversized posterior with eyes and ears (passive laity— sitting, watching and listening). Most of the body's parts would be missing or underdeveloped due to a lack of use.

INFLEXIBLE AND IRRELEVANT FORMS

As the church lost its sense of mission and purpose, it increasingly entrenched itself in patterns that distanced it from the people it is called to evangelize. Consequently, it became powerless to shape the beliefs, pursuits and attitudes of the masses of people being influenced by secularism.

In comparison to secular pastimes, the church seems burdensome and boring to attend. An astonishing statistic indicates that only 16 percent of Americans believe that the church is sensitive to the needs of non-Christians. Even worse, only 9 percent of non-Christians believe that the church is sensitive to their needs.[26] This was my own early experience.

When I was thirteen, my parents began attending a liturgically-oriented church. I attended out of respect, but my mind and heart were somewhere else. I did not understand much of the service. I was terribly bored.

Sunday morning worship was somber. Everyone was very serious and quiet. The pastor's garb (a robe and backward collar) seemed strange, the ceremony and the music foreign to my tastes.

The ritual of church had no personal meaning as far as I could grasp. The most difficult time for me was communion. I never knew the correct procedure in taking the bread and wine. After my turn, I just returned to my seat and knelt with my parents until everyone else finished communion. My knees and back ached from kneeling and the palms of my hands hurt from my fingernails as I desperately tried to overcome drowsiness. It seemed like an eternity! (The thought of eternal life was not very appealing).

Church music was another test of my endurance. The hymns dragged, the beat was slow, the verses complicated and pitched in a

Only 16% of Americans believe that the church is sensitive to the needs of non-Christians.

key that caused me to strain my voice to get high enough or deepen my voice like my father's. I learned to lip-sync in church! Outside of church my friends and I listened to contemporary music: ballads, country-western and rock 'n' roll.

The church's preaching didn't move me either. Even though I sat through hundreds of sermons and attended confirmation classes, I don't remember what was taught. Although the message that "Jesus is salvation to everyone who believes" was probably offered in at least one of the churches I attended, it was not presented in a way that I could understand. Unfortunately, when I think of my early experience in churches, one of the main things I recall is the sound of my stomach growling and the scandal when the married choir director ran off with the organist.

ALIENATED YOUTH

One reason given for the decline in church attendance is aging membership.[27] English church-growth expert Peter Brierley notes the church's failure to attract youth.[28] Some of the reasons for this disinterest is revealed in responses to a questionnaire by a Christian Fellowship in Arizona. *What don't you like about church, or what turns you off in the churches you have been to?* was asked of young people. The following answers are listed in order of importance:

1. Church services are too impersonal, formal and traditional (including the way you are expected to dress), and consist of

too much unnecessary ritual and pomp.

2. People at church seem unfriendly, and unwilling to accept those who do not follow the cultural image of a "Christian" (appearance, dress, terminology, etc.).

3. The church is centered on its own program, needs, accomplishments and attendance records, rather than on the Lord and the needs of individual people.

4. The church has too many sermons about and emphasis on money and tithing.

5. Congregations are hypocritical and plastic. Christianity is only a "religion game," not applicable to everyday life. Christians do not practice what they preach.

6. Teaching and preaching is irrelevant and does not meet personal needs.

7. The church is more concerned with social issues and social reform than it is with reaching the world with the gospel of Jesus Christ.

8. The teaching and preaching is based upon legalism, which exhorts a Christian to live in response.[29]

This information is particularly depressing in light of other surveys that consistently indicate that more than two-thirds of all adults make a decision to accept Christ before the age of 18.[30]

ANEMIC INFLUENCE

The crushing blow that led to today's nominality in Europe stems from the First World War. Before that war, church attendance was close to 39 percent.[31] The First World War was a slaughterhouse marked by hand-to-hand fighting and gas warfare. Unclear moral issues and the alignment of church and state caused many to lose faith in religion. Those who were fortunate enough to return from the battle field did not return to the church. Churchgoing became mostly a matter of individual decision chosen only by a minority.

The first half of the 20th century was a nightmare in Europe. Thirty years of war, from 1914 to 1945, pogroms and brutal purges brought the death of more than 50 million. The noted French theologian, Jacques Ellul, said that in the First World War France lost her body; in the Second World War she lost her soul. The same analysis applies to most European countries.

The question for many was (and still is), *Where is God in all of this?* Thus far, the church has not provided a convincing answer. To most people, the church appeared not only powerless to prevent such carnage but was actually a party to it.[32] It is no wonder that to some, secular society is a liberation from the domination of an irrelevant hierarchical church ruled by fear.

CALL FOR RE-EVANGELIZATION

Much of Western Europe must be regarded as de-Christianized. Secularization can have a functional purpose — forcing Christians to a radical realism. It may be one of the ironic ways that God is calling the church back to its true spiritual nature — the proclamation of Christ's Kingship over all realms of life.[33]

At the same time, secularism and nominalism are a rebuke to the church. For some time the church has lost vitality because of fatal long-term dynamics.[34] Fresh forms of the church are needed to reverse the self-absorption and pitfalls of institutionalization.

The revitalization of existing churches and the planting of new ones is the only way to re-evangelize the Western world.

> **Secularism can have a functional purpose— forcing Christians to a radical realism.**

Many who have remained in traditional churches (and most of those who have dropped out of church) still regard themselves as Christians.[35] These nominal, or notional Christians, lack a vital personal relationship with Christ and need to be evangelized and renewed in their faith.

The style of Christianity that has been rejected or ignored is a poor reflection of the dynamic faith found in the pages of the New Testament. The church of Western Christianity has been constrained by culture, institutional structures and political expediency. It has been more concerned with preserving its traditions than in proclaiming the gospel. It has neglected being Christ's witness in the world.

There is a desperate need to evangelize the millions of un-churched who have turned to non-Christian religions, or pagan and sub-Christian beliefs. In addition, the church cannot ignore the millions who have deserted Christianity. The unchurched masses want a faith that meets their needs. They wait for the Good News that God was in Christ, reconciling the world to Himself. This message will go unheeded unless the church reorganizes its ministry in a fresh way, relevant to modern culture.[36]

HOPE ON THE HORIZON?

While much of the above analysis is discouraging, there are some hopeful trends indicating God is at work. The decline in attendance and the nominality of the church can be reversed. The Western world can be won to Christ. Churches of all stripes with a vision for evangelizing the unchurched are making *some* headway. Ironically, Europe and her cultural offshoots are once again pre-Christian, not merely post-Christian.

In addition to the fact that the Christian heritage is still strong in some countries, there has been growth in evangelical, Pentecostal and charismatic churches.[37] In America, church growth expert, Lyle Schaller estimates that 3,000 churches die each year but 3,500 to 5,000 are planted. Thus, 500 to 2,000 more churches are being planted than are dying.[38] Researcher and author George Barna states that if existing plans are carried out, there will be a net increase of 50,000 new congregations in this decade in the United States.[39]

Perhaps the most positive trend is the increasing number of growing, vigorous churches world-wide. These high-impact churches are characterized by dynamic worship, loving fellowship, and coop-eration between clergy and laity. They show zeal for God's Word, personal experience of the Holy Spirit and an eagerness to plant new churches.

The West has great potential resources to mobilize for Christ. There are vast leadership, technological and academic resources to contribute to the cause of Christ around the globe. The affluent West has financial resources that can be used to further the kingdom of God. The United States, Canada and several European countries have continued to be missionary-sending countries, aided by the fact that many Europeans are now multi-lingual. There is also a tremendous spiritual openness in Eastern Europe which may have a positive effect on the West.

All of this is preparation for what God wants to do in the world. The Holy Spirit is preparing the hearts of hundreds of thousands of people to respond to the gospel. People everywhere are looking for something that will satisfy and give meaning to their lives.

Alongside the overall secularization and decline of the church in Western Europe, God is speaking to the hearts of Christian leaders. A fresh approach to the church is needed. The unchurched and nominal Christians will not be reached, nor will the Great Commission be fulfilled, if the church maintains the status quo. High-impact, new and renewed churches are needed that demonstrate "breakthrough thinking."

3

BREAKTHROUGH THINKING

*The church doesn't just need a minor tune-up;
it needs a major overhaul.*

BRAINSTORMING!

About twenty church leaders gathered in Pitlochry, Scotland, to grapple with "Managing Change." We talked about weighty issues that hang over the church like a cloud. These include the secularization of society, breakdown of social structures, disaffection toward the church and the internationalization of metropolitan cities. Our leader, Dr. David Cormack, church and business consultant in Scotland, pointed out that people both inside and outside the church resist change because of tradition, fear, complacency and self-interest.

With a flourish, Cormack scattered several boxes of Scrabble (alphabet letters embossed on wood chips) and some dictionaries out on the long seminar table top. What could we possibly grasp about "managing change" with Scrabble pieces?

Cormack had a plan for "hands-on learning." He quickly divided us into three teams and gave us a challenge: "Produce as many four-letter words as possible in one minute." We had five minutes to think and plan before the starting whistle.

Our group started out timidly — perhaps because it was primarily British. But we quickly had a plan of action: Two would call out words at random, two would search a dictionary and two others would organize the tiles. We raced the clock and came up with 104 words.

We were surprised that the other groups beat us (although not by much). Then Cormack challenged us again. Another five minutes to plan, and one minute to produce *twice* as many words as the first round.

We took off at a feverish pace. Between the starting and ending whistle we produced 194 words, almost, but not quite our goal of 208.

Then Cormack outlined what seemed an impossible task — five more minutes to put together 1,500 words. We thought we had worked to the limit of our abilities to come up with nearly two hundred words, how could we ever achieve more than a thousand?! It would take all six of us spelling four words per person per second. This was impossible. No way could we reach that goal.

What to do? Get discouraged and give up before we began? Do our best, even if we knew we would never succeed? Maybe complain? Argue the absurd? We knew the goal was illogical with the approach we had used before. Ah, that's it. *A new approach was needed!*

Brainstorming led to a breakthrough in our thinking. We had been limited by a particular perception of how we *thought* we were to proceed. We had just assumed we were required to use the Scrabble tiles to form words.

We reviewed the assignment with new eyes: "Produce as many four-letter words as possible in one minute," Cormack had said. He did not say we had to use the Scrabble to produce the words; we only *assumed* that the little wooden pieces were necessary. This assumption caused us to *believe* the assignment was impossible. After this breakthrough, we were revitalized and enthusiastic. We quickly discovered a variety of ways to produce more than 1,500 four-letter words in one minute.

Cormack didn't need to say much to make his point: Breakthrough thinking is needed to overcome the enormous problems facing the Western church. The church's mandate to carry the gospel into all the world can only be carried out by breakthrough thinking!

Unfortunately, many church leaders — like our word-producing teams that day in Scotland — blindly believe they can use only traditional forms to carry out the Great Commission. They equate the maintenance of the institution with the mission of the church. Narrow thinking limits the church's avenues of reaching modern, secular people with the gospel.

WHAT IS BREAKTHROUGH THINKING?

Breakthrough thinking is the ability to accomplish seemingly impossible goals through new and creative approaches. This requires letting go of entrenched perceptions, configurations and patterns of thought, behavior and organizational structure that bind us to the mundane and keep us from reaching our goals.

John F. Kennedy's challenge to put a man on the moon before the Russians demonstrates a powerful example of breakthrough thinking. NASA (National Aeronautical and Space Administration) engineers had told President Kennedy that this goal was impossible in the time frame he specified. Undaunted, Kennedy sent his planners back to the drawing board with the instruction to persevere until they came up with a workable plan and acceptable schedule. They succeeded! Often it is not the goal that is impossible; the real limitation is our way of approaching the problem.

Over the centuries, breakthrough thinking has been the pivotal point of change. In the 1500s, Nicholas Copernicus conceptualized the universe in a new way. This founder of modern astronomy argued that the earth was constantly spinning and rotating, causing the sun to *appear* to rise and set each day. Prior to this, the opinion that dominated scholarly thinking was Greek astronomer Ptolemy's view that the earth was the center of the universe. Despite great opposition, Copernicus finally broke through the established pattern of perceiving the universe. The 16th century church's persecution of Copernicus illustrates how the church has been tied to traditional thinking, limiting it from new possibilities.

WHY DO WE NEED BREAKTHROUGH THINKING?

Secularism and Nominality

The Western church can no longer continue a status quo approach to its mission to spread the gospel throughout the earth. Breakthrough thinking is needed to regain persons who have been captured by secularism and to reach modern Western culture with God's Good News.

Western countries (from which Christianity spread nearly two centuries ago) do not match the church growth occurring in other parts of the world. The annual growth rate of Christian adherents in the former USSR, Latin America, Asia and Africa is increasing; the rate in Europe and North America is declining.[1]

The Western world is not experiencing vital Christianity. Millions who consider themselves Christians are little different in their morals and life styles than non-believers. The church is losing its grip on those who are nominally Christian in the West—particularly Europe. Western Europe has more nominal Christians than the rest of the world.[2] (America has a fair share, too.)

Traditional approaches to evangelism and discipleship are not accomplishing the goal of the Great Commission. Breakthrough thinking is needed in Europe and North America to evangelize those who are not yet Christian and to re-evangelize and disciple those who call themselves Christian. With these changes in place, the church in the West could be an important model for the church in other parts of the world where nominality is also increasing.[3]

Urbanization

One of the most dramatic changes during the 1900s was the urbanization of the world. By 1990, 47 percent of the world lived in urban areas.[4] Between 50 to 70 percent of the world's population will be urbanized by the year 2000.[5] The majority of the population of the United States and Europe is already urban. That trend will continue: 94 percent of the U.S. and Canada, 82 percent of Europe, and 80 percent of Russia will live in cities by the turn of the century.[6]

Urbanization has led to "world class cities" — cities with a population of more than one million people.[7] In 1986, there were 290 such cities, by 2000 that number will grow to more than 500. Another 2,400 cities have at least 100,000 residents.[8]

Rapid urbanization has staggering implications for city and social planners. It also presents a tremendous challenge to the church. The majority of city dwellers are unreached and unchurched. How can they be brought to Christ and incorporated into Christ's Body, the church?

While the phenomenon of urbanization represents a challenge, it is also an opportunity. Whoever wins the city wins the world. English church leader Ray Bakke says in his book, *The Urban Christian*, "The Lord seems to be shaking up the world. 'Go and make disciples of all nations.' Now we know where all the nations are — in the big cities. God has brought all the nations to wherever your big city is."[9]

Cities are strategic because urban centers dominate areas much larger than just the inner city. Urban culture spreads out and colonizes suburbs, small towns and even rural areas. Thus, cities are centers of influence — they dominate surrounding areas. "The city is less of a place and more of a process, taking its franchised outlets to the small towns, and its standard newspapers and television broadcasts to the remotest rural village," writes Bakke.[10]

Millions of people migrate to cities looking for job opportunities, providing a golden opportunity for the Christian church to witness. Studies show that people are most receptive to the gospel shortly after they have moved to the city.[11]

New migrants to the city are a prime target group for evangelism as Christians reach out to them, help them acclimate, and present the gospel. In turn, these new Christians are likely to be in contact with former friends and families still in villages and rural areas. They can become a mission force to carry the gospel back to the frontier and other unreached people groups.

> **The phenomenon of urbanization is a challenge and an opportunity. Whoever wins the city wins the world!**

This is a strategic way to reach the so-called "10/40 Window," the area that extends from West Africa to East Asia, from the latitudinal lines ten degrees north to forty degrees north of the equator. This area is often called the resistance belt because it encompasses the majority of the world's Muslims, Hindus and Buddhists—the "final blocs of resistance to world evangelization."

Luis Bush, International Director of the AD 2000 and Beyond Movement, says that 97 percent of the people who inhabit the least evangelized countries live in the 10/40 Window and believes that this makes this area of the world the first priority for world intercessors.[12]

Unfortunately, many of these countries are also the most resistant to missionaries. People from those 10/40 countries, however, can be reached in the cities of the West where many have immigrated due to the economic struggles of the 10/40 countries and the opportunities and attractiveness living in Western countries affords. Those reached can be trained and sent as missionaries to their own countries.

Psychology of the City Compared to Rural Life

Breakthrough thinking is needed, not only because of the masses of people living in cities, but because the psychology of the city is different than a rural area. The way to reach people in urban areas is unique. The city is more than a place; it is a mindset.

City dwellers, in contrast to rural uniformity, view change as a way of life. Cities have distinct pluralistic values and cultural expressions. And urbanites easily tolerate disparate life-styles.[13]

Another difference is the way in which people identify themselves. In rural areas, the extended family and neighborhood networks keep close ties — everyone knows everybody. In cities, relationships are secondary and casual. The nuclear family often has only one parent. Peer and vocational networks are the main source of identity.

Most city people do not know their neighbors, and their relatives often live across town or in another city, state or country. The absence of extended families and close neighborhood networks result in a reduced sense of "connectedness" for city dwellers. Many people have no network for emotional or material support.

Because personal value is defined by the ability to contribute to the goals of the state or nation, urbanites also experience a diminished sense of worth. When they are unable to produce due to economic recession or personal limitations, they feel useless. Urbanites perceive their welfare to be dependent on the benevolence of an impersonal state.[14]

BREAKTHROUGH ATTITUDES

The Western church has not adequately responded to the challenge to reach the city. While there are some exceptions, most metropolitan churches — particularly in Europe — have been ineffective in reaching the unchurched. In the United States, there has been a phenomenal growth in the numbers of evangelicals, but a broad subculture has developed that makes it easier for evangelicals to isolate themselves from the rest of society.

The church has been hindered by looking only to traditional perspectives to carry out its mission. To effectively reach the city, out-of-date perspectives need to be replaced with breakthrough attitudes. These important shifts are needed:

Parish to Pursuit

Churches rooted in the parish concept consider everyone in proximity to the local church automatically a member. Similarly, many people equate church affiliation with faith, regarding persons as Christian because they belong to a particular church or denomination. These assumptions contribute to mass nominality.

Nominality weakens the understanding that one becomes a Christian by personal faith in Jesus Christ. Where churches do not emphasize conversion and have little concept of discipling their parish members, stagnation sets in. An emphasis on evangelism and renewal of faith within their own constituency can result in revitalization and growth for nominal churches.

The parish concept has contributed to territorialism and a resistance to starting new churches. Persons in an area where there is already a church are considered "reached." Negative, sometimes even hostile responses are common from older churches to the idea of starting a new church in their locale — even where surveys show that as many as 90 percent of people in the targeted area are not actively connected with *any* church.

God has called Christians to "go into all the world." Therefore, we reach out in every direction and pursue lost people for God. We take the gospel to urban cities and suburban communities, never assuming that parish districts are already fully evangelized. Even if people profess to believe in Christ, we know that it may be a nominal faith. Those attending church may still be searching for God.

Property to People

For centuries, the Western church has been dominated by its buildings. Many cathedrals and churches have become empty shells rather than nurturing and equipping centers to promote and spread the faith in the midst of secularism and nominality.

Equating the church with its buildings and institutions has contributed to a fortress mentality and a passive spectatorism — that people must come to a particular building for ministry and worship. Many churches are poorly equipped for the kind of activities needed to reach and minister to contemporary people.

The maintenance of property often saps resources that could be used in more vital ways. Comprehending the church as the people of God who are called to minister in the world restores meaning and purpose.

The church is the Body of Christ. It is made up of living stones. The church is located wherever the people of God gather. I am not against a church owning buildings. Indeed, it is hard to have ministry without facilities. But, the church is *people*, not property. Buildings, like liturgy, are a means to an end, not an end in themselves. A healthy church's focus will be on building Christ's Body and reaching the lost, not preserving property.

Performance to Penetration

Historically, the church perpetuated a medieval cleric-centered model where the pastor or priest was held in high esteem as the best educated, best read, and best traveled person in the community.[15] The title "minister" meant that this person did most, if not all, of the ministering.

This model still prevails in Protestant, Catholic, Evangelical and Pentecostal churches today. The leader of a pastor-fo-

> # The focus of the church must shift from platform ministry to mobilizing thousands of non-professional ministers.

cused church is the one who is expected to be informed, articulate, charismatic and in touch with God. The role of members is not to minister, but to give financially and be ministered to in return.

The primary place of ministry in the cleric-centered church is the pulpit or platform where the pastor and a small cadre of performers carry out ministry. A good deal of the energy of the platform-focused church is spent on performance, program and promotion. Eighty percent or more of the people who attend the "performance" watch as passive observers.

If the church is going to reach the masses of unchurched people living in cities, the focus of the church must shift. Emphasis on platform ministry needs to decrease as thousands of non-professional ministers begin to penetrate their communities with the gospel. An alive, vibrant church will mobilize and train its people for ministry.

Form to Function

While it is not always the case, many older denominational churches are so liturgical-centered and tradition-bound that they place more emphasis on preserving past forms than they do on communicating the message of the gospel. Liturgy can give form to worship, or it can engulf and obscure the gospel so that form replaces substance.

Historically, liturgical symbols visually communicated spiritual truths to non-literate congregations. In the West, where people are modern, urban and largely literate, these forms seem archaic and unrelated to the everyday lives of most people.

One liturgical-centered church I attended was led by a pastor who faithfully followed a prescribed order of service from a prayer book each Sunday, yet declared that he did not believe in the miracles, deity or Resurrection of Christ. This pastor, dominated by the traditions of the church, strips the gospel of its true power by replacing substance with form.

Tradition, like liturgy, can serve to preserve essential values and forms, or it can coat fresh expressions of faith with non-essential cultural forms. Many church members resist much needed change and renewal with the statement: *We never did it that way before*!

A liturgical and/or tradition focus emphasizes the *way* of doing things, rather than the *purpose* for doing them. A purpose focus asks, *What are we trying to accomplish and how can we best accomplish it?* Breakthrough thinking realizes that liturgical forms are the means to an end, and not the end in themselves.

Survival to Strategic

Survival-focused churches are dominated by the goal of mere self preservation and maintenance. This is common where churches have existed as a minority in the shadows of another dominant religious or philosophical group. The faith and perseverance of the persecuted church is to be commended, but the survival thinking accompanying it frequently endures long after the threat is gone.

The survival church identifies itself by its history and accepts smallness as the norm. Even though the historical conditions may have changed, it is hard for a church with survival mentality to change its inward focus and grasp hold of mission opportunities. A church's prior conditioning makes change difficult.

Both aging churches (bound by tradition) and mission churches (without vision) can be survival oriented. A lack of strategy, or an inability to contextualize the church's programs to relate the gospel to people's needs, produces this situation. These churches are locked into a small-church model.

I received a sad letter from a man, a believer who is a committed member of a survival-mentality church. His church has not grown for 20 years and averages between 24-32 people each Sunday. He writes, "The church is still the same — six pianos, one grand piano and an organ, a full supply of color crayons, Elmer's glue, chairs and tables — everything needed for Sunday school except children and people."

This survival church is in desperate need of breakthrough thinking that sees the unlimited resources of Christ and strategizes with the view that obstacles to God's purposes can be overcome through them. In contrast to the church that merely subsists, the high-impact church trusts God for empowerment. It looks through the grid of His power and His resources and expects a great return for the kingdom of God.

Maintenance to Multiplication

An estimated 85 percent of American Protestant churches are either stagnant or in decline.[16] The situation is equally adverse in Europe. Maintenance-oriented churches resist change and shun risk. An institutional focus and a failure to distinguish between the non-negotiable gospel and culturally negotiable forms, cause degeneration. Churches rooted in centuries of tradition are prone to stagnation.

Churches that "just maintain" place greater value on stability than on innovation. They fear venturing out to try new ideas and methods.[17] Suggested change produces staunch resistance.

Many people see the church as a guardian of the status quo rather than as a critical agent of spiritual and social change. Excerpts from a letter I received from a pastoring couple in a maintenance-oriented church expresses their frustration:

> Many families want to keep their little ones in the sanctuary during the service. We hope to eventually convince them to hire someone to baby-sit, but that usually isn't done here.

> The music is traditional hymns and a few choruses, and this has taken us some getting used to. (Neither of us have worshipped with an organ for a very long time!)
>
> Most of the members have grown up in the church. There are only a few new Christians and never any visitors. This church has a reputation for having problems with its ministers—many people in town know about that!
>
> There's a great variety of opinions within the congregation. A few are highly conservative and have already disapproved of some of our ideas. Many of those who are active in the church still refuse to become members. In many ways, it is like entering into a new culture.

In the maintenance-focused church, newcomers are treated with suspicion or (perhaps unconsciously) rejected because new people represent a threat to the status quo. Such a short-sighted church is simply focused on perpetuating existing relationships and organization.

When a church endeavors to move from a maintenance focus to a multiplication focus, its leaders and members comprehend that Christians are more than conquerors—through Christ. The high-impact church does not hide the mission God has entrusted to it, but breaks through in the adventure of multiplication. Christians are mandated to build the kingdom of God. That commission demands risk-taking change.

Successful to Spiritual

The success orientation of our culture has clearly infected many churches. This has even corrupted the principles of church growth.[18] Some churches are so enamored with numbers that all the criteria of success are materialistic. If a pastor has a big congregation, big building and big budget, he is considered successful. Churches abound in the realm of popular culture that concentrate on breadth of audience to the neglect of spiritual depth and truth.

The so-called electronic church is very successful, but is there an underlying biblical integrity and genuine spirituality? It is more and more difficult to differentiate between what is really of eternal value and what is only temporal. We need churches that are more concerned with kingdom building than with empire building; we need church leaders whose values are more shaped by God's Word than by good advertising.

The greatest need that people have in the West is not material success but spiritual truth — liberation from the deceptions of dark forces that bind people and

> **Some churches are so enamored with numbers that all the criteria of success are materialistic.**

cultures and even creep their way into the church. Prayer is crucial to defeating these forces, opening the eyes and hearts of believers to comprehend the truth of God's Word and experience the love of God and power of the Holy Spirit.

Doubt to Dare

Anglican evangelical theologian and author John Stott warns against "Europessimism," the conviction that European churches cannot grow.[19] This warning applies to all churches mired in negative expectations and sceptical outlooks. Indeed, some churches doubt whether Scripture is more than a book of myths. Such churches have redefined mission in line with their doubts.

Evangelical churches are likewise characterized by doubt. Overwhelmed by obstacles and difficulties in reaching their communities for Christ, they overlook creative opportunities and divine resources. Jesus beckons His disciples to, "Open your eyes and look at the fields!" Fields of lost people are ready to harvest.

The Psalmist said, "Come...magnify the Lord with me." The Greek word for magnify means "to make great." When we magnify the Lord and His promises we move from doubt to faith. By focusing on the greatness of the Lord, human problems become small in comparison. By breaking through old patterns and taking risks for God, we are filled with faith that moves mountains. With the "greatness of the Lord," breakthrough Christians can daringly reach the masses of lost people in our world.

Guilt to Grace

Lifeless churches are known more for what they oppose than what they stand for. They stress the "don'ts" and the prohibitions of Christianity, rather than the grace, hope and possibilities in Christ. The church has been negative and overly concerned with creeds — known more for what it prohibits than what it promotes. Charles Swindoll comments,

> Bound and shackled by legalistic do's and don'ts, intimidated and immobilized by others' demands and expectations, far too many in God's family merely exist in the tight radius of bondage, dictated by those who have appointed themselves our judge and jury."[20]

The winsome and biblical message of hope and grace is the vibrant alternative. The high-impact church rejects the "grim-faced character of religion." Instead of a negative focus, it encircles a positive, expectant focus that radiates God's grace.

A lack of positive and credible models of Christianity — particularly in Europe — characterizes today's church. A healthy church model that grows and thrives is critical to reverse the negative impressions about Christianity and the church.

BREAKTHROUGH PERSPECTIVES OF THE CHURCH

What kind of churches are needed to reach cities? What kind of churches will attract unchurched people to Christ and reverse the decline? What kind of churches will overcome negative perceptions? To impact urban centers of the Western world, the church must change. Consider the high-impact church profile:

- *Purposeful and Expectant* — commits to reaching the lost by cultivating praying, worshipping, caring, equipping, witnessing bodies of believers.
- *Faithful and Flexible* — honors the mandate of mission rather than man-made tradition. The high-impact church is innovative and flexible, yet never violates the authority of Scripture.
- *Gracious and Relational* — emphasizes God's love, acceptance

and forgiveness and fosters relationships so people can meaningfully share their lives together.

- *Attractive and Engaging* — creatively programs ways to capture the interest of contemporary urban people.
- *Loving and Caring* — demonstrates equal concern for the needs of believers, and for those not yet saved.
- *Joyful and Celebrative* — worships God for His holiness, obediently relates to Christ's Lordship and actively draws from the power of the Holy Spirit.
- *Vital and Dynamic* — equips people to discover and use spiritual gifts and empowers people to minister to others.
- *Growing and Reproducing* — facilitates the growth of believers. The high-impact church breaks through barriers which limit church growth and multiplies itself by supporting other new witnessing churches.

The high-impact church includes breakthrough concepts of ministry and mission. Breakthrough thinking begins with a fresh realization of the greatness of God. When Christians are filled with an understanding of God's power and a realization of the unlimited resources He has made available to us, expectations change. Breakthrough thinking transforms negative expectations into positive ones, counters discouragement, and leads to creative initiative. I am convinced this is the key to reaching the Western world for Christ. ◪

4

PART II

THE CORE OF THE HIGH-IMPACT CHURCH

Life-Giving Spiritual Dimension

4

SPIRITUAL VITALITY

*I have come that they may have life,
and have it to the full.*
—John 10:10

WHAT IS THE LIFE-GIVING CORE
OF THE HIGH-IMPACT CHURCH?

A t the Church on the Way in Van Nuys, California, I saw an unusual sight—a line of people waiting to get in a half hour before worship. I later learned that the church had seven services on Sunday and *all* were filled! As people exited from one service, others rushed to find seats in the next.

In 1969, The Church on the Way began with only 24 people meeting in a 200-seat auditorium. But, Jack Hayford, the pastor, had a plan for a ministry-minded church: The Lord Jesus Christ, at the center; the Word of God as the foundation; and the Holy Spirit filling the church so it reached outward with the kingdom life of Jesus.[1]

Spiritual vitality characterizes the Church on the Way and other high-impact churches. What makes a church radiate the vitality of the Spirit of God?

To return to the analogy of a bright and shiny apple (noted in the Introduction), the high-impact church has three parts: a life sustaining core, a substantive interior and an attractive exterior. The supernatural life of the Spirit—the core—is essential to Christ's church and His people. To experience this, churches today must model the New Testament church and draw upon the principles found in the book of Acts and in the Epistles (letters to New Testament churches).

THE VITALITY OF EARLY CHRISTIANITY

Christianity was born in obscurity on the remote fringe of the pagan Roman Empire. Within a few decades, vital churches had been planted in Palestine, Lebanon, Syria, Turkey (Asia Minor), Greece and Macedonia. The New Testament church even penetrated the heart of Rome itself. By the fourth century, the Roman emperor Flavius Constantine professed Christ and declared Christianity as the official religion of the Empire, winning him his title, "Great."

Early Christians paid an enormous price for spreading their faith. They were called "atheists" because they didn't believe in multiple gods. They were assailed by false accusations such as holding disorderly meetings, murdering their children, and cannibalism. Christians, persecuted by false witnesses and corrupt magistrates, were burned, scourged, stoned, hanged, tortured, imprisoned, fed to wild animals, thrown off cliffs, and crucified.

Yet the Christian movement continued to spread from city to city and from country to country. St. Justin, a second century philosopher and early Christian martyr, summarizes this growth: "From Jerusalem there went out twelve men into the world; they were unlearned and had no ability in speaking; yet by the power of God they proclaimed to every race of men that they were sent by Christ to teach to all the Word of God."[2]

The key to the rapid spread of Christianity was the vital faith of those early Christians. In his *Letters to Young Churches*, British author J.B. Phillips comments on the vitality of these Christians:

> The great difference between present-day Christianity and that of which we read in these letters is that to us it is primarily a performance, to them it was a real experience. We are apt to reduce the Christian religion to a code, or at best a rule of heart and life.

To these men it is quite plainly the invasion of their lives by a new quality of life altogether. They do not hesitate to describe this as Christ 'living in' them. Mere moral reformation will hardly explain the transformation and the exuberant vitality of these men's lives....

We are...driven to accept their own explanation, which is that their little human lives had, through Christ, been linked up with the very Life of God.[3]

What characterized these Christians and the new churches they planted? How can we reproduce the dynamics of the first century church and impact our world as they did theirs?

A CHECKLIST OF SPIRITUAL VITALITY

The first few chapters of Acts illustrate the dynamic nature of the early Christian church. Although the birth of the church was a unique event, the same spiritual ingredients are essential today. The rest of this chapter portrays the spiritual core of a high-impact church. Use it as a checklist to gauge the vitality of the church in the Western world.

☑ Unshakable Confidence in the Resurrection of Jesus

A church will only be as vital as the degree to which its leaders and members have a dynamic relationship with Christ. Without this commitment, a church becomes a mere human institution, losing power and effectiveness. This power-filled relationship is based on an unshakable confidence in the bodily Resurrection of Jesus.

The Resurrection of Jesus Christ is the foundation of Christianity. The faith of the early church was undergirded by this historical reality. Belief in the Resurrection assured Christians they were forgiven and accepted by God, giving them the courage to persevere during times of persecution.

The physical resurrection of Jesus Christ had a transforming effect on His followers. They were emboldened and could not stop speaking about what they had seen and heard. They testified with great power to the Resurrection of the Lord Jesus and did everything in the name of a living Jesus. Christian martyrs faced death with confidence in the "Son of Man standing at the right hand of God."[4] No matter what happened to these early believers, they knew their future was secure.

The church's message remains yet today: "Christ died for our sins...He was buried, He was raised on the third day according to the Scriptures, and He appeared...."[5] The apostle Paul said that if Christ was not raised, then our preaching and faith are useless. (Even worse, those who preach this are false witnesses because they testify to something that did not occur.)[6]

☑ Kingdom Orientation

The early Christians had "kingdom eyes" and "kingdom hearts." (These characteristics are discussed more fully in the following chapters). Before His death, Jesus taught His disciples to seek first the kingdom of God. In the forty days following His resurrection, Jesus continued to speak about the kingdom.[7]

This kingdom orientation became the bedrock of the first church. Paul argued persuasively about the kingdom of God and widely preached that message. And Christians in the first century understood that the "gospel of the kingdom" was to be preached throughout the whole world.

The spread of the church and the message of the kingdom went hand-in-hand. Paul spoke of three synonymous tasks in his missionary endeavors: serving Christ, raising up vital churches and laboring for the kingdom of God.[8]

The high-impact church likewise commissions zealous missionaries who risk everything to spread the kingdom and send Timothy-like workers charged to preach the Word, correct, rebuke and encourage new converts with great patience.[9]

☑ Obedience to Jesus as Lord

Jesus called those who obeyed His commands "friends." He expected the believing band of faithful friends to be obedient to His teachings. The disciples obeyed because they trusted Jesus as Lord and King![10]

Teaching others to obey Jesus' commands was an integral part of the disciples' task in the Great Commission. He told them, "go make disciples of all people, teaching them to obey everything I have commanded you."[11]

Still true today, obedience is critical to assure God's blessing for the church. Vitality in the church can come only from wholehearted obedience to the Word of God. Christians' willingness to obey rests on the conviction that Jesus is Lord and He is worthy of our complete allegiance and loyalty.[12]

✔ Persistent Prayer

The church described in the Book of Acts was born in prayer. The followers of Jesus constantly joined together in corporate petition. They were devoted to prayer both before and after Pentecost. Paul, an anointed apostle, prayed for the early churches and asked believers to pray for him. In Paul's Epistles, he urges Christians to keep praying—"to pray about everything and to devote yourselves to prayer."[13]

Throughout the Book of Acts and the Epistles we see that a vital Christian is a praying Christian. And a vital church is a praying church. No church today better illustrates dependence on prayer than The Full Gospel Church of Seoul, Korea. This church has a prayer mountain where thousands come to pray daily and as many as 50,000 people attend an all-night prayer meeting each Friday.

Pastor David Yonggi Cho[14] prays two to three hours a day because he believes that only in prayer are Christians anointed with great power. Indeed, the vitality of a church depends upon prayer.[15]

✔ Power of the Holy Spirit

The Holy Spirit is the life force of the church. Jesus instructed His disciples not to leave Jerusalem but to wait for the gift of the Holy Spirit which the Father had promised.[16] When the Holy Spirit came, He created, filled, baptized, grew, led, emboldened, and sent out the early Christians.

The terminology for the church's experience with the Holy Spirit is different from one place to another in Acts. Nonetheless, we see a consistent emphasis on an encounter with the Holy Spirit. He empowered the New Testament Christians and gave them vitality to multiply the church.[17]

The Book of Acts is the story of the Holy Spirit working in and through Christ's followers to spread the gospel and build the church. It was the Holy Spirit who opened people's hearts to believe the message and be saved. Through the Holy Spirit the disciples healed many people and performed miraculous signs. Christians were strengthened and courageous leaders were called to lives of ministry and service. Sometimes Christians were led through trials and supernaturally delivered. At other times they faced persecution and death with spirit-filled power. The early disciples cast out evil spirits, brought pagan groups to faith in Christ and started new churches—all through the power of the Holy Spirit.

Churches without the Holy Spirit are "dry"—like clouds without rain. To be "alive" in Christ, Christians are to be filled and empowered by the Holy Spirit and are neither to grieve the Spirit, nor put out the Spirit's fire.[18] Ignoring the Holy Spirit or spurning His gifts quenches Him. Believers who open themselves to the Holy Spirit expect Him to work. A church becomes vital when members appropriate the ministry of the Holy Spirit in their lives.

☑ Spiritual Gifts

On the day of Pentecost, the Holy Spirit imparted new spiritual gifts. Believers were filled with the Holy Spirit and were enabled by Him to speak in other tongues.[19] Peter quotes the Old Testament prophet Joel and parallels Pentecost with the gift of prophesy that God had promised in the Old Testament to one day pour out on His people.

Other gifts besides tongues and prophecy appear in the Book of Acts: the gifts of apostleship, evangelism, teaching, healing, miracles, discernment, leadership and martyrdom. The Books of Romans, 1 Corinthians, and Ephesians give additional lists of spiritual gifts.

Spiritual gifts are given sovereignly by God for the common good and are to be exercised in love to build up the Body of Christ.[20] Today, as in the New Testament times, a spiritually vital church recognizes the essential role that spiritual gifts play in the life and ministry of the church and organizes itself so that those gifts can be exercised.

☑ Strong Leadership

The Book of Acts and the Epistles reveal that strong leadership was important in the early church. Jesus invested three years in training and preparing a group of disciples to lead His church. When one of these disciples fell away, another was chosen to take his place.[21]

Soon after the beginning of the church, seven more men, known to be full of the Holy Spirit and wisdom, were chosen for positions of service in the early church. Other gifted leaders emerged like Barnabas, Ananias and Paul.[22] Both men and women in leadership were crucial to the spread of Christianity and the growth of the church.[23]

Strong, gifted, wise, spiritual and faithful are qualities of those called to lead. Potential leaders are to exhibit gifts and prove themselves trustworthy through service before being entrusted with authority. Strong, authoritative (not authoritarian), dedicated leadership is essential for a church to be vital and to serve, teach, guard and equip a growing body of believers.

☑ Persuasive Proclamation

The church at Pentecost declared the wonders of God to unbelievers in Jerusalem. (This was the purpose of the gift of tongues in Acts Chapter 2.) So began the fulfillment of Christ's promise that the disciples would receive power to be His witnesses in Jerusalem, Judea and Samaria, and to the ends of the earth.[24]

The early Christians were not content to merely preach the gospel — they were intent on *persuading* people of its life-changing message.[25] Wherever Christian missionaries went, they delivered their message with conviction and the power of the Holy Spirit. The gospel persuaded people to repent, believe in Christ and be saved from sin and eternal death. The Christian message soon spread from Jews to Gentiles, and from Jerusalem to the uttermost parts of the known world.

Like the New Testament church, when modern churches prioritize discipleship and evangelism, they experience continuous growth. A spiritually vital church is one that mobilizes it members to witness and creates many opportunities to present the gospel.

☑ Supernatural Intervention

The record of the early church documents God's supernatural intervention. With the birth of the church, the gospel was accredited by God through miracles, wonders and signs.[26] The cause and effect of history is interspersed with acts of God on behalf of His people. Numerous miraculous interventions characterized the church: Believers spoke languages they never learned; a crippled beggar was healed; a deceitful couple was struck dead; Saul was supernaturally converted; Peter received a vision; Cornelius was addressed by an angel; an angel released Peter from prison; and Elymas was struck blind.

Along with these dramatic interventions are more "common, everyday" manifestations of the saving work of God: answers to prayer; men and women brought to faith; God saving, healing and transforming peoples lives; the Holy Spirit giving gifts, guiding, providing and empowering believers. The ministry of the early followers of Christ radiated a sense of expectancy of the manifest presence and power of God.

An attitude of expectancy makes followers of Christ willing to attempt the impossible—believing in God's supernatural intervention. This perspective is reflected in the daring statement, "I would rather attempt something great for God and fail, than attempt something insignificant for God and succeed."[27] A spiritually vital church expects God to act supernaturally.

☑ Growth and Multiplication

At Pentecost three thousand people were added to the early church at one meeting—that's explosive growth! Afterward, many more heard the gospel and the church grew daily. Following Peter's healing of a crippled beggar at the entrance to the Temple in Jerusalem, the church swelled to over five thousand men (the method of counting excluded women). These numbers, recorded by Luke in the Book of Acts, signify that numerical growth is part of God's purpose for His church.[28]

Although threatened from within and without, the church continued to grow. The Holy Spirit strengthened the church so that it grew geographically as well as numerically. It spread throughout the city of Jerusalem, then to Judea and Samaria, Damascus, Caesarea, Phoenicia, Cyprus and to Antioch in Syria.[29]

The church in Antioch organized a strategic mission to the Gentiles. An apostolic band of disciples was commissioned to preach to unbelievers in other lands. At this point, Christianity shifted from a Jewish sect to a cross-cultural, world-wide movement. A vital church grows through conversions and then multiplying congregations of believers.

☑ Devotion to Apostles' Teaching

After the influx of new believers at Pentecost, the church "devoted itself to the apostles' teaching." While Jesus was still with them, the apostles had been commissioned by Him to lead and teach the church after His ascension to heaven.[30] Spiritual guidance by these faithful disciples formed the basis for Christian faith and practice and assured the stability of the emerging church.[31]

New Testament apostles, like prophets of the Old Testament, spoke out messages from God as they were guided by the Holy Spirit. Their teaching was God-breathed and useful for teaching, rebuking, correcting and training in righteousness.[32]

The apostles devoted themselves to the ministry of the Word from the Holy Scriptures. Devotion to biblical preaching and teaching is likewise essential for the vitality of the church today.[33]

☑ Caring Community

The early church also devoted itself to fellowship. The word "fellowship" (koinonia) means to share together. Believers shared a relationship with God as Father; with His Son, Jesus Christ; and with the Holy Spirit. Because of their love for God, New Testament Christians drew together — a community of believers in fellowship with each other.[34]

This fellowship was not only spiritual, it was also practical. Early Christians were concerned for each other's needs. Believers gathered together regularly, broke bread together (probably like a pot-luck) and voluntarily sold property so that no members were destitute.[35]

Close fellowship symbolized the life of Christians in the early church.[36] Their communal spirit was an outward expression of God pouring His love into the hearts of believers through His Holy Spirit. Genuine fellowship or koinonia in a church continues to manifest the life of God.[37]

☑ Joyful Praise and Worship

The early Christians met together frequently. With glad and sincere hearts they praised God. In both large and small gatherings there were formal and informal expressions of praise and worship.[38]

Joyful praise and worship demonstrated the vitality of the early church. As believers, filled with the Spirit, they spoke to one another with psalms, hymns and spiritual songs. They made music in their hearts to the Lord, giving thanks to God for everything in the name of the Lord Jesus Christ.[39]

They were always joyful, reflecting whatever was excellent and praiseworthy. They worshiped by the Spirit of God and gloried in Christ Jesus, putting no confidence in the flesh. The vitality of the church, yet today, is linked to the spirit of its praise and worship.[40]

☑ Baptism and Communion

Early Christians were baptized as an expression of their acceptance of the gospel. Baptism, a response to faith in Christ, became an outward sign of incorporation into Christ's Body. Baptized believers shared in the blessings of the gospel and participated in ministry to the saints. Water baptism mirrors the spiritual baptism of the Holy Spirit occurring when a person trusts Christ.[41]

The New Testament word "fellowship" (*koinonia*) also means communion. Communion is a sign that we share in the life of Christ. The celebrating of communion remembers Christ's broken body and shed blood, and the Lord's Supper is to be practiced by His followers until His return.[42]

Communion was most likely celebrated in homes, not in the temple. Jesus Himself broke bread for communion in a home, a private and intimate setting. Emphasizing the spiritual significance of baptism and communion contributed to the vitality of the early church.[43]

HOW DO YOU GENERATE SPIRITUAL VITALITY?

Can we expect the same substance in the church today as we see in the church shortly after Pentecost? I believe we can. Throughout the book of Acts and the Epistles, Christians are told that these vital elements shall characterize the church throughout *all* ages. The components listed above are meant for the entire church age. Pentecost was a unique historical event, but the same Holy Spirit can break forth in revival and power at any time.

Spiritual vitality is a mark of a dynamic high-impact church. God is the One who imparts spiritual life and vitality. Yet God works through human means to inspire a spiritual vitality as Christians exercise their faith by believing in and acting on His Word. When believers have a dynamic relationship with God's Son, Jesus Christ, they receive the life-giving Holy Spirit as an inner gift. The spiritual life that God bestows on the inside then begins to radiate outward.[44]

Spiritual Vitality Checklist

Use the list below to check the spiritual vitality of your own church:

- [ ] **Unshakable Confidence in the Resurrection of Jesus**
- [ ] **Kingdom Orientation**
- [ ] **Obedience to Jesus as Lord**
- [ ] **Persistent Prayer**
- [ ] **Power of the Holy Spirit**
- [ ] **Spiritual Gifts**
- [ ] **Strong Leadership**
- [ ] **Persuasive Proclamation**
- [ ] **Supernatual Intervention**
- [ ] **Growth and Multiplication**
- [ ] **Devotion to Apostles' Teaching**
- [ ] **Caring Community**
- [ ] **Joyful Praise and Worship**
- [ ] **Baptism and Communion**

There is a correlation between our faith and the vitality of the church. God promises that as we draw near to Him, He will draw near to us. As we place confidence in the Resurrection of Jesus, develop a kingdom orientation, obey Jesus as Lord, and pray persistently, spiritual vitality is generated.

5

KINGDOM HEART

But seek first his kingdom....
—Matthew 6:33

KENSINGTON TEMPLE

On Kensington Park Road near Notting Hill Gate in London, the Kensington Temple radiated a heart for the kingdom of God. The large auditorium was packed. People smiled (even to strangers), shook hands and welcomed me. As the service began, worshippers sat on the edge of their seats with expectancy and joy. Faith and love exuded from every corner of that congregation.

The Sunday service reflected Kensington Temple's fervor for worshipping God and spreading the kingdom. After the lively worship, I met with a group led by Pastor Reverend Colin Dye. He reviewed the growth of Kensington Temple—from 500 to 5,000 members. He described the church's ministries, including a 150-student Bible school which emphasizes spiritual dynamics and practical theology.

Kensington Temple has a sweeping vision to extend the kingdom of God through church planting. In addition to starting churches, Kensington nurtures these new churches so they in turn "birth" additional churches. In one decade, Kensington Temple launched 50 churches. Kensington has set an ambitious goal of launching 2,000 churches by the end of the 20th century. These faithful Christians are likely to exceed their aspirations as they average one new church planting per week!

WHAT IS THE HEART OF THE HIGH-IMPACT CHURCH?

Kensington Temple is a church with a kingdom heart. The heartbeat of the high-impact church is a passion for the kingdom of God. Jesus taught His disciples to seek first the kingdom of God and His righteousness;[1] everything else is secondary. Only when the kingdom of God is Christians' most precious treasure can the church profoundly impact the world.

> **Jesus taught his disciples to seek first the kingdom of God and his righteousness; Everything else is secondary.**

The passion to pursue the kingdom of God is not just "pie in the sky...by-and-by...when you die." A church that is "so heavenly minded that it is no earthly good" misses the point. Jesus taught His disciples to pray for the kingdom to "come on earth, as it is in heaven." Seeking first the kingdom of God includes the present, as well as the future.

Nothing else compares in value to God's kingdom. Jesus said the kingdom of God is a treasure so valuable that we should be willing to sell everything we have to obtain it. Other treasures may be stolen, become rusty and moth-eaten; God's kingdom cannot. Christians, in harmony with the heartbeat of God, make the kingdom of God their foremost priority. They are consumed by a passionate desire to initiate God's kingdom into human history—in the here and now.

The Western world's quest for earthly treasures—such things as money, sex and power—ultimately does not satisfy. Those who aim "to gain the whole world," end up with empty hearts and lost souls.

When I was attending graduate school in Vancouver, Canada, a realtor friend told me that divorce was the main reason homes were for sale in an affluent West Vancouver suburb. Wealth and success were not enough to keep families together. Money cannot secure heart treasures.

People in the Western world are constantly assaulted by the pressures of their culture's values and attitudes. Fortunately, a consuming desire for the kingdom of God enables Christians to overcome the enticement of worldly philosophies, internal fleshly lusts and subtle spiritual forces including counterfeit religions. Gripped by a passion for the kingdom of God, Christians can transcend earthly desires that would otherwise ensnare.

HOW DO YOU RECEIVE A KINGDOM HEART?

Like many people who are not yet Christian, Ellen was having a difficult time "finding herself." She jumped at the opportunity to leave New York and work in Geneva. But being thousands of miles away from home didn't make much difference in Ellen's inner being—emptiness had become her constant companion.

My wife and I met Ellen and invited her to a home-fellowship group. As Christians shared how Jesus made a difference in their lives, she was curious and wanted to know more. Ellen had attended church in New York, but never heard about a personal relationship with Jesus Christ. Ellen began to see that it wasn't "herself" she was seeking—it was God. Soon she opened her life to Christ and received a kingdom heart.

Receiving a kingdom heart is possible only through God's grace.[2] It is a gift from above and is received in faith by those who, like Ellen, are often worn out and burdened by life's struggles. A kingdom heart is given to those who "become as little children," putting simple trust in God's gracious provision.[3]

A kingdom heart is based on repentance and faith in Jesus as Savior and Lord.[4] The basic meaning of repentance is to turn around or reverse the direction of one's thinking and action. Repentance acknowledges that a life without Christ is headed in the wrong direction. Saving faith confesses that Jesus is Lord and believes that

God raised Him from the dead.[5]

Ellen recognized that she was going in the wrong direction and turned her life around by receiving Christ. Her new faith pointed her in the right direction. The basic requirement for a kingdom heart is to willingly receive Jesus and yield to His dynamic reign as Lord and King.[6]

> **A kingdom heart is based on repentance and faith in Jesus.**

Ellen was the first person to accept Christ as we planted a new church in Geneva. Now, years later, she still writes us expressing a deep gratitude for showing her how to enter the kingdom. Ellen is a transformed person. Because of her new life in Christ, her spirit has been set free from the snares of a difficult childhood and despondent young-adult years.

HOW DO YOU SPOT A KINGDOM HEART?

A passion for experiencing and advancing the kingdom is what grips and motivates the Christian. A kingdom heart exhibits passion for kingdom fruit, kingdom love, kingdom values and kingdom authority.

Passion for Kingdom Fruit

Jesus said that the kingdom is for people who bear its fruit.[7] Christians are called to bear the fruit of righteousness. This cause transcends any level of human attainment.[8]

Elsewhere we are told that kingdom fruit includes answered prayer and lips that confess the name of Jesus; goodness, righteousness and truth; the growth of the church world-wide; and the fruit of the Holy Spirit—love, joy, peace, patience, kindness, goodness, faithfulness, gentleness and self-control manifested in our lives.[9]

God bestows kingdom fruit upon us when we receive Christ and trust His dynamic reign in our lives. It is only by God's power—as we abide in Christ's love and allow Him to abide in us—that we are able to bear the fruit of righteousness.[10]

Through Christ's perfect sacrifice on the Cross of Calvary, God credits Christians with His righteousness. This purity is a judicially declared fact and a progressively experienced reality of the spiritual life. The righteousness of God permeates the thoughts, motives and attitudes of believers who depend upon Christ. This righteousness generates concern for the well-being of others.[11]

God not only credits Christians with righteousness, He begins to manifest its fruit in the Christian's life. When I was just a new Christian, my marriage was on the verge of breaking up. Whenever my wife, Sharon, and I had a conflict I would vent whatever I felt. I expressed my feelings loudly and forcefully! Sharon, on the other hand, held in her feelings.

After each argument, I calmed down and even forgot what the problem had been. For me, it was over. I had a hard time understanding why Sharon would still be cool toward me several days later. When I finally asked her to explain, I discovered that she could recount our conflicts in minute detail—every stormy word I blurted out.

I felt at a disadvantage because I could not remember details, and Sharon could. So, I began to keep a list of grievances against my wife. After an argument (there were many), I would document everything I thought proved the conflict was her fault. I hid my "gripe list" in a small wooden cigar box beneath some papers in my desk.

> **A kingdom heart permeates thoughts, motives and attitudes.**

Fortunately, I became a Christian before our relationship deteriorated to the point of divorce. When I understood that God had forgiven all my sins and accepted me unconditionally, the Holy Spirit began to soften my heart. I discovered a renewed love for Sharon. I wanted to rid myself of resentment toward her. In an act of faith, I took the wooden box from my desk drawer and tore up the list. God was growing within me a desire to bear kingdom fruit!

Passion for Kingdom Love

A love for God and others is the clearest evidence of a kingdom heart. Before we come to a point of faith, we are separated from God and spiritually alienated from one other. But, when we enter the kingdom, we are drawn to the loving heart of God and reach out with loving hearts.

When Natalie came to live with us, we had four young daughters running around with endless energy. Our home was a lively place! Surely it wouldn't be any more frenzied if we hosted a sixteen-year-old girl for several months, we reasoned. Besides, Natalie needed a home. As an opportunity to tangibly show God's love, Sharon and I decided to invite this young woman into our hectic family.

Natalie came from a broken home and was not a Christian. Her family was quite wealthy. Natalie had lived in a beautiful house and had many material things, but she lacked loving family relationships. Natalie had artistic talent and one day revealed her intense inner pain through an artistic analogy. She spit out how she wished she could erase from her life all the people she had grown up with—her mother, father, brother and aunts and uncles.

A love for God and others is the clearest evidence of a kingdom heart.

Our love for Natalie grew, and the few months she had planned to stay with us turned into two years. During that time, we nurtured a caring relationship with Natalie that drew her into our family circle. Although expressing and receiving love was especially difficult for Natalie, she slowly began to believe in God's love for her and finally gave her life to Christ.

When Natalie went on to university, it was difficult for her to say good-bye. I can still picture the warm September afternoon, when she hesitantly stood in our front doorway loaded down with a final arm load of drawing equipment, books and high school mementos. Natalie just couldn't get out what was on her heart, so she slid into her car and drove off.

Five minutes later Natalie was back on our doorstep. She said "thank you," but it was obvious that she wanted to say more from deep within. We again said good-byes and she drove away.

We assumed that Natalie was well on her way to San Francisco when she appeared for the third time. This time, she didn't hesitate. Instead, she said what had been so hard for her to express. "I love you," she warmly said with teary eyes. Then, she added, "I've never told anyone that before." I felt a lump in my throat as we hugged Natalie tightly before she drove off for the last time.

Natalie had come to us with a hunger for loving relationships. When she received a kingdom heart, she developed a passion for kingdom relationships and service.

During college years, Natalie worked with Jr. High students, helping them to understand God's love just as she had done a few years earlier. Her life bore kingdom fruit. Today, she and her husband continue to share God's love, ministering to others in need. Natalie's pilgrimage illustrates that a kingdom heart results in a transformed life.

Passion for Kingdom Values

A kingdom heart also leads to a passion for kingdom values. Worldly pleasures are like cotton candy, fluffy stuff which is sweet, but does not sustain. Only kingdom life truly nourishes and satisfies our inner soul.

Belonging to the kingdom turns our world upside down.[12] Life in the kingdom is full of joyful, baffling surprises. The least become the greatest; the immoral receive forgiveness; the poor are blessed; and servanthood is the path to prominence. Kingdom life is filled with paradoxes: It is hard, but easy; it costs everything, yet it costs nothing; it brings death, but it brings life.[13]

Gary, a dentist friend who specializes in plastic surgery, lives an upside-down life because of his kingdom heart. In the United States, he would be making hundreds of thousands of dollars every year as a maxilla facial surgeon. Instead, he travels around the world on a Christian mercy ship and contributes his skills to serve the poor.

When Gary is based in Third World countries, he works long days to repair facial deformities on young children. Thousands of people around the world have been the recipient of his dental and medical skills. Gary's kingdom life reflects a Christ-centered concern for others. He is driven by a passion to show the mercy and love of Christ.

This dedicated surgeon takes seriously Jesus' admonition to use worldly goods to make friends for the kingdom.[14] Gary realizes that kingdom life means that everything he has belongs to God.

In the kingdom life, eternal values supplant the malnourishment of man attempting to live by bread alone. Mercy and generosity are the yardsticks of success. Restoration, forgiveness and redemption take precedence over economic gain and profit. Even enemies are treated as friends in the kingdom.[15]

Passion for Kingdom Authority

I first met Scott in my weekly Bible class. He sat in the back of my class and hardly said a word. Then, a mutual friend invited us both to breakfast one morning. When our host failed to show up, Scott and I got acquainted. Although a relatively new Christian, I found that Scott has a passion for the kingdom of God.

An executive in a large corporation, Scott is responsible for several hundred employees and millions of dollars of business. His spiritual priority, however, is to serve God and grow as a Christian. He took a two-year sabbatical from his profession to spend time strengthening his family life and to help Christian Associates International plant a church in Geneva. Scott has a passion for God's authority and power in his life.

Spiritual power is entrusted to those who submit to the authority of Jesus the King and are willing to become the least among men. The greater the submission, the greater the power. When the kingdom of God consumes a Christian, there is a passion for kingdom authority rather than earthly authority.

Jesus entrusted authority to His disciples to drive out evil spirits, heal diseases and overcome the power of Satan. Paul spoke of the authority given him to "build up and pull down" and he instructed the missionary preacher Titus to encourage and rebuke with all authority.[16]

Christians' spiritual authority is from Christ. When Christ is Lord of our lives, we can be victorious in earthly battles against sin. In all things we are "more than conquerors." Christians believe that all things work together for the good of those who love Christ and are called according to His purpose. We can never be separated from the love of Christ. Death itself is swallowed up in victory.[17]

A passion for kingdom authority in our lives allows Christians to stand firm even in suffering. Victory and suffering are not incongruous. Both are testimonies that we live in the midst of two kingdoms.

Passion to Advance the Kingdom

As believers, our desire is to use our authority in Christ to liberate those who are in bondage to the powers of darkness. A Christian's life purpose is to advance the kingdom of God toward its ultimate goal of rescuing the lost so that every tongue confesses and every knee bows before Jesus as Lord, to the glory of the Father.[18]

The biblical parables of the "lost sheep," "the lost coin," and "the prodigal son" illustrate God's heart to find the lost. These stories of a shepherd's concern for one lost sheep, a homeowner's concern for one lost coin, and a father's concern for a wayward son focus on

> **A Christian's life purpose is to advance the kingdom by rescuing the lost.**

Christ's compassion. Jesus summed up the purpose of His own ministry with the words: "The Son of Man has come to seek and to save that which was lost."[19]

Jesus also called His disciples to be evangelistic—to become fishers of men for the kingdom of God. Jesus commissioned His disciples to extend the realm and influence of God's kingdom. Luke's last description of Paul in the book of Acts documents Paul's preaching about the kingdom of God and his teaching that Jesus is Lord of that kingdom.[20]

I met Lance on a basketball court in California. A young Jewish university student from the east coast, Lance was ensnared by alcohol and drugs and was just drifting through life. He was a large man with a big frizzy blond Afro hair style. Sharon laughed when he would ask, "Can Linus come out and play?" (I was 28 years old, married and had three children at the time).

As we played one-on-one basketball, Lance became acquainted with my family. He observed something in our lives that was different and was intrigued when I told him about our personal relationship with Christ. For a while Lance went to New York where he again got caught up in a debased life-style. Then, as he was driving back West, he had many hours to think. Lance saw that his life was like a traveler without a road map. Lance remembered that Sharon and I had told him that "Christ wanted to give him new life." Right there, driving down the highway in his Volkswagen Bug, Lance decided to give his life to Christ.

After Lance graduated, he went on to study for the ministry. He volunteered to lead a youth ministry while he was in seminary. And, yes, he played basketball with those young people and told them about Christ, the Captain of the game of life.

Eventually, Lance pastored a church of several hundred people. One Sunday, he was praying and saw a vision of a map of New York with a fire burning in the middle of it. Lance was gripped with a passion to advance God's kingdom, right where he had grown up. Now he's in New York, where God is using his kingdom heart to plant churches and to fulfill the Great Commission.

Christians need a kingdom heart in order to impact the world with the gospel. People like Colin, Ellen, Natalie, Gary, Scott and Lance make seeking the kingdom of God their number one priority. Their passion to live out the truths of the kingdom and seek its advance is the heartbeat which pumps life into the church and is the force that energizes the high-impact church — to the praise and glory of Jesus Christ.[21]

6

KINGDOM EYES

The kingdom of God is near you.
—Luke 10:9

A CLASH OF KINGDOMS

I 'll never forget a particular Sunday morning service at the Crossroads International Church of Amsterdam. The Christian Associates International staff had carefully planned a "seeker-sensitive" worship time—everything designed to help visitors feel at ease.

The prelude music was contemporary and upbeat. A special "welcome" drew in guests, and a humorous drama allowed people to laugh and feel comfortable. It was amusing to see three soldiers stiffly marching onto the stage in their fatigues, all the while being riddled by their commanding officer about guerrilla warfare.

But the skit had a serious point, too. The actors visually demonstrated how the "enemy" disguises himself and attacks when believers are least prepared for spiritual warfare.

Then, Pastor Dan McConnell preached about how Christians are called to be vigilant, know their enemies' tactics and help one another in the fox holes of life. In his message, "The Believer's Battle," he explained that *anyone* could be the target of "spiritual assassins"—unseen demonic forces. He cautioned against skepticism and fanaticism and described the enemy's deceptive strategies to gain footholds in our minds.

Although McConnell typically had a clear, easy to understand delivery, that day he seemed to be stumbling and forgetful. I wondered if he was unprepared. My wife, Sharon, whispered and asked if he was ill. Something was definitely amiss.

The situation worsened. McConnell's every word became a struggle. He hemmed and hawed, seemed puzzled, and stammered, "The enemy's desire is to plan thoughts...and...and...and...and to overwhelm...our...our...our mental resistance. But...God says that we can resist the devil; we can resist these thoughts and temptations. You know the strategy of the enemy...of the enemy...."

"Excuse me...I feel a bit dizzy...."

McConnell sipped some water and tried to stand tall, but I noticed sweat dripping from his brows. Finally, he spoke again, but his quaking voice sounded like a record slowly running down, or a cassette player with a low battery. "The strategy...of the enemy...is to...is to...establish...mental...strongholds...in our mind."

As McConnell's body drooped over the lectern, several staff members rushed to steady him. Although he was wide-eyed, he did not seem to recognize familiar faces. I tried to help him sit down, but his knees were stiff and rigid. His whole body was temporarily immobilized.

When McConnell's wife dashed up front and spoke softly to him, some people thought this must be another skit—but it wasn't. By the time we loosed his tie, took off his jacket, unbuttoned his shirt, unbent his body and sat him down, our preacher of the morning looked as if he had been through a fight. Our carefully planned, seeker-sensitive service came to an abrupt halt.

At first, people were perplexed. Then, a thoughtful, take-charge member of the congregation suggested, "Let's pray." He began: "Dear God, surround Dan with your love. We acknowledge your sovereignty and control. Lord Jesus, we claim your guidance, wisdom, and comfort for your servant, Dan."

Then, someone else prayed: "Forces of darkness, we speak to you in the Name of Jesus. The word that Dan is teaching this morning must go forth. We are equipped to battle against you. We claim the power of the Word of God and the Holy Spirit. We rebuke the evil one, in the name of Jesus. We command you to depart from this place...in the name of Jesus."

All around the congregation, small groups hovered together to pray. The music team began singing soft worshipful songs.

As people prayed and worshipped, McConnell gained composure. He wanted to return to the speaker's stand to explain that he had just been through a spiritual battle—not unlike what the whole church is up against.

The preacher, who a quarter hour before had been weak and faltering, was now revived! McConnell told how a dark cloud had settled over his mind so that he felt confused, forgot where he was, and felt as if he were losing control of his body. The message about the power of evil had become a reality in his own life that morning.

The service ended on a positive note, as a quartet sang Keith Green's, "The Victor." The chorus rang in triumph:

> *It is finished!*
> *He has done it!*
> *Life conquered death.*
> *Jesus Christ has won it!*

Others who acknowledged a struggle with evil forces in their lives stayed after this service for special prayer. The power to release, conquer and protect believers is in the name of Jesus!

KINGDOMS IN CONFLICT

What happened at the Crossroads International Church exemplifies a power encounter between the kingdom of God and the kingdom of Satan. Nothing like that had ever happened to McConnell before. (And, several years later, he has had no similar attack.) Three doctors who assisted McConnell that eventful morning each concluded that there was no medical cause for his disorientation.

We all wrestle against forces of darkness that seek to overcome our minds and establish control. Satan does not usually reveal himself in open conflict, like he did with McConnell. Instead, he infiltrates our minds in more subtle ways. We encounter day-by-day struggles with thought patterns such as bitterness, lust, anger, doubt and discouragement.

The leadership of Amsterdam's Crossroads International Church reasoned that pastor McConnell's attack was a desperate attempt by evil forces to disrupt, confuse, intimidate and destroy our efforts to reach unchurched people through our new seeker-friendly format. Satan did not want the Crossroads International Church to impact Amsterdam with the gospel of Christ.

But Satan did not succeed. Quite the contrary, Christ was lifted up and the church was strengthened. Instead of being discouraged and giving up on seeker-sensitive Sunday celebrations, the Crossroad's staff resolved all the more to develop a high-impact church in that large, secular city. Satan had overplayed his hand. The Crossroads church was re-energized with zeal for the Savior.

SEEING WITH KINGDOM EYES

Sometimes, as in Pastor McConnell's one-time experience, evil forces can be dramatic and obvious. Most of the time, however, they are quite subtle. To effectively accomplish God's will, Christians need kingdom eyes to discern the unseen. Relational, emotional, economic, and cultural struggles are only surface problems. There is also a supernatural dimension to these conflicts.

Believers who seek to advance the kingdom of God can expect satanic battles. When God's people make inroads into Satan's domain, he counterattacks. But kingdom eyes keep us on the alert.[1] Everyday we are in conflict with our human nature (the flesh) and the non-Christian views around us (the world). Supernatural forces (Satan and his demonic hoard) crouch unseen. All about us a cosmic conflict rages between the kingdom of God and the kingdom of darkness.

Humankind's involvement in this conflict began with Adam and Eve. When Satan deceived them in the Garden of Eden and they turned away from God, they severed ties with spiritual authority. Humanity was imprisoned by sin[2] and came under the rule of the evil one.[3] Sin twisted human nature, and warped the world.[4]

From overt forms of Satan worship—such as witchcraft and occult practices—to more subtle forms of violence, greed and immorality,[5] evil pervades our world. The source of evil is an intelligent, powerful, arrogant, cunning, determined, implacable foe of God who wants to taint everything that is good and lovely.[6]

Satan is the thief that Jesus spoke of coming to steal, kill and destroy.[7] The Bible warns Christians that Satan— the god of this age— can blind the minds of

> **All about us a cosmic conflict rages between the kingdom of God and the kingdom of darkness.**

unbelievers, preventing them from seeing the light of the gospel and coming under the rule of God.[8] The origin of evil in the universe is traced to Satan's own willful rebellion against God and then his deception of Adam and Eve.[9]

Several years ago, while having breakfast in a busy restaurant with some friends, I had an inner urge to ask the waitress if she knew that God loved her. My friends and I came to this restaurant each week and I was sure that the waitress observed us enjoying an informal Bible study while we ate. After some small talk about the beautiful morning, I swallowed hard and asked, "Patty, has anyone ever told you that God loves you more than anyone else in the whole world?"

Patty had been through some tough times. Quickly she told us that her 15-year-old son was in prison for murder, and that her husband had abused and deserted her. She'd lost her home and was now trapped in a job she didn't like. As Patty scurried to another table she asked, "How can I believe that God loves me after all this?"

While Patty was busy with other customers, I had a few minutes to think about an answer. When she came with coffee refills, I told this disheartened woman, "The problems you have are not because of God. There is an evil spiritual person in our world whom the Bible calls Satan. He is trying to destroy you. Satan has masterminded the evil things that have happened in your life. But the Bible tells how to overcome Satan. God is not the one who has caused evil things.

Instead, God sent His Son, Jesus, to come to your aid...He loves you!"

Before we left the restaurant, I invited Patty to come to our church. Later, she began attending our home fellowship where we fervently prayed for her son in prison and began corresponding with him. The group rejoiced with Patty when a letter from her son told how he had trusted Christ as Savior.

KINGDOM EYES AND JESUS

Kingdom eyes recognize principalities of evil in the world, yet remain focused on the redemptive and liberating power of Jesus Christ. Believers are in an intense spiritual battle—but it is not between two equal forces. The warfare is lopsided, weighted for God. "Greater is He who is in us [Jesus] than he who is in the world [Satan]."[10]

Victorious living is assured as Christians focus on the person, power and purpose of Jesus Christ. Jesus proclaimed that the "rule of God," which the faithful in the Old Testament hoped and prayed for, indwells Him.[11] Jesus is the true King of the kingdom. He is the One who destroys the works of Satan and liberates believers from bondage.[12] Jesus establishes this kingdom in the hearts of

Kingdom eyes remain focused on the redemptive, liberating power of Christ.

all who, by faith, receive Him. He delivers each believer out of evil darkness into the kingdom of God's Son.[13]

The gospel is "Good News" that the King has come to earth bringing His kingdom with Him—the kingdom of God's dear Son, the kingdom of Christ. Jesus preached the message of the kingdom and revealed the reality of the kingdom through His life, death and resurrection.[14] Through the message and the earthly mission of Jesus, the kingdom of God invaded history. His coming was the dawn of a new era which will never be fully overcome by darkness.

Jesus Himself is the chief representative of the kingdom of God. He in turn mediates this kingdom to His disciples—the people of

God.[15] As Christians embrace Jesus as loving Savior, living Lord and reigning King, they unlock the power of the kingdom. Faith in Christ taps us into God's incomparable, great power.[16]

KINGDOM EYES AND THE CROSS

Kingdom eyes behold the Cross as the way God brought His kingdom on earth. The message of the kingdom is the gospel of salvation declared by Paul in 1 Corinthians 15:3-4: "...that Christ died for our sins according to Scriptures, that He was buried, that He was raised on the third day according to the Scriptures...."

In the Old Testament, Jesus had been foretold as the Suffering Servant (Isaiah chapter 53 with Psalm 22) who suffered and died on the Cross for the sins of the world. In the New Testament, Mark 10:45, Jesus identifies Himself as the Son of Man, One who came as a ransom for many.[17]

The Cross, the foundation of the new covenant, bestowed the kingdom with power. Through the Cross, Jesus gained victory over sin, Satan and death. The apostle Paul preached "Christ crucified,"[18] telling the Jews and Gentiles alike that because of the Cross sin is atoned and believers are reconciled to God.

Seeing with kingdom eyes leads to changed attitudes. The message of the Cross declares Jesus' perfect sacrifice and summons followers to servanthood in the kingdom. Christians are called to a kingdom of the meek and lowly in which leaders are willing to be "last of all and servant of all."[19] The arrogance of the world exhibits a sharp contrast to the kingdom of God.

The Cross, however, is not the ultimate proof of God's divine power – the empty tomb is. The Resurrection demonstrates God's final victory over sin, Satan and death. Thus, the Christian has hope even in the midst of suffering, because infinite victory is in the death and resurrection of Christ.

KINGDOM EYES AND THE CHURCH

Before embarking on a particular church planting project, I remember feeling inadequate and overwhelmed. I knew how complex and difficult the task would be. I needed to stay tuned in to God's Word.

In my prayers, I meditated on Jesus' words, "I will build my church and the gates of hell will not overcome it."

As I read these words, I realized that Jesus described the church as a power-filled church. Christians can do more than just "hold out" against evil, they can *assault* the gates of hell and overcome the forces of darkness. The gates of hell cannot stand against the attack of the church marching in the power of Christ.

Some weeks later, when I was praying again, God allowed me to see our church planting ministry in Europe with kingdom eyes. In my mind's eye, I saw Christians attacking a fortress. Some were wounded before reaching the stronghold and some were attacked while scaling its walls. Others fought through the defenses and liberated the captives.

I was greatly encouraged! I sensed that our European ministry would be used to either liberate men and women from the forces of darkness or at least support others who would plunder the "strong man's house."[20]

Kingdom eyes see the church as God's agent of liberation in the world. Jesus preached the kingdom and gathered the church.[21] However, the church (and all of its structures and forms) is not equal to the kingdom of God. Church history proves that the church is not a pure reflection of the kingdom of God. Although the two are closely related, the kingdom of God stands over and above the church, beckoning it to a higher calling.

Therefore, there is a distinction between the kingdom and the church.[22] Too close an identification between these two blinds us to the shortcomings of the institutional church; too sharp a distinction erodes the calling and mission of the church. In his writings, the Apostle Paul does not merge the church and the kingdom; neither does he separate them as two distinct entities.[23]

Jesus Christ is the connecting apex between the kingdom and the church. He is both King of the kingdom and Head of the church. Jesus called the twelve disciples, carefully taught them, and sent them out as heralds of the kingdom. He established these ambassadors as the new people of God—His church.[24] The church is God's agent, proclaiming Jesus, the crucified and risen Savior. In His name alone, sins are forgiven and the Holy Spirit bestowed.[25]

Kingdom eyes understand that the people of God are intimately related to the the kingdom of God. Christians are God's instruments to establish His kingdom on earth. Every book in both the Old and New Testaments professes this conviction.[26]

When the Bible refers to God's kingdom, it always refers to His reign and His sovereignty. The kingdom of God is the dynamic rule of God in people's lives.[27] It is not a physical, spatial or geographical realm but the sphere of authority in which God exercises His rule.

> **The kingdom of God stands over and above the church, beckoning it to a higher calling.**

God seeks His authority "on earth as it is in heaven." His vehicle is the church— the "people of God" who voluntarily submit to Him and proclaim to others His saving grace. The kingdom of God is the master plan, the master purpose, the master will of God that gathers everything up into itself and pours out redemption, coherence and purpose.[28]

KINGDOM EYES AND THE HIGH-IMPACT CHURCH

If a church wants to impact modern Western culture and reach urban centers for Christ, it needs to see itself as God's agent on earth. And as a church promotes the kingdom of God, it must prepare for inevitable counterattacks from Satan.

The Western world cannot be won for Christ without warfare from reigning principalities and powers. Jesus said that no one can enter a strong man's house and carry off his possessions unless first he ties up the strong man.[29] The high-impact church binds "the strong man" through prayer and relies on spiritual armor to overcome forces opposed to the gospel of Christ. Through the Cross of Christ and the power of the Holy Spirit, the church is assured of victory. The high-impact church faces conflicts with the confidence that Jesus is Lord and King. He will pour out His power on those who trust Him alone and see the world with kingdom eyes. ◼

7

CULTURALLY ATTRACTIVE

Collectively we have lost our attractiveness.
—Peter Brierley

GUNTER THORSTEN

When Gunter Thorsten of Frankfurt, Germany, turned 20 years old, he packed his bags, said good-bye to his parents and bought a one-way ticket to Maui. Deep inside, Gunter had a nearly unbearable emptiness. Thoughts of suicide flashed through his mind, but even that act seemed meaningless. Adrift in his spirit, Gunter headed for the white, sandy beaches of Hawaii.

Maui, a mecca for body surfers, wind surfers and people who just want to laze around in the sun, seemed the perfect "escape" to Gunter. For awhile, he enjoyed bumming the beaches during the day and ending up in a booming bar at night. But before long, he felt depressed again.

While windsurfing, Gunter met some other singles from Maui's Calvary Chapel. Late one afternoon, when the breakers were too high to risk, he joined in as they sat under a palm and watched the

Pacific roar with a pending storm. Before he knew it, Gunter had accepted an invitation to a mid-week worship service. *Now, that would be different!* he thought.

And, different it was. Gunter was surprised with the church's friendly and informal atmosphere. He met other surfers there. Together they sang songs with a contemporary beat, clapped to the music, and laughed at a silly skit. This church wasn't anything like the rigid, somber church he remembered from boyhood days in Germany.

Gunter discovered that worshipping God can be exciting. He also found what had been missing in his life—an engaging personal relationship with Jesus Christ. During the four years that Gunter stayed in Hawaii, he grew spiritually in the fellowship of Maui's Calvary Chapel.

THE NEED TO ADAPT

The greatest barrier to the gospel is not theology; it is culture. A major issue facing the Western church is making the gospel message intelligible and attractive to people unfamiliar with the church. People receive the Good News of Christ when it is presented in a culturally appropriate manner.

> **The greatest barrier to the gospel is not theology; it is culture.**

Breakthrough thinking allows a church to attract unchurched people from various cultures. Creative programs using popular music, lovingly taking time to listen to questions, understanding another's point of view, relating to their burdens, and communicating in their language are some of the ways that the church can breakthrough to those unfamiliar with Christianity.

Cultural attractiveness is what missionary experts call "contextualization."[1] To carry out the Great Commission the church needs to keep the gospel biblical in content, culturally significant in form.[2] In the first century A.D., the New Testament church contextualized and adapted its message and structures to reach unbelievers. This same approach will attract people living in the cities of our modern Western world.

CULTURAL ADAPTATION OF JESUS

People were attracted to Jesus Christ not only because of His unique teaching and character, but because He fit into Judea's cultural milieu. Jesus grew up in a normal way, culturally-speaking. He participated in a family, worked at a job, attended social functions, was a guest at weddings and dinner parties, and worshipped in the synagogue.

In public ministry, Jesus spoke the local dialect. His teaching was sprinkled with familiar stories about fishing, farming, business and management, international politics, and every day occurrences. Jesus asked questions that drew listeners into dialogue with Him. Always, His parables were applicable and relevant to people's lives.

CULTURAL ADAPTATION OF THE EARLY CHURCH

The New Testament church, born at Pentecost, was also culturally attractive. The primary appeal of the early church was its spiritual vitality,[3] but people were also drawn to the church because it adapted its message and structures to the local culture. Consider the following examples:

- The earliest followers of Jesus continued to attend temple and synagogue services. There, they had many opportunities to tell about their new-found faith in the context of common Jewish practices.[4]
- At Pentecost, believers spoke in many different dialects so that Jews visiting Jerusalem from various countries could hear about the Messiah. God set the precedent of communicating the gospel in the language (and culture) of the hearer.
- The Apostles chose seven Hellenistic Jewish-Christians to oversee the distribution of food to widows. The Antioch church understood the need for multi-cultural leadership and sensitivity to all people.

The early church was painstaking in adapting God's message of salvation to non-Jewish cultures. From the conception of the church at Pentecost until the dispersion of the Greek-speaking Jewish Christians in Acts Chapter 8 (about 15 years), followers of Christ kept close ties with their Jewish heritage and culture.

Stephen was the first to break through the cultural shackles binding the Jerusalem church. This martyr for the faith (Acts 7), understood that the gospel was not confined to any one culture.

After Stephen's death, other Christians began to spread the gospel to non-Jews. Philip went to Samaria and the Greek-speaking cities of Palestine. Those who were forced to leave Jerusalem spread the Good News wherever they went. The persecuted church scattered throughout the known world and brought a great number of Gentiles to the Lord. The first predominantly Gentile church was established at Antioch in Northern Syria.[5]

CULTURAL ADAPTATION OF PAUL

The Apostle Paul adapted his message to both Jewish and Gentile audiences. He spoke to fellow Jews in familiar terms, identifying with their customs and practices wherever he could. He appealed to the Old Testament in an attempt to convince them that Jesus was their promised Messiah.

And, when he addressed the Athenians, he communicated in a manner befitting his Greek audience. Instead of using Jewish concepts and terminology, he began with the premises of Greek philosophers.

In his first letter to the Corinthians, Paul explains his approach to different audiences:

> To the Jews I became like a Jew, to win the Jews. To those under the law I became like one under the law (though I myself am not under the law), so as to win those under the law. To those not having the law I became like one not having the law (though I am not free from God's law but am under Christ's law), so as to win those not having the law. To the weak I became weak, to win the weak. I have become all things to all men so that by all possible

means I might save some. I do all this for the sake of the gospel, that I may share in its blessings.[6]

THE LIFE CYCLE OF A CHURCH

The ministries of Jesus, the early church, and the teaching and writing of the Apostle Paul illustrate the importance of adapting and contextualizing the gospel message to the culture. That same cultural adaptation is crucial to the life, growth and survival of churches today. This reality is demonstrated by the typical life cycle of a church. Most churches experience a predictable 50-60 year life-cycle as follows:

The Life-Cycle of a Church

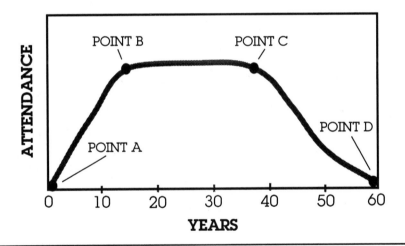

Point A: Birth

Point A—a new church is launched. Leaders of new churches usually believe that their church is needed in a particular community. This conviction energizes a church to reach out in culturally relevant ways. Attitudes are positive toward newcomers—members are eager to draw new people into fellowship.

The first few years of a new church are the most crucial. The church's vision to reach people forces it to be culturally sensitive in outreach and ministry. Consequently, a church usually grows during its first few years. Generally, if a church makes it past its third year, it will likely continue another 60 years, or more.[7]

When cultural sensitivity is structured into a new church's strategy, it will continue to grow. Unfortunately, institutionalism often stifles a church's original vision.

Point B: Plateau

Point B—a church begins to reach a plateau. Members become comfortable with the status quo. Leaders focus on holding to tradition (to placate old members) and new growth slacks off. A church at Point B is no longer a zealous pioneer.

When a church becomes institutionalized it loses touch with unchurched people. This church gradually forgets its original purpose. It resists change. Members look back with fondness on "the good old days." Few programs, if any, appeal to newcomers who are con-

Unless a Point B church renews its vision and restructures for growth, it will continue to plateau.

sciously or unconsciously resisted because they are a threat to the status quo. Unless a Point B church intentionally renews its vision and restructures for growth, it will coast for another thirty to forty years.

All churches experience plateaus—periods of consolidation and preparation for the next stage of growth. Too often, however, plateaus mark the beginning of decline and the eventual demise of churches with lost vision. Church growth expert Win Arn notes that, "In the normal life cycle of churches, there is birth, and in time, death. Many churches begin a plateau and/or slow-down around their 15th-18th year." He adds the shocking statistic that 80-85 percent of America's 350,000 churches are on the down-side of this cycle.[8]

But plateaus can alert a church to renew its vision. Through renewed faith of pastor and people, a church can be restored. New programs, organizational changes and contextualization of message and methods bring new life.

Point C: Decline

Point C—a church's attendance begins to decline. This decline may not be rapid, but it is noticeable. Faithful members move away or are deceased. Old-guard members resist change—their attitude is, *We've never done it that way before.*

Generations succeeding founding members show less interest in the church because its ministries are no longer culturally relevant. Volunteers are difficult to recruit (10 percent of the members do 90 percent of the work). Programs dissolve due to lack of leadership.

As attendance continues to decrease, survival becomes the primary goal of a Point C church. Zeal for outreach has vanished; few programs are attractive to the unchurched. Outsiders look at these aging congregations as relics of the past.

Point D: Death

Point D—one of two things happen: A church continues to exist indefinitely on artificial life support—a denomination, endowment, or the state may fund the church. Or, this church ceases to exist. Either way, spiritually, a Point D church is defunct.

Churches perish because they fail to attract and assimilate new members. When a church begins to turn inward and focus on self perpetuation instead of the unchurched in need of Christ, that church is in trouble.

PATH TO NEW LIFE

To entice the lost, high-impact churches reach beyond their walls and extend God's love to others. These churches develop ministry programs that meet the needs of those outside the church.

God's love motivates Christians to open up and reach out to others so that they, too, can hear the Good News. When a church exudes care, warmth and contagious love, newcomers are attracted. And visitors spread the word that they felt welcomed, loved and accepted. An alive church is a genuine, caring body of believers.

A life-giving, supportive church loves enough to become involved in the lives of the people in its community. A caring church adapts itself culturally so that non-members feel welcomed and comfortable. This leads to revitalization and growth in a church.

CAN THESE BONES LIVE?

Calvary Community Church of Westlake Village, California, returned from near extinction. The church began in the 1930s, the oldest church in northern Los Angeles. Initially a house church, it joined the Missionary Church denomination in 1956 after it had grown to more than 100 members. But after the church moved into a building it stopped growing.

By 1972 the church had only sixty members. The shriveled congregation had lost its purpose, vision and cultural attractiveness. Older members ran out of energy to keep the church alive and attendance continued to decline. When a handful of members concluded that there was more to "church" than just maintaining a worship schedule, there was hope for change.

In the late 1970s, three concerned Calvary Community families attended a seminar on church growth to learn how to help their ailing church. Energized about the possibility of ministry in the surrounding Conejo Valley, this church decided to risk trying some innovations. They called Larry DeWitt, an imaginative pacesetter, to lead their now tiny, 21-member congregation.

DeWitt's love for unchurched people, and his vision for growth, introduced significant changes in the church's strategy. Boldly, they relocated to a large, well-known restaurant just off a busy L.A. freeway. To identify with the Conejo Valley, the church took a new inclusive name—"Calvary Community." A modern translation of the Bible was adopted and services switched to a contemporary format. For example, "worship" was dubbed a "celebration."

New ministries targeted the interests of different age groups. Sermons related to people's real-life needs. "Growth Groups" began in homes and special events reached out to the community. The revitalized church grew rapidly. Fifteen years later, Calvary Community Church has led hundreds of people to Christ. Their average Sunday service attracts more than 3,000.

CAN A LEOPARD CHANGE ITS SPOTS?

Holy Trinity Brompton in the Kensington district of London is another example of an older church that dared to change. An

Anglican church, it dates back to 1822 and originally seated 1,505 people. (More than half of the pews were rented and 600 were free of charge.) In Victorian days, the church was attended by ladies and gentlemen from the area who usually walked to church. Worship followed the 1662 Common Prayer Book and the church had a reputation for forceful preaching. The church was also known for beautiful music with a professional choir and a skilled organist.

During World War II, Holy Trinity Brompton was filled, but as with most Anglican churches in Great Britain, attendance drastically declined after the war ended. Changes in demographics in London drew the Kensington district into the urban center.

Attendance at Holy Trinity dwindled to 100 people at morning worship (mostly older women), and only a half-dozen at evening services. The vicars were semi-retired, older men. The church was a hollow relic; it faced bankruptcy.

But in 1976, two significant changes occurred. John Collins, a charismatic evangelical became the vicar of Holy Trinity. When nearby St. Paul's went bankrupt, about 120 young people from that parish joined Holy Trinity. This influx of younger, energetic members brought the nucleus for revival.

Holy Trinity's evening service was redesigned so that it targeted young adults. Contemporary, instrumental music resounded throughout the cathedral where worshippers lifted their hearts in joy-filled services. In fact, the Sunday evening worship was even so popular that TV monitors in the balcony accommodated overflow crowds.

Exuding a new vitality, Holy Trinity Brompton began to draw from outside the immediate parish. By 1985, Holy Trinity had grown to 1,000 members! Then, this church took another bold step of faith — it sent a staff person and a hundred of its members to revive nearby St. Barnabus. Seven years later, that church grew to 700 members.

In 1987, Holy Trinity commissioned another 50 members to revive a deteriorated church in Clapham — only six people in a sanctuary that seated 600. In five years, this church grew to 300 members.

In 1990, 200 Holy Trinity members re-opened St. Paul's. Today, the congregations of Holy Trinity Brompton, St. Barnabus, St. Mark's and St. Paul's are all thriving. Together, they total around 2,700 members, all because one church dared to change its ministry and reach out to newcomers.

In the program at Holy Trinity Brompton, newcomers read: *Welcome! As a growing church, we love seeing new people.* Current vicar Sandy Millar writes and preaches with clarity—no Christian lingo. Newcomers come to an open house and meet the church staff. The church's overall goal is expressed in its desire to create a "GLOW-ing church"—generous, loving, obedient and warm.

Calvary Chapel in Maui, Calvary Community Church of Westlake Village, California, and Holy Trinity Brompton are examples of churches that understand the need for cultural attractiveness. All three churches are making an impact on modern, secular people. Both revitalization and new growth in churches are linked to contextualizing ministry styles.

8

FRUITFUL AND GROWING

*And we pray this in order that you may live a life
worthy of the Lord...bearing fruit...growing....*
—Colossians 1:10

COMMITTED TO GROWTH

In 1979, while a student at Seattle Pacific University, Doug Murren began Eastside Foursquare Church in Bellevue, Washington with only eight people. He had a vision to reach the unchurched community by mobilizing laity for ministry. In just two years the church grew to 100 members.

Doug, an avid reader and researcher, studied the "baby-boom generation."[1] He had a passion to reach "Baby Boomers" for Christ and wanted to know as much as he could about the American generation born from 1945 to 1964.

The motto of the Bellevue church: "Excellence in All Things" reflected Murren's intense commitment to quality. He scrutinized the music, curriculum, graphics, teaching, tapes, facilities and presentations of the church, making sure they were of high caliber. The atmosphere of the church's contemporary celebration service was one of acceptance, love and forgiveness.

Doug Murren led with the conviction that "If we ever level off, we're dying."[2] When the Eastside's attendance reached 1,000, some members said, "We're big enough." But, Doug said, "We must get to the next level or we'll die."[3]

As goal after goal was reached, more members caught their pastor's vision. They trusted in Murren's foresight as they set more ambitious goals. (However, the church lost some staff who were overwhelmed by the church's risk-taking ministry.)

Today, this church continues to strive for ever more excellence in ministry. Every part of Bellevue's Eastside Foursquare Church is geared toward growth and fruitfulness. When a program doesn't work, it is eliminated. Murren stretches staff and lay leaders to set new goals and keep growing instead of giving in to the temptation to just relax and maintain the status quo.

The staff and leaders of the Eastside Foursquare Church forged ahead by anticipating and planning for growth. Now, with an attendance of 4,000 (and goal of 10,000), it has expanded its cell structure to more adequately incorporate and care for new people. This fruitful and growing church continues to effectively proclaim the gospel both to the greater Seattle area and around the world.

CALLED TO BEAR FRUIT

Jesus called the church to bear much fruit. His vision was for quality and for quantity.

Christians bear qualitative fruit as they grow to maturity and Christ-likeness. Christ-like character demonstrates the qualitative fruit of the Holy Spirit. Jesus told His disciples that the pathway to bear much fruit was to abide in His love. He promised that in Him their joy would be complete and that they would know His peace. These three qualities—love, joy and peace—are the kinds of qualitative fruit which God wants His people to bear.[4]

Christians are also to bear quantitative fruit—to grow numerically. In John 15, Jesus explains how a farmer prunes in order to bear more abundant fruit. When a branch is pruned, both the quality and the quantity of the fruit are enhanced. Quantitative fruit is depicted in new believers being added to the church.

I recently visited a sixteen-year old church that had not grown for several years. The 40 worshippers that nearly filled the small building seemed comfortable with their size and their warm, cozy fellowship.

After the service, I chatted with a church leader who knew about my concern for church growth. He began on a defensive note: "I am familiar with church growth, but I don't think we should be in the numbers game. It's better to lead one believer to spiritual maturity than it is to emphasize numbers." I did my best to convince him that Jesus was interested in both quality and quantity in the church.

> **When a church grasps Jesus' plan for the church, it will grow numerically.**

When a church grasps Jesus' plan for the church, it will grow numerically. Without a scriptural impetus for growth, some churches are content to stay small. Other churches want to grow for selfish reasons, instead of growing to reproduce believers. Jesus' mandate is for the church to grow both qualitatively and quantitatively.

JESUS' VISION FOR NUMERICAL GROWTH

Jesus' teaching is charged with the expectation of numerical church growth. He expected the gospel to be preached throughout the whole world. Jesus illustrated His perception of the church when He told the disciples to cast their nets into the water — and they caught so many fish that the boat began to sink! Then, Jesus told these same disciples (the nucleus of the church) that from then on they would be fishers of men. He expected them to be fruitful witnesses.[5]

Many parables of Jesus point to the large quantity of fruit His followers will bear. In the above parable, a fishing dragnet is cast into the sea and *becomes full*. The parable of the sower teaches that good soil reproduces seed *one hundred fold*. The parable of the mustard seed points out that although the kingdom starts small it grows to a *huge size*.[6]

Other places in the Gospels Jesus spoke of the *great extent to which the yeast permeates* bread, a banquet host inviting the masses from the streets, alleys, roads and country lanes to *fill the banquet hall*, and *rewards being meted out based on the size of return on an investment.*[7]

Jesus' judgment on the barren tree was due to its failure to reproduce. He also taught that when a grain of wheat falls onto the ground and dies, it produces *many seeds.* In these passages we catch glimpses of Jesus' expectations for His church — measureless growth.[8]

The early church in the Book of Acts showed quantitative growth. Gospel writer Luke documented the numerical growth of the early church from the calling of the first four disciples, choosing the twelve disciples, the mission of the seventy-two, gathering one hundred and twenty in the upper room, the conversion of three thousand on the day of Pentecost, and the growth of the church soon thereafter to five thousand believing men.[9]

> **The church is the pilgrim people of God. It hastens to the ends of the earth to call all humanity to be reconciled to God.**

Luke traces the expansion of the church and demonstrates God's plan for numerical growth. First, the gospel spread among the Jews. The Lord added to the church daily those who were being saved. Common men and women believed in the Lord and many priests also became obedient to faith in Christ. So, the number of disciples in Jerusalem increased rapidly.[10] Then, the church spread to Samaria, Judea, and throughout Asia into Europe, including Rome, the capital of the pagan empire.[11]

Paul's Epistles also evidence that quantitative growth is part of God's plan for His church. In Rome, Paul told Christians that their faith was talked about throughout the world. He commended the church at Thessalonica for its faith which was known everywhere.[12] Paul wrote to the Colossians describing the fruit and growth that the gospel was producing over the known world.[13]

THE EMERGING CHURCH

God has designed the church to be a missionary or "emerging" church. To "emerge" is to bring into view something that has been concealed.[14] The high-impact church is an "emerging church" which develops as it was designed — discovering its full potential.

The church is commissioned to have a forward-looking, outward, growth-oriented attitude. A church cannot afford to be complacent or stand still, taking the attitude that it has arrived, either spiritually or numerically. An emerging church remembers its destiny, calling and mission.

> **The high-impact church gives no room to a maintenance or status quo mentality.**

The church is the pilgrim people of God. It hastens to the ends of the earth to call all humanity to be reconciled to God. It always anticipates the end of time when the church will meet its Lord.[15] The church carries out Jesus' charge: "You will receive power when the Holy Spirit has come upon you; and you will be my witnesses both in Jerusalem, and in all Judea, and Samaria, and even to the remotest parts of the earth."[16]

The growing and emerging church is an ever-widening, mushrooming group of witnesses who individually and collectively desire to grow into Christ-likeness. The people of God are in process of emerging numerically, culturally, geographically, structurally, organizationally, theologically, architecturally, musically, economically and spiritually.[17]

The church emerges as it grows qualitatively and quantitatively, over time. The missionary or emerging church doesn't limit itself to the present but, by God's grace, always sees more possibilities. It gives no room to a maintenance or status quo mentality. It is dynamic, growing and ever-changing. It is connected to the past, yet always pressing on toward the future.[18]

The emerging church pushes forward striving toward its God-given design, yet realizes that the church will never achieve perfection. The church's own understanding is not complete, uncorrupted, deep enough, nor wholly transparent.

Jesus beckons the church to look at the "ripeness of the harvest." I have seen pastors' complacency change to enthusiasm when they realized that the vast majority of people within their locale were unchurched. Stirred by this vision, they began praying for innovative ways to reap their share of the harvest for God.

North River Community Church of Duluth, Georgia is an example of a church with a missionary, emerging spirit. Even before the church officially started, its founding pastor proposed an outline of the kind of church needed in Gwinnett and North Fulton Counties. His vision is that North River Community Church would become:

- A culturally relevant church, enabling believers to reach the unchurched.
- A church whose members would enthusiastically bring their friends to celebration services. The worship style would be casual, creative, marked by excellence, sensitive to seekers (people who normally do not attend church) and would challenge people to follow Christ.
- A church that genuinely cares for people in small group ministries — support groups that allow eight to ten people to be loved, encouraged and prayed for. In a safe context, people can develop accountable relationships and learn to apply Biblical truth to real life.[19]

COMPLEMENTARY DYNAMICS OF GROWTH

A church's spiritual vitality affects its quantitative growth. If the spiritual life of the church is weak, unbelievers will not be attracted and the church will not grow. When spiritual growth is neglected numerical growth diminishes.

The quantitative growth of a church is connected to both spiritual and strategic factors. The church has a dual nature — it is both human and divine. A church is a mysterious creation of God that comes into existence wherever the Holy Spirit pleases to blow. At the same time, it develops along well-defined sociological lines.[20]

Paul teaches in his letter to the Colossians that church growth comes from God. The Body grows as it is nourished and knit together by Christ. Because of this, Paul admonishes the Colossians to "hold fast to the head."[21]

Paul explains that there is also a human dimension of growth. Spiritual growth comes when Christians allow the Word of Christ to dwell in them, teach and admonish one another, and sing psalms and hymns with thankfulness in their hearts.[22]

Growth takes place as Christians are knit together in corporate thanksgiving and service and as they express kindness, humility, gentleness, patience, forgiveness and love toward one another. As the Body holds fast to its head — Christ — in these faith responses, He in turn nourishes the Body. Another act of faith that influences the Body's health and growth is how each person fulfills familial and economic obligations.[23]

The quantitative growth of a church is connected to both spiritual and strategic factors.

The church grows both naturally and supernaturally, sociologically and spiritually. The church is a human entity, yet exists by the will and impulse of God. The building of God is constituted through human hands, though it is not made with human hands. The essence, purpose, relation to the world and role of the church are established by God but carried out by men. The natural and supernatural elements are inseparable and occur at one and the same time.[24]

People join churches for many social, demographic, cultural, political and economic reasons — yet no one *joins* the church who is not called, elected, justified, adopted by Jesus Christ and baptized into His Body — the church — through the Holy Spirit.

The church grows through a dynamic interaction between God and believers. On one hand, the church is totally dependent on God, who gives the growth. On the other hand, it grows as goals, strategies and plans are implemented by and through church leadership. And it grows through membership and administrative programs.

THREE DIMENSIONS TO GROWTH

God's charge to the church is to grow and be fruitful. This might be interpreted as growing up, growing together and growing out.

Growing up and growing together point to qualitative growth. Growing out refers to quantitative, or numerical growth.

However, a word of caution about the focus of growth: If a church is preoccupied with growing up, elitism and isolation occurs. If a church is preoccupied with growing together, introversion occurs. If a church is preoccupied with growing out, super-ficiality and worldliness occur.

The high-impact church grows up as it embraces spiritual truth, worships God and appropriates supernatural power. It grows together as Christians care for one another in close-knit fellowship and commit themselves to build Christ's Body. It grows out as its members live as Christ's witnesses in the world. Only this three-dimensional growth allows a church to be healthy and bear good fruit for Christ.

In high-impact churches, qualitative and quantitative growth are equally important.

3-Dimensional Growth

1. Growing up

2. Growing together

3. Growing out

Christ's design calls for both. The high-impact church resists polarization. It does not choose between "qualitative vs. quantitative" nor "supernatural vs natural." Instead, it incorporates all of these characteristics and is fruitful and growing, fulfilling the church's divine commission.

9

PURPOSE- AND VISION- CENTERED

Not much happens without a dream. And for something great to happen there must always be a great dream.
—Robert Greenleaf

CALVARY COMMUNITY CHURCH

People aren't used to a church meeting in a restaurant—but, why not? It's a non-threatening environment familiar to the unchurched. Large restaurants are centrally located and easy to find. Hotels, schools and warehouses are good, affordable locations, too. Hotels have few conventions scheduled on Sunday morning, so banquet rooms are easy to rent. Also, there is no upkeep during the week. Schools have auditoriums and classrooms that sit empty on Sunday and warehouses can be subdivided to meet the needs of a new and growing church.

When Calvary Community Church of Westlake Village, California, reorganized, they chose a restaurant for their sanctuary. They started with 35 people, but by their fifteenth year, attendance topped 2,000 and they were forced to move into a warehouse. Today they are bursting at the seams and looking to relocate again. This high-impact church obviously meets real needs.

When Sharon and I first visited the church meeting in a restaurant, we found comfortable seats in the large, attractively decorated room. Persons of all ages streamed in — singles, families, older couples. Some were dressed in suits and ties, most much more informally. Four brightly-colored banners behind the speaker's stand proclaimed the purposes of the church: Celebrate, Cultivate, Care and Communicate.

Different parts of the service highlighted and alluded to each of these purposes. The same four objectives stuck out on the front page of the Sunday morning bulletin and on the church's brochure — "Commitment to the Body."

Newcomers were invited to a "church chat" that evening where Pastor Larry DeWitt talked about Calvary Community and answered questions. At this meeting, Sharon and I felt welcome in the warm, intimate atmosphere and met some of the church staff and other recent newcomers. DeWitt's talk centered around Calvary's four purpose words. He clearly stated that the purpose of Christ, as expressed in the words celebration, cultivation, care and communication, was the number one priority of the church. Before we left, we were asked to indicate whether we had made a commitment to Christ and if we wanted to also commit ourselves to strengthening this Body of believers.

Later we found that the church is even organized around the four purposes. There is a Division of Communication, a Division of Cultivation, a Division of Care and a Division of Communication. Elders and staff evaluate every program in the church on the basis of whether or not it fulfills one of these purposes. A program that does not do so is either refined or discontinued.

PURPOSE-DRIVEN CHURCH

The Calvary Community is a purpose-centered and purpose-directed church. Unfortunately, many churches in the Western world have lost their sense of purpose. One reason for this is a turning away from the authority of the Bible. Churches that turn away from the authority of the Bible lose their reason for existence. A loss of purpose causes a church to lose vitality and often it dies.

Robert Raines describes churches that lose their purposecenteredness and merely accommodate themselves to the cultural climate:

> The church is not enabling her people to live with a purpose in a world without purpose. The average church member has little sense of mission in the world. The people believe in God and support the institution of the church and enter into its activities, but they do not believe they are chosen to be salt, light and leaven in the world...the average church member and the typical local church has lost its sense of mission...."[1]

More failures come about in the church due to ambiguity of purpose than for any other reason.[2] An ingrown church asks, *What functions should we perform that fit our existing structure and organization?* In contrast, the purpose-driven church is driven by the question, *What structure will best enable us to carry out our purposes?*

PRIORITIES: FIRST THINGS FIRST

A purpose statement unifies church members, motivates them, gives direction, and generates driving power and energy. The number one task of leadership is to clarify and communicate the purpose and vision of the church.

A statement of purpose is not just a hoped-for target; it is the church's reason for being and the foundation for healthy ministry programs. When churches stray from being purpose-driven, they slip into becoming centered around the problems of people, program and property.

People-Centered

Traditional churches that focus primarily on people or social issues lose members. Less traditional churches that allow their members to decide the church's agenda likewise do not grow.

A seasoned pastor told me with candor, "For the past five years, my priorities have been wrong. I thought that the most important role of the pastor was to teach and counsel. Instead of leading the church to carry out Christ's purpose, I have been consumed with counseling neurotic people. I've made people my first priority and I've ended up with a neurotic, problem-centered church." Fortunately, this pastor decided to refocus his priorities.

People matter to God, but they're not the first priority of the high-impact church. The most important question for a church is not, *What do people want?* but, *What does Christ want to have happen in people's lives?* Only as Christians claim Christ's purpose for the church will ministry be in accord with His will.

Program-Centered

Many churches are program-centered, relying primarily on their activities and traditions. These churches become time and culture-bound and lose their relevance in contemporary society. They are program-centered, without the flexibility and ability to adapt to changing cultural situations.

Such churches become so fixed in their ways that they become relics of the past—irrelevant guardians of the status quo! This will happen to every church that makes program rather than purpose its priority.

To counter this program-centered inertia, the question must continually be asked, *What kinds of programs will best help us accomplish Christ's purpose in the lives of our people?*

Property-Centered

Many churches are dominated by property issues. Because it is a large budget item, property can consume a majority of leadership efforts for fund-raising. Through the ages, the church has erroneously been identified with its buildings.

There are seasons in a church's growth when significant attention must be given to the church's facilities, but not at the expense of purpose. One pastor friend undergoing a church relocation due to the need for expanded facilities expressed his frustration over the attention this demanded of him saying, "I should have gotten an M.B.A., a realtor's license, and been a contractor. I'd be better prepared for the demands of the pastorate." Even when the need is legitimate, it is easy to get sidetracked by property.

The most important question to ask about property is, *What kind of property do we need to facilitate our programs designed to carry out*

Christ's purpose in people's lives? The issue is not architecture of the building, but how it suits needs. Buildings are tools, not temples. They are a means to an end, not an end in themselves.

Problem-Centered

Churches commonly become focused on their problems. Problems are inevitable and can be expected in every area (people, programs and property) of a church's life. It is necessary to deal with problems, but the focus and energy of the church cannot be diverted from carrying out its purpose.

Churches that become people-, program- or property-centered, or focused on problems, eventually lose their direction and vitality. The antidote is to remain purpose-centered in Christ.

DISCOVERING THE PURPOSE OF THE CHURCH

The first step in starting a new church is to *define* its purpose. The first step in revitalizing a church is to *redefine* its purpose. Both beginning and renewing the church means agreeing with the purpose Christ revealed in Scripture—to follow the biblical passages about the church.

Scriptures teach that the church—those who follow Christ—have been chosen as Christ's instrument to manifest His glorious life and carry out His mission of reconciling the world to Himself. God's glory is revealed through Christ in His people.[3]

Many churches have only a limited understanding of the church's purpose. At Lausanne II, an international congress held in Manila in 1989, I was fascinated by contrasting perceptions of the church's purpose.

Dr. Robert Schuller, pastor of the large Crystal Cathedral in Garden Grove, California, began a workshop by proclaiming that the number one purpose of the church is "a mission station to reach the lost." At this same conference, Jack Hayford, pastor of Church on the Way in Van Nuys, California, opened another session with the statement that the church's number one priority is "the worship of God."

Which statement is true? Both! At the same time, however, each is incomplete.

Biblically, four things are highlighted as Christ's purpose for His church: worship, fellowship, nurture and evangelism. Not all churches see these as equally important. Many churches emphasize one or another of these purposes, ignoring or de-emphasizing the others. Leadership in one church insists that the primary purpose should be worship, in another that it should be Christian education, still another fellowship, and so on.

Many times these conceptions are subconscious impressions that come from past church experience. They become unconscious standards that Christians use to measure the orthodoxy of others. Church splits often occur when leaders and members do not understand that the purpose of the church is multi-faceted.

> **It is a mistake to assume that church members or staff understand an unstated purpose for the church.... Over and over, the church must reclaim its purpose.**

In Scripture, the overarching purpose of the church is to glorify God. But Christ also revealed several other specific purposes for His church. Worship, fellowship, nurture and evangelism are all biblical and important ingredients for the church. Each characteristic is honored in a church that glorifies God.

It is a mistake to assume that church members or staff understand an unstated purpose for the church. Mobility in Western society and large turnover rates mean that purpose must be continually clarified. Over and over, the church must reclaim its purpose.

ELABORATING THE CHURCH'S PURPOSE

The purpose of the church needs to be meaningful and challenging to modern Western culture. British theologian John Stott, in an exegesis of Acts 2:42-47, lists the four primary characteristics of a vital church:

- Worship that expresses the reality of the living God and joyfully celebrates Christ's victory over sin and death.
- Preaching and teaching that faithfully expounds the Word of God while relating to the burning issues of the day and to the pressing needs of people.
- Caring and supportive relationships between individuals, Christ and one another.
- Outreach into the surrounding community that is imaginative, sensitive and compassionate.[4]

A clearly stated, relevant, challenging purpose of the church allows both leadership and members to easily develop a strategy and plan that effectively carries out their purpose. The statement will be broken into measurable and achievable goals. While a mission statement may seem trite to some, it does help people remember the church's purpose and relate themselves to it.

A good purpose statement needs to be specific about each targeted thrust of the church. The Crossroads International Church of Amsterdam, a church planted by Christian Associates International, alliterates its purpose statement in many ways so that members become familiar with the church's mission. The primary purposes of the Crossroads are: Exalt, Establish, Equip and Extend.

These four purposes stand out on banners hung high above the platform to remind people as they celebrate in worship. The purposes are further elaborated in the church's literature and are the basis of instructing members. Each repetition reinforces what the church is all about.

The Crossroads International Church exists to:

1. **EXALT** God the Father, Son and Holy Spirit through:
   a. Praise, prayer, worship and celebration of God's glory, holiness, truth, beauty and love.
   b. Communion with Jesus Christ as the loving, powerful Savior, Lord and King.
   c. Oneness and praise created by the presence of the Holy Spirit and expressed corporately through the Spirit's fruit and gifts.

2. **ESTABLISH** a caring community of believers through:
    a. Encouraging an environment of love, acceptance and forgiveness.
    b. The development of warm, caring and supportive relationships.
    c. Service and sacrifice to meet each other's needs.

3. **EQUIP** believers for effective ministry through:
    a. Preaching and teaching that faithfully expounds the Word of God while relating to the issues of the day and the need of the people (as per Stott above).
    b. Teaching, discovery, recognition, development and use of the gifts of the Spirit by each believer.
    c. Ministry training and equipping believers to know Christ's will, to experience Christ's power and to do Christ's works.

4. **EXTEND** the Good News of Christ to the world through:
    a. Outreach into the surrounding community that is imaginative, sensitive and compassionate using creative forms of evangelism and communication, proclaiming that people should repent, confess Christ, put their trust in God through Him, accept Him as Savior and serve Him as their King in the fellowship of His Church.
    b. Concern for the whole person by ministering to emotional, physical, social and spiritual needs and bringing them to wholeness within our community.
    c. Commitment to church planting and the revitalizing of the church throughout the world.

It is helpful to sum up the purpose statement in a single phrase, something that people can easily remember. The purpose of the large Saddleback Valley Community Church of Mission Viejo, California, appears each week on the church's bulletin: "A great commitment to the Great Commandment and the Great Commission." Members and visitors alike are aware of the goal of the church.

Statements like the above provide a framework to help churches remain focused and purpose-centered. However stated, these four elements — worship, fellowship, nurture and evangelism — are the critical to a church that glorifies God. They are mandates for all believers. The high-impact church keeps these purposes before its people, enlisting the members of the body in activities to match the goals.

A DEEPER LOOK INTO THE CHURCH'S PURPOSE

Worship/Celebration

A comprehensive definition of worship is found in Archbishop William Temple's *Readings in St. John's Gospel*. Temple defines worship as:

> The submission of all our nature to God. It is the quickening of conscience by His holiness, the nourishment of the mind with His truth, the purifying of imaginations with His beauty, the opening of the heart to His love, the surrender of the will to His purpose — and all this gathered up in adoration, the most selfless emotion of which our nature is capable and therefore the chief remedy to that self-centeredness which is our original sin.[5]

Worship acknowledges that God is the all powerful Creator and Sustainer of all things, that Jesus is the King of kings and Lord of lords and that the Holy Spirit is the Comforter, Teacher and Guide. Worship allows us to experience intimacy with God as our loving Father, with Jesus as our Brother and Friend and the Spirit as the One who empowers us and guides us into all truth.

One of the main objectives in worship is to draw people into a more intimate relationship with God. This intimacy is the heart of being a Christian. God draws near to believers as they draw near to Him in worship and devotion. This results in a deep sense of spiritual nourishment, healing and wholeness.[6]

Often a sense of closeness to God will accompany or be accompanied by physical expressions in worship. Clapping, lifting hands, bowing down, praising, shouting and dancing are all biblical expressions of worship. Unfortunately, this kind of enthusiasm is virtually nonexistent in many American and European worship services.[7] Western Christianity has equated expressiveness with emotionalism, leaving an overemphasis on the cerebral dimension of the Christian faith. The same enthusiasm expressed in other social settings (e.g., sporting events) is restrained in worship.

Expressiveness in corporate gatherings of the church may threaten some but have the effect of enlivening an otherwise dull service and drawing people closer to God. The widespread influence of Pentecostal and charismatic churches has helped people to more easily accept outward expressions of inner faith.

The degree of expressiveness and appropriateness of expression will depend upon the purpose of the service, who is being ministered to and who is doing the ministering. When the Body of Christ gathers together for worship, all things are to be done decently and in order and are to be subject to the leadership of the church. Setting guidelines based on Scripture helps minimize attention-seekers, extremes and the inappropriate — but encountering God in worship frequently leads to expression of emotion.

Personal encounters with God are one of the most powerful means God uses to transform and heal us. When we experience His presence or some aspect of His character, we no longer perceive Him as some distant God or abstract idea; He is real, living, powerful and near.

Worship in the high-impact church engages the cognitive, emotional, volitional and spiritual. It is intelligent, creative and inspirational. Jesus said that God the Father seeks worshippers who come to Him in spirit and in truth.

Fellowship/Caring

A second facet of the purpose of the church is fellowship. Christian fellowship (or community) is essential to strengthen believers and assure the success of the church's mission. The regular gathering of believers is necessary for Christians to grow and be spiritually nurtured. Hebrews 10:24-25 admonishes Christians not to forsake the assembling of ourselves together (as the manner of some), but consider ways to stimulate one another to brotherly love and right conduct.

The term *koinonia* is used both to describe the intimate relationship that we have with God through Christ and to describe the reciprocal relationship we have with one another as members of the Christian community.[8] The concept of *koinonia* is fundamental to the caring function of the church.

> ***Koinonia* answers the heart cry of today's men and women living in an impersonal society.**

A conscious experience of community (*koinonia*) is especially needed in today's society where people are lonely and alienated. Western society has severed individuals from their natural inter-relationships of family and neighborhood. Urbanites frequently move from place to place, job to job, acquaintance to acquaintance, and often from mate to mate with minimal commitment.

Building relationships, ministering to one another with spiritual gifts, meeting practical needs, and establishing caring, loving, healing fellowships are all part of being the people of God. *Koinonia* answers the heart cry of today's men and women living in modern, secular, individualistic, and—more often than not—impersonal society.

The caring Body of Christ is the opposite of the prevailing individualism and fragmentation of Western society. The church's cell group structure encourages the kind of fellowship, community and caring that Christ intends for His Body. (Cell groups are explained in a later chapter.)

Nurture/Training

A third facet of the purpose of the church is nurture—discipleship of believers. The word *disciple* is used 233 times in the Gospels, 30 times in the Book of Acts, but never in the Epistles. Instead, the terms *saint, brother, servant* and *witness* are used in the Epistles to identify followers of Christ.

Saint points to the new character of the disciple—that a disciple has a new relationship with God. *Brother* points to the new redeemed communal relationship of discipleship—that a disciple has a new relationship to other Christians. *Servant* points to the new motivation of discipleship—that a disciple has a new motivation to serve Christ instead of him or herself. *Witness* points to the missionary responsibility of disciples—that a disciple has a new relationship to the world. The shift from the use of the word *disciple* in the Gospels to the terms *saint, brother, servant* and *witness* in the Epistles indicates that the early church saw discipleship as a multi-dimensional, church-based corporate activity.

God's primary agent of discipleship is the church—from leading people to Christ, to developing Christ-like character, to restoring relationships, to serving Christ, to witnessing for Christ. Both cell groups and larger gatherings of Christians are important dimensions of nurture and discipleship. Large gatherings provide celebration, teaching, inspiration and unity and have an impact on the surrounding community. The small group, however, is the primary place where believers are nurtured, discipled, equipped and given opportunities to minister.

Evangelism/Outreach

The fourth facet of the church's purpose is evangelism. Evangelism is "to so present Christ in the power of the Holy Spirit that men come to put their trust in God through Him, accept Him as Savior, and serve Him as King in the fellowship of His church."[9] God wants the lost found, saved and incorporated as responsible members of His church.

When a passion to find the lost is missing, the church is no longer true to its purpose. A missionary spirit longs for the lost to be found, assimilated into Christ's Body, and for believers to grow and use their spiritual gifts.

God is a missionary God. Just as the Father sent the Son to find the lost, so the Son sends His church. In mission, the church discovers her God-given nature. If the church fails her missionary obligations, she is no longer a living church.

Missionary work is not just a church activity, but the impetus for all outreach. The church is called to be a witness and to summon the whole world to faith in Christ.[10] The people of God are called to be together, but they are also called to go outward in mission.

The church is called by God to carry out Christ's purpose of advancing His kingdom on earth. It is called to profess Jesus as the Christ, obey His commands and preach the gospel throughout the world. Mission includes evangelism, discipleship, church growth and social service.

FROM PURPOSE TO VISION

The high-impact church is not only purpose-centered; it is vision-centered. The clearly articulated purpose of the church needs a vision statement that more specifically defines the unique ministry and tasks of that church and the means to accomplish them. Purpose asks, *Why do we exist?*; vision asks, *What needs do we feel deeply burdened about and uniquely qualified to meet?*[11]

Author George Barna defines vision as "a clear mental picture of a preferable future, imparted by God to His chosen servants, based upon an accurate understanding of God, self and circumstances."[12] Purpose plus today's world equals mission; purpose plus tomorrow's world equals vision. The distinction between purpose and vision is like the difference between the tracks of a railroad and the destination of the train. Purpose is what guides us along the path and vision is where we are headed.

Vision + Today's World = MISSION!

Vision + Tomorrow's World = VISION!

Vision distinguishes a strong church from a weak one. Every successful organization has a shared sense of direction unifying the members of the organization. For a church to impact society and reach the city, it must have both a clear purpose and a clear vision.[13]

My friend Barney Hamady, pastor of Bethany Church of Sierra Madre, California, quotes Helen Keller who wrote that there is only one thing worse than being blind, "...being able to see, but having no vision." Hamady's conviction is that vision demands a certain boldness from us and calls forth a lively courage that is faith induced. It requires that we truly trust God with our futures.

Hamady's bold vision for Bethany Church hangs on a plaque in his office and reads:

> GOD HAS CALLED BETHANY TO BE CULTURALLY RELEVANT IN THE APPLICATION OF TIMELESS, SCRIPTURAL TRUTH IN ORDER TO REACH SECU-LAR, UNREACHED PEOPLE, THEN DISCIPLE AND UNLEASH THEM TO FULFILL THE GREAT COM-MISSION LOCALLY AND GLOBALLY.[14]

Fellowship Bible Church of Park Cities in Dallas, Texas, is another church that is purpose- and vision-centered. The church defines its purpose as:

- *Celebration* — gathering together to praise God.
- *Caring* — biblical instruction, serving each other, and building supportive relationships.
- *Communication* — spreading the Good News about Jesus and taking His compassion to the world.

However, Fellowship Bible Church's pastor, Bill Counts, realized that his church needed a vision statement that was more specific than its purpose statement in order to reach its cultural target group. So, the church adopted a specific statement of vision:

> To reach out to people through a contemporary style of ministry, to help them restore an authentic relationship with God through the healing love of Jesus Christ, to enable them to relate to each other in Christian community and small groups and to release them to serve others through using their God-given abilities.

This large Dallas church targets young professionals in the North Dallas metropolitan area who are not being attracted by other evangelical churches. The vision of the church drives its strategy and contemporary style of music, messages, ministry and organization.

Now, more than 1,500 of these people have been attracted to the culturally–appropriate ministry of Fellowship Bible Church.

REACH THE CITY!

Pastor Rich Marshall of the Community Church at Foothill in Los Altos, California, has a target of reaching the entire Santa Clarita Valley of which Los Altos is a part. Marshall says, "The average pastor's vision is to fill his building, my vision is to reach the city."

Marshall's strategy to accomplish this is to plant churches through the Santa Clarita Valley where members know how to share their faith, have an area of service, participate in a small group where there is accountability and co-ministry, support the church through prayer and giving, and regularly attend the celebration service.

Fellowship Bible Church of Dublin, Ireland, is another church with a clear vision to reach its city. FBC was set up in 1977 with a vision to see "new communities of God's people set up in every neighborhood of our city and townland as models of the coming kingdom, making Jesus visible and displaying His character and loveliness to all around." FBC's strategy includes Home Groups (the principle caring units of the Fellowship), Ministry Groups (where men and women are trained and equipped for the specific ministry tasks of evangelism, worship, children's work and social action), Congregations (larger gatherings which meet each Sunday for worship, prayer and teaching) and Celebrations (held once a month to praise God in a large venue).

Each of the churches above is vision-directed. The church with keen purpose and vision is on the way to becoming a high-impact church. The high-impact church has a multi-faceted purpose to glorify God through worship, fellowship, nurture and evangelism — and a targeted, specific vision to reach the city.

PART III

THE SUBSTANCE OF THE HIGH-IMPACT CHURCH

Mobilized Ministry of Believers

10

STRATEGIC STEPS TO REACH THE CITY

Listen! The Lord is calling to the city....
—Micah 6:9

UNDERSTAND THE CITY'S DIVERSITY

I n 1800 only 2.4 percent of the world's population lived in cities. But by the year 2025, 60 percent of the world's 8 billion people will likely be urban dwellers. As masses of people move to the city, the church's mission of reaching the unchurched is an ever greater challenge.

To win the city, we must understand its diversity. A common culture has given way to multiple subcultures. Cities are made up of diverse subcultures that have different interests and life circumstances. Cities are pluralistic societies with teeming multitudes of peoples, cultures and languages. People from vastly different places live close together. Not only are people diversified in ethnicity and language, but also in life-style and life-stage.

The world-wide phenomenon of internationalization now impacts every major city in the West. Oslo, Norway, has 116 different people groups. The 11 million residents of Paris include one million immigrants. Amsterdam, The Netherlands, a city of approximately 800,000 people, has 115 different nationalities, including 44 different ethnic neighborhoods.[1]

Los Angeles may well be today's most prodigious example of internationalization. The Los Angeles Times predicted that L.A. will become the "ethnic salad bowl of 21st-Century America." Already this teeming cosmopolitan city is home to more people of Mexican descent than any other city outside Mexico, more Koreans than any other city outside Asia, and more Filipinos than any city outside the Philippines. Minorities in L.A. are collectively the majority of the population: 33 percent Latino, 15 percent Black and 10 percent Asian-American. Whites comprise only 41 percent of the population.[2]

> **Cities are made up of diverse subcultures that have different interests and life circumstances.**

The world seems to shrink as people from many nations flock to big cities. This urbanization is a tremendous opportunity for the advance of the gospel. At the Crossroads International Church in Amsterdam, we have noted as many as thirty nationalities at one Sunday service.

In past decades, people in rural areas or small towns (in the Western world) looked to the church as the socially integrating vortex of community life. For many living in big cities, that is no longer true. As multiple cultures blend, people tend to become more eclectic. They begin to question the validity or necessity of previous patterns and let go of old cultural and religious practices. This cultural metamorphosis is especially true for second and third generation immigrants who integrate into mainstream culture.

Mobile Western society causes people to be uprooted — disconnected from a traditional framework of friends, family and faith. They often leave behind cultural and religious patterns as they become engulfed in the demands of economic survival. This is both good news and bad news. The bad news is that many leave behind their faith; the good news is that displaced persons are usually receptive to a fresh presentation of Christianity.

BREAK THE CITY INTO SUBGROUPS

Bodies of believers that relate the gospel in culturally relevant ways are needed to fulfill the Great Commission. Jesus commanded His followers to make disciples of "all peoples."[3] "All peoples" includes the multiple subcultures in the megalopolises in the Western world.

The pluralistic diversity of cities demands a different approach to evangelism and ministry than in more homogeneous small towns and rural areas. For the church to reach the city, it must carefully design strategies to reach diverse subcultures.

A subculture is a group of people bound together by a similar world view. Common values, codes, behaviors and perceived needs produce a unique group identity. The church needs to penetrate each segment of society and express God's truth in ways that make sense to the subculture it is trying to reach.

PENETRATE SUBCULTURES; DON'T BECOME ONE

Instead of penetrating city subgroups with the love of God, many churches have themselves become subcultures, separating themselves from the very people God has called them to reach.

Church subcultures develop distinct vocabularies, standards of dress and social behavior that mark members from surrounding subcultures. Many Christians tenaciously hold to standards not mandated by Scripture. Superficial expectations of ingrown churches can cause Christians to confuse cultural choices with Biblical norms.

Many believers are so involved in Christian activities that they have lost touch with non-Christians around them. This unintentionally happens in some churches; in others, it is deliberate elitism. The latter are fearful of losing their subcultural identity. They are comfortable with their traditional forms and styles, so they resist change and contact with the unchurched.

My friend Asbjörn was hired by his church to disciple Christian young people and to evangelize youth in the community. Asbjörn was effective at both. He led Bible studies and prayer times for the Christians and organized fun-filled activities that attracted non-Christians. However, Christian parents feared that having contact with non-Christian youth was a negative influence on their children.

Traditional Church

The church is called to reach Subgroup A and Subgroup B, but instead it often becomes its own subgroup ("C"), characterized by a culture that separates itself from the groups it is called to reach.

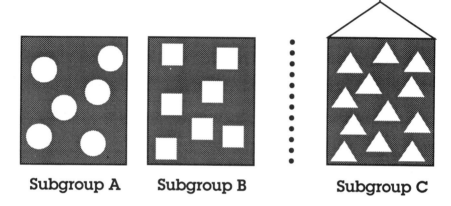

Subgroup A   Subgroup B   Subgroup C

The High-Impact Church

The high-impact church responds to God's calling by serving as salt and light within the networks of friends, relatives, neighbors and colleagues. It penetrates subgroups rather than becoming a subculture of its own.

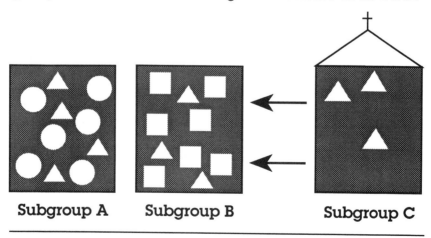

Subgroup A   Subgroup B   Subgroup C

The Christian subculture prevailed on Asbjörn to curtail outreach activities.

In many ways, churches can become more concerned with preserving cultural values than reaching surrounding subcultures. In one church, a proposed change to a modern translation of the Bible was delayed for years because a major donor in the church objected. The wealthy donor insisted that pew copies of the King James Bibles (she had donated) could not be replaced during her life time. The church was forced to wait until she died (of natural causes!) to use other translations.

PICK A TARGET

While the high-impact church desires to reach as many subcultures as possible, to be effective it must begin by targeting a primary subculture and design a culturally relevant strategy for that group. Various subcultures overlap with cultural similarities, so several subcultures within a city may have enough in common to make them responsive to a single church strategy.[4]

When Christian Associates International founded the Crossroads Evangelical Church of Ferney Voltaire, France (a suburb of Geneva, Switzerland), it selected English-speaking internationals as its primary target group because of the strategic potential of the multinational composition. The Crossroads, however, has attracted people from a variety of cultures. As many as 40 different nationalities are now part of this church.

The majority come from Western Europe and North America, but a growing number of Africans, Asians and Latin Americans educated in Europe and North America are also members. Most work for international organizations and multinational corporations in the greater Geneva area. They are well educated, cosmopolitan business and professional people and students who have been influenced by modern, secular Western culture.

The primary ingredient these nationalities have in common is the desire to speak English. Even when English is their second or third language, they believe it's very important for them (and for their children) to learn. Because of this common ingredient, people of various cultures respond to the Crossroads strategy.

HOW DO YOU DEFINE THE TARGET?

Select a target group by defining a city in terms of its geography, demographics, culture and spiritual makeup.

Geography

Determine the make-up of those persons living within one, three and five mile radii of the church. *Where does the target group live?* Most urbanites consider travel time, not distance, when choosing a church. Another question to ask is, *What percentage of the target group attends any church?* In most Western cities, even those who claim church affiliation do not attend church regularly and are candidates for outreach.

The effective urban church understands that the customs of neighborhood churches are but a legacy of the former rural life. In villages and small towns there was a neighborhood consciousness — people lived and worked and spent their leisure time together. Public and private spheres of society merged as did different generations and people with various professions and trades. Today, many outdated programs and practices found in urban churches are leftovers from the heritage of neighborhood churches.[5]

The high-impact church assesses its calling with a regional viewpoint. Churches that want to impact their geographical area will discard the parochial mind-set and look at the city regionally.[6] City dwellers do not see their residential neighborhood as the primary focus of their social identity. Urbanites are accustomed to travel and have wide networking relationships. Public transportation and the abundance of automobiles have made mobility a way of life, thus reducing the appeal of the small neighborhood church.

Demographics

Define people by ethnic group, age breakdown, marital and family status, income bracket, education and occupation. This information can be gathered from census bureaus, libraries and city planning offices.

In most cities, social networks often supercede geographical boundaries.[7] The church needs to analyze the constituency of persons living in a geographical area. Who does the church want to target — the majority ethnic group or a minority one? Is there a broad age spectrum or a narrow one? If a particular church tries to reach everyone, it may not reach anyone. To be effective, a church needs a specific strategy that addresses the unique needs of a targeted group.

Culture

A high-impact urban church understands the life-styles, values, fears, interests and mind-set of the unchurched. Knowing what captures the attention of various cultural groups enables a church to minister effectively.

Cities are made up of "life-style enclaves" — fragments of society that maintain similarity. Urban people usually relate to those who share their life-style and status and distance themselves from others.[8] The church needs a strategy to reach these various enclaves.

The Church Information and Development Services has developed a Vision Area Profile classifying the U.S. population into 50 life-style groups — such as White Picket Fence, Metro-Ethnic Mix, Good Family Life, Successful Singles, etc. Each group has a descriptive name and a summary of characteristics.[9]

Spiritual Make Up

What does the target group understand about God and the gospel? All people are not at the same place spiritually; they need to be met where they are.

AIM YOUR STYLE AT YOUR TARGET

Once a church selects and defines a primary target group, the next step is to develop a strategy of ministry that fits the group's cultural patterns. The styles of worship, music, preaching, leadership and programs need to be culturally contextualized to fit the targeted unchurched.

Too many churches are inflexibly locked into patterns and behaviors that do not contribute to the church's calling to make disciples of all people groups. To reach the diverse subgroups of the city, the patterns, forms, style and structure of the church must be culturally relevant. Only then can the church effectively reach the unchurched, assimilate them into fellowship and lead them to Christian maturity.

The way evangelism is developed in a church is especially important. Urban people are more open to developing relationships than being part of a social or religious institution. Thus, in big cities, relation-centered evangelism works better than an institution-centered approach.

Urbanites are wary of strangers and protect themselves from superficial and manipulative relationships. They want high quality and long lasting friendships.[10] Thus, door-to-door visitation is largely ineffective.

Urban people are less friendly to strangers than are people in villages and in farming communities. To prevent psychological overload and reduce the constant bombardment of sales messages, urbanites are more selective in their relationships.[11] In the city, the church needs a contextual approach to evangelism that encourages friendships.

The Crossroads Evangelical Church of Geneva has effectively reached a diverse international community because its evangelism program is non-confrontational. The friendship approach is accepted by Geneva's international business and professional community—where most people are wary of strangers and a hard-sell approach.

The Crossroads' low-key evangelism allows people to develop relationships and become involved in activities before they are asked to make a profession of faith. (Leadership, however, is reserved for committed Christians.) This tactic contrasts with churches that require theological conformity before a newcomer is integrated into church activities.

Gary Edmonds, the Crossroads' pastor, explains that Jesus is the church's model for evangelism: "The disciples did not have all the answers before following Christ. They followed, then got the answers." A Crossroads' convert revealed the effectiveness of this practice when he commented, "You evangelized us by not evangelizing us. You included us."

KEY ON NETWORKS

Once a subgroup is targeted, the next step to reaching the city is to realize that every subculture is made up of multiple networks. Three types of networks are geographical, social and personal. The high-impact church develops a strategy to reach each of these networks with the gospel. Ichthus Christian Fellowship targets the geographical boroughs of London with a cell multiplying strategy designed to win the city to Christ (see Chapter 12).

Social networks can be targeted by encouraging Christians to establish a presence in the various social organizations that bring people together. Several women in the Crossroads International Church of Amsterdam attend the American Women's Club regularly and have developed friendships resulting in entire families coming to Christ and becoming a part of the church.

> **Social networks or "households" undergirded the explosive growth of the early church.**

The most effective strategy to reach a city is to train Christians to reach their personal networks. Most people have a personal network of 20-30 people they regularly relate to and trust. Family, neighbors, friends and associates form an interlocking social system. In the city, networks are predominantly made up of friends and associates exclusive to a life-style enclave.

Social networks or "households" (the Greek biblical term *oikos*) undergirded the explosive growth of the early church. Jesus commanded new believers to return to their "households" (network of family and friends) to tell them the Good News. The same principle is seen in the Apostle Paul's ministry when the households of Lydia and the Philippian jailer became believers and were added to the church.[12]

These networks are what the late Donald McGavran of the Church Growth Movement at Fuller Seminary called "the bridges of God." The church needs a strategy to encourage believers to develop positive relationships with the unchurched in their network of family and friends. It is unfortunate when Christians avoid or isolate themselves from the non-Christians around them.

One of the bridges of God in my own life was the relationship with my father-in-law. Six months after my conversion I had a chance to share the gospel with him as he witnessed the changes that Christ was making in my life. New Christ-like attitudes were evident in my relationship with his daughter—my wife, Sharon.

My father-in-law had resented the way I had treated Sharon and I'd been alienated from his friendship. But Sharon (and her mother and grandmother) had been praying for both of us to become Christians. I knew the bridge was open when he said, "If Christ can change Linus, He can change anyone." Because of this, Sharon's father was receptive and received Christ.

DIFFERENTIATE TYPE A AND TYPE B UNBELIEVERS

Strategies to reach unchurched urban dwellers must differentiate between "Type A" and "Type B" unbelievers. Author Ralph Neighbour classifies unbelievers into two categories—those who are "near" (Type A) and those who are "far" (Type B) from salvation.[13] Those who are near to salvation are open to the truth about Christ in Scripture; those who are far away are negative or ignorant of the gospel message.

These two types of unbelievers must be approached differently. The Type A unbeliever already believes in God, accepts the Bible, understands that Jesus is the Son of God, and has some understanding of biblical facts like the death and Resurrection of Christ. These may be church members who have been inactive, or people who have just never understood the need for personal commitment. Type A unbelievers are open to attending a church-sponsored event such as a Sunday service, Bible study or discussion group.

Alan and Lorna, a Scottish couple, occasionally attended church before moving to Amsterdam. They considered themselves Christians, but their faith was nominal. As Type A unbelievers, they were not opposed or resistant to the gospel. After a community survey, Alan and Lorna began attending church and a cell group. In the small group they learned how the gospel related to them personally. After several weeks, this couple opened their lives to Christ.

Type B unbelievers are much more difficult to reach. They seldom attend church and have little or no desire to do so. They do not believe in God, Christ or the Bible. They have little interest in attending a church-sponsored event, Bible study or discussion group.

I recently met a Type B person who spoke of the church's "medieval language, music and bureaucracy" and went on to describe the church as "disciplinarian, intolerant, hypocritical, persecuting and self righteous." In light of his negative attitude, I thought it unwise to invite him to attend church until we were better acquainted.

Most Type B unbelievers have little awareness of the gospel. Instead, they are steeped in secular or non-Christian beliefs. Other Type B unbelievers may have heard the gospel, but are not receptive because of their distorted concept of Christianity. Still, others might be receptive to the Good News of Christ, but they have not encountered vital Christianity.

The key to reaching both Type A and Type B unbelievers with the gospel is first to build relationships and then to meet felt needs. Type A unbelievers are easily reached through cell groups and fellowship events. Type B unbelievers can be reached through visitor-friendly events, and discussion groups. The latter require more time and patience.

DESIGN FELT-NEED MINISTRIES

Felt-need groups are the church's "root system" allowing it to penetrate the world around it.[14] The more a church can identify and minister to felt needs, the more effective its outreach will be. Understanding felt needs contextualizes ministry and connects the believers with the interests and life stages of unbelievers. While felt need groups begin with a focus on a common interest, they ultimately move to deeper spiritual needs as well.

Unbelievers in cities have many needs. Urban people hunger for security, significance, belonging and meaningful relationships. Ministering to these needs shows that the gospel is relevant to the urban dweller.

Alan and Lorna were reached because of their felt need to identify with other Christians and learn more about Christianity. The felt need ministry aimed at these Type A unbelievers was a home fellowship group (cell group) with a series of discussions designed for seekers to consider the basis of belief in God, the Bible and Jesus Christ.

Social issues are another area of felt-need ministry. These include helping refugees, providing counseling and feeding the poor. Also, special life-situation ministries like divorce recovery, substance abuse support groups, outreaches to the homeless and crisis pregnancy care meet felt needs.[15] Social scars due to poverty, crime, violence, drug and alcohol abuse, prostitution, joblessness and family breakdown are openings for the love of Christ and the power of the gospel to touch lives in both urban and suburban areas.[16]

> **The more a church can identify and minister to felt needs, the more effective its outreach will be.**

Mike Breen began his new role as vicar of All Saints Church, Brixton Hill by talking and listening to the people of his community. Soon after arriving, along with some of the church members, Breen surveyed the area to know what was happening locally as a prelude to evangelism. People were asked to name the three best things and the three worst things about the community. This revealed a surprising need. The worst thing which polled the most votes was the litter and rubbish on the streets. All Saints responded by organizing "praise and litter" marches to clean up the rubbish. This led to opportunities to talk with people about the kingdom of God.

Another major problem that the Brixton Hill survey revealed was housing. All Saints took constructive action by organizing a "care and repair" program to help people in the community with household repairs and decorating. A care and repair team leader organized a small team of helpers who set about to meet needs they knew existed among the friends, neighbors and families of the congregation, prioritizing the elderly and single parents.

This very practical demonstration of the church's concern for the needs of the community is a reflection of Breen's "theology of incarnation." God sent His Son Jesus to identify with us and demonstrate His love for us in order to complete the rescue plan that would save us and draw us back to Him.[17] When we address the needs of people, we open a window for them to understand that God cares for them and that knowing Christ makes a difference.

Felt-need ministry groups are effective in reaching both Type A and Type B unbelievers. Special seminars can also be used as an effective response to the felt needs of contemporary urban people. For example, special seminars can be offered to help people strengthen marriages and relationships, manage finances, develop parental skills and explore the reasons for faith in God.

The Crossroads International Church of Amsterdam has successfully used a felt-need communication seminar to reach out to couples in the Netherlands. Many Dutch are fluent in English and have married English-speaking mates. While the Dutch culture has much in common with other Western English-speaking cultures, there are significant differences bringing tension and strain.

An interest in better communication skills brought Charlie and Claudia into contact with the church. Both Type B unbelievers, they have become our good friends. Instead of urging them to attend Sunday morning celebrations at the Crossroads, we, along with other members of the church, reached out to them at a point of their felt need.

We invited Charlie and Claudia to attend a six-week couples communication seminar. They were grateful for their new skills and new friendships. In fact, when the class ended, it was they who suggested the group continue to stay in touch to encourage one another.

Although they were not immediately responsive to the message of Salvation, they were receptive to the messengers. Claudia has since warmed up to the message, and Charlie is not as defensive as he first was. We believe that meeting the felt needs of this couple provided a groundwork for the gospel.

The Crossroads Evangelical Church of Geneva also emphasizes meeting needs to reach its target group. Such ministries as "mothers of toddlers" groups, aerobics classes, children's programs, junior-high and high-school activities, support groups and counseling services are offered that appeal to the different needs of the diverse cultural subgroups of that church.

Felt-need preaching also effectively reaches the unchurched. The Crossroads pastoral team focuses on addressing the tensions, pressures, loneliness and alienation that characterize the international community living abroad. Preaching and teaching themes are life-related and applicable to the needs of ex-patriots living under pressure. One grateful church member declared, "Most of us were taught that the church needed us. As we've moved around the world, we've come to realize that we need the church."

HOW DO YOU START A FELT-NEED MINISTRY?

The felt-need ministry must begin, of course, by determining what the felt needs of the unchurched are. Before beginning specific groups, it is important to find out whether the group will attract healthy or hurting unbelievers. Will participants be in crisis and struggling with deep problems, or will they be healthy and interested in relationships based on a common interest? Both kinds of ministries are needed. However, in a new church it may be wiser to focus on reaching relatively healthy, stable persons who, when evangelized, can strengthen the church so it will be able to target the acute needs of prisoners, substance abusers, the homeless, etc.).

When a felt need is defined, the ministry should not be started without a motivated and capable leader. An aborted program due to inadequate leadership leaves everyone more frustrated and disappointed than before the group was launched. Wait until the right person is found to initiate a quality program.

Those whose knowledge and skills match the needs of the specialized ministry make the best leaders. The church grows spontaneously when gifts are identified and used. Unfortunately, Christians are sometimes recruited without matching gifts to needs. This results in "burn-out" and frustration. Gift-based programming takes longer, but is more effective in the long run.

A felt-need ministry should have another name besides "Bible study" so it doesn't sound threatening to Type B unbelievers. The primary goal of a felt-need ministry is to build relationships and community. Once a sense of community is established, there will be greater openness to discussing spiritual things.

The mothers of toddlers program of the Crossroads International Church of Amsterdam bustles with both Christians and non-Christians. During social get-togethers, the women enjoy making crafts, studying parenting and developing relationships based on Christian principles. If the meetings were billed as Bible study, many of the non-Christians might not come.

Felt-need ministries are scheduled for a prescribed length of time. Six to eight weeks is adequate for the group to bond. Then, the group can decide whether they want to continue with a format that ponders the spiritual life.

The city is the most strategic mission field in the world today. The unreached (but reachable) masses of people living in and around cities can be won to Christ through a fresh approach to the church. In addition to revitalizing existing churches, thousands of new churches are needed as new churches are generally more motivated to penetrate metropolitan subcultures. (Church growth expert C. Peter Wagner of Fuller Seminary states that "New church planting is the single most effective evangelistic methodology known under heaven."[18])

Whether new or renewed, high-impact churches are needed that differentiate between cultural norms and biblical absolutes. The high-impact church strategy is based on penetrating the diverse cultural subgroups of cities. Once a primary target group is chosen, the church's ministry is contextualized to reach both Type A and Type B unbelievers. The key to reaching them is for Christians to build friendships with them and to relate to their felt needs. A harvest awaits those churches who use this strategy.

11

MINISTERING THROUGH CELL GROUPS

Feed my lambs...take care of my sheep.
—John 21:15-17

HOW TO GROW A CHURCH

The 600,000 members of the Yoido Full Gospel Church of Seoul, Korea—divided into more than 60,000 cell groups—have truly impacted that crowded city.

It seems simple, doesn't it? However large a church congregation wants to become, it divides that number by ten (the average size of a cell group), and that's the number of cell groups the church finally establishes. But some critics are skeptical about the cell group strategy working in Western culture. They argue that the cell group success in Korea is due to factors unique to a regimented Asian society.

PORTLAND AND LONDON: IT WORKS HERE TOO!

Dale Galloway, pastor of New Hope Community Church in Portland, Oregon, disputes the contention that successful cell groups are restricted to certain cultures. Portland is called the "most unchurched city in America."[1]

Before launching New Hope, Galloway had a clear-cut vision that the new church could attract unchurched thousands in the city of Portland.[2] Today, the church has grown to more than 6,000 members in "Tender Loving Care" groups adapted from Cho's community home cell group strategy.

Other critics have said that even though the cell group model might work in Asia and the U.S., it cannot work in Europe. In London, England, however, Ichthus Christian Fellowship has adopted a successful cell group strategy of church planting.

The high-impact church goes beyond merely *having* cell groups to *being* a cell-structured church.

First started in 1974, Ichthus has employed a "checkerboard pattern" of deliberately forming cells in targeted sections of the city and then challenging those cells to penetrate their adjacent neighborhoods.

Cell groups in each section (called boroughs) come together weekly in congregations, and all cell groups meet together monthly for a large celebration. At last count, Ichthus Christian Fellowship had 200 cell groups making up 32 congregations in London using this strategy.

The Yoido Full Gospel Church, the New Hope Community Church and Ichthus Christian Fellowship prove that the community penetrating cell group strategy is not unique to any geographical location. Cities in both East and West can be reached this way.

Cell groups are absolutely essential to the high-impact church. This goes beyond merely *having* cell groups to *being* a cell-structured church. The high-impact church is cell structured; that is, the basic organizing principle of the church is for people to be in cell groups. It is built on the premise that basic Christian community occurs in the small group. Rather than having small groups to complement the large group ministry, the large group ministry complements the small groups. It is a different way of looking at the church.

CELL GROUPS EVANGELIZE

Dr. David Yonggi Cho, pastor of the Full Gospel Church of Seoul, Korea, has a strategy to penetrate the city of Seoul. His home cell group plan for evangelism was instituted because he believes that confrontational door-to-door evangelism induces resistance and the low response rate is frustrating for witnessing Christians.[3]

Cho believes that cell group evangelism is more effective:

> When a home cell meeting is full of life, and people are happy and sharing their faith and witnessing to what the Lord has done in their lives — other people are drawn to them. Unbelievers become curious. They want to know why this little group of Christians is so joyful when all around them there are so many troubles.[4]

A cell-structured church is the most effective way to saturate the different subcultures and networks of a city. Jesus Himself sent His disciples in pairs into towns and villages with the instruction to search for a worthy person and stay in their house. They were to do kingdom work in one household at a time.[5]

The apostle Paul employed this same evangelistic strategy. He joined together with others like Barnabus and Silas, to search out responsive households as the foundation of his church planting.[6]

CELL GROUPS MAKE DISCIPLES

The best place to make disciples is within the intimacy and trust of a small group. In the cell group, newcomers can form relationships, discover gifts, meet needs, heal hurts, kindle hope and build faith. A cell-structured church provides the infrastructure for Christians to grow, be nurtured, develop leadership, and extend the kingdom of God.

The cell group ministry establishes a vital, healthy church body. The cell group infrastructure promotes maturity, nurturing, discipleship, life transformation and accountability for the believer. The intimacy of small groups encourages the development of godly character. In this context, people can discover faith, grow, and become committed to Christ's Body and to the world.

Small groups also provide practical opportunities for service. Providing food during crises, helping a family move, and offering transportation are just a few of the countless ways to minister to one another through small groups.

CELL GROUPS DECENTRALIZE PASTORAL CARE

In the high-impact church, cell groups fulfill the biblical mandate to evangelize and disciple all people. In a growing church, the pastoral staff is strained in its ability to provide primary pastoral care. A decentralized caring structure is needed to insure that everyone's needs are met. The role of the pastoral staff should shift from being the *providers* of pastoral care to *equipping* lay members to provide it.

Cell groups led by non-professional shepherds allow the church to provide care and community for every believer. Lay-pastoral care is provided as members use their gifts to minister to one another. Serious counseling needs should be referred to professional Christian counselors, but most pastoral needs can be met through cell groups.

The cell group structure is an ideal vehicle for providing the fellowship, and the caring needed to bring people to maturity in Christ. As a new believer, I attended numerous training seminars that helped me grow as a Christian. But the thing that impacted me most was coming together each week with two other new Christians to share needs, study the Bible, and pray.

My first cell group was Dennis, Tom and me — students at Oregon State University. Each of us wanted to grow as new Christians and discover ways to live out our faith in Christ. As we met together weekly, I felt a camaraderie and deep sense of acceptance that I had not had known as a non-Christian.

Dennis, Tom and I read passages of the Bible together and discussed personal applications to our lives. Our time together was life-transforming as spiritual truth became real to each of us. I also discovered the power of praying with and for others — even though one of us usually fell asleep.

Caring groups draw believers together with love and commitment for Christ and for one another. The cell group (or home church) provides a loving environment with an inward focus (mutual care, education, edification and discipline); an upward focus (worship, adoration, praise and intercession); and an outward focus (evangelism and service). The result is qualitative and quantitative growth of the Body of Christ.[7]

TYPES OF CELL GROUPS

The cell structured church organizes all of its ministries on the basis of the cell multiplying principle. Several types of cell groups are possible:

- **Geography** — People living in the same geographic area. These groups can be inter-generational or based on similar life-stage. Not everyone can be expected to be involved in geographical-based small groups. People with wide variations of personality, life-stage and expectations are not necessarily bonded just because they are neighbors.
- **Affinity** — Those who have similar interests. This is a sharing group based on similar life stages (singles, youth, children, women), or activities (sports, recreation, music).
- **Need** — Those who have similar needs (compulsions, addictions) or problems (crises, concerns).
- **Task** — Those who come together for a set period of time to accomplish a mutually agreed upon task (musicians, ushers, greeters, children's workers). Each of the ministries of the church that performs some job can organize as a cell group and carry out the essential functions of cell group ministry. Ichthus Christian Fellowship's cell multiplying strategy is task oriented.
- **Language** — Those who speak a common language. A church that wants to reach the city must plan for an ethnic minority and/or multi-lingual cell group strategy.

A high-impact church offers a variety of groups covering a wide range of interests, expectations, activities and themes. The kinds of groups depend upon the gifts and interests of cell group leaders, the needs of people and the vision of the church.

ESSENTIAL GOALS OF A CELL GROUP

All cell groups are integrated into the overall vision, strategy and leadership-training structure of the church and have four essential goals:

1. Edification

The primary goal of cell groups is edification—the building up of the members of the group. A cell group ministry is structured so that members nurture and care for one another, helping one another to grow to maturity in Christ. This is a joint ministry of all believers as they are directed by the Holy Spirit.

The cell group represents the extended family of God. Here, true community occurs. Men and women are incorporated into Christ's Body—the church—and there discover redeemed relationships with God and with others.[8] Interpersonal commitments form and people develop a sense of sharing and belonging. They also learn to minister to one another.

Cell group edification is rooted in and draws from biblical teaching. The primary purpose of the cell group, however, is not Bible study. A Bible study focus intellectualizes Scripture and externalizes faith. Cerebral groups shrivel up and die. In contrast, cell groups that emphasizes the edification of believers through *an application* of the Bible, grow. The goal of a cell group is not Bible information, but life transformation.[9]

2. Leadership development

As a high-impact church grows, more and more cell groups will be needed. Consequently, leaders must be multiplied. Leader multiplication occurs in the context of the existing cell groups. Alongside the cell group leader, each cell group should have an apprentice leader. Once trained, an apprentice takes on the role of cell group leader for a new group.

The cell group leader does not need an extensive theological background. The primary qualifications are spiritual maturity, relational strength and leadership skills. He or she should display the same qualities as those of an elder listed in 1 Timothy, Chapter 3. Cell group leaders should exhibit the fruit of the Spirit and evidence a visible life of faith.[10] They should enthusiastically participate in church outreach and ministry and complete all training for cell group ministry.

The multiplication of quality-led cell groups assures that the community surrounding a high-impact church can, indeed, be reached for Christ.

3. Evangelism

The third essential function of a cell group is evangelism. While the primary purpose of a cell group is edification, it is important that cell groups not become ingrown and preoccupied with themselves. Cell groups must remain open to newcomers and continually reach out.

To accomplish this, each group must set measurable outreach goals. In a receptive spiritual climate, it is recommended that each group have the goal of winning at least one new family or person to Christ every six to eight months.

4. Multiplication

Cell groups need multiplication goals, as well as addition goals. Cell groups multiply as they develop and send out trained leaders to start new groups. Again, assuming a receptive spiritual climate, it is recommended that each cell group have a goal of multiplying itself approximately every six to eight months.

In one church, my admonition to establish a goal to multiply cell leaders and groups was challenged by a cell group leader who argued that the goal was unrealistic. He faced some difficult personal circumstances which limited the time he could give to his group. I suggested that rather than give up the goal because of obstacles, he try to overcome the obstacles and grow into the vision—the goal of multiplication should stand. (Affirming that these goals are realistic, another cell group leader at this same meeting told how his group had multiplied three fold in a six-month period.)

Conducive circumstances and a receptive climate assist the multiplication of cell groups. More important are the faith, vision and skills of the leader. Cell leaders will go through a learning curve and as they do so their effectiveness will increase.

It is wise to start small when transitioning a non cell-structured church to a cell group ministry. Hand-pick those who are most receptive to the cell group concept and train them by gathering them together to experience cell group life. These can then start other cell groups and extend the cell ministry of the church.

The hardest part of such a transition will be getting the first wave of successful groups. Of the ten N.C.A.A. (National Collegiate Athletic Association) basketball championships that coach John Wooden achieved at the University of California at Los Angeles (no other university has come close to that record), the hardest was the first. After that initial success, players gained confidence that his coaching system would work, and more readily applied themselves to it.

HOW DO YOU FORMAT A CELL GROUP?

Prepare

Periodically, the cell group leader meets with the apprentice leader and a cell group host(s) to pray, plan and set goals. The leader delegates the responsibility for contacting persons, hosting, setting up, refreshments, and so on.

Praying for the formation of the group is critical. The success of a cell group depends on the power of God, not just human effort. The cell group leadership team intercedes for those being invited to the group.

The leadership team arrives 15-20 minutes before a cell group to pray and to make certain that everything is ready so that ministry can focus on people, not things. Arrangements are made ahead of time by the hostess for child care for young children. A greeter welcomes and introduces people. For the first few meetings, name tags may be helpful.

Share (First 10-15 minutes)

To help people get acquainted, ice-breaking questions such as telling about vocations, birthplace, size of family, favorite food or other personal trivia are helpful (one theme per meeting). As the level of trust increases in a group, people will naturally be more willing to share intimate needs and spiritual concerns.

It is good to train leaders to think of "tying shoe-laces" — connecting people together in a group. No one should be left to stand alone. A goal of each meeting should be on building friendships — encouraging everyone to feel they belong.

Clarifying where the group is going and what can be expected builds security. The cell group leader introduces the goal of cell groups: "This is a time to encourage and share Christ's love with one another by applying the Bible to our lives and to use the gifts God has given to us." It is important to create a friendly and safe environment by role modeling friendliness, love and acceptance. (Love will speak more powerfully than words.)

Praise (15 minutes)

The praise time (prepared in advance) begins with a brief conversational prayer where the group leader shifts the focus of the group from each other to praise and worship of God. If a gifted worship leader is present, he or she can lead this portion of the meeting. Even though the praise time may be delegated, the cell group leader still carries the responsibility for oversight.

Worship is an important dimension of edification. It is the key to opening ourselves to the work of God in our lives. Worship breaks down barriers and allows love and acceptance to flow. It also facilitates the healing and empowering work of the Holy Spirit. Through worship Christians minister to the Lord and the Lord ministers to them.

Praise time incorporates songs of celebration and joy. Start by singing about God (who He is, what He has done, and who we are before Him). Then move to more intimate songs sung to God. There is a distinction between music leading and worship leading. Worship leaders evidence the reality of worshipping God in their own lives.

Praise time can include testimonies, reports about answered prayer, and thanks to God for what He is doing in people's lives. The focus is upward to God—reaffirming and reinforcing an identity and relationship with Him.

Apply (20-40 minutes)

During the application time the cell group leader encourages group discussion through questions. These are prepared in advance and carefully emphasize edification of the group members through application of the Bible to everyday life. It is best to keep discussion about the meaning of Bible passages short and very practical. The goal of the cell group is life transformation and living effectively under the lordship of Christ.

It can be helpful to link the cell group discussion to the teaching of the previous Sunday Celebration. This encourages a unified direction and focus and allows the body to grow together. It also reduces the amount of time necessary for leaders to prepare. (Some potential leaders are intimidated by the amount of time needed to prepare.) Groups are free, however, to pursue topics of common interest.

Application is not a teaching time, it is a time of interaction and group participation. Application means: *What about me – how does this affect my life? What commands am I to obey? Where do I need to change? Are there scriptural promises for me to hold on to?*

Group intimacy occurs by creating a positive atmosphere of acceptance. People will not share if they feel criticized or judged. Generally, it is more important for a person to feel free to speak than to be absolutely accurate. The cell group leader accepts people in process and is cautious about correcting (unless someone is promoting obvious error).

Minister (20 minutes)

Ministry time is the "one another" portion of the meeting. In Scripture, Christians are admonished to pray for one another, encourage, love, edify, care and comfort one another.[11] During the ministry time, struggles are shared and biblical promises are applied to life situations. The cell leader's role is to model this to the group.

Members share what they feel that God is saying to them. Ministry time is fruitful only if the members of the group are led into fellowship with the Holy Spirit. Edification flows from sensitivity to the Holy Spirit. Many personal issues, needs and hurts are so deep and complex that only the Holy Spirit can decipher and minister to them. Members will take some risks in ministering to each other, but should not exceed the Holy Spirit's guidance.

The ministry time includes praying for one another. God is always present, but He may seem distant from a perceptual point of view. He draws near to us as we draw near to Him. During intercessory prayer, God's presence will be sensed and encouraged.[12] Through prayer, the Holy Spirit gives Christians insight into the needs of those being praying for. As the Holy Spirit ministers through each member to meet the felt needs of others, deeper needs may surface.

Members may become emotional as they allow the Holy Spirit to speak and minister His healing touch. This is often an indication of the Holy Spirit's work. The group leader should seek to identify what the Lord is doing and affirm the Spirit's work, yet be alert to discern and deflect anything that may be a product of the human flesh or of a counterfeit spiritual source.

Leaders should not presume to provide easy solutions to people problems or claim to know the root causes for traumas. The focus of the group should be on God's power, grace and love—not on fixing people's problems. Unless someone asks for advice, leaders must be cautious in volunteering counsel.

Conversational prayer is the primary form of prayer in cell groups as it encourages Spirit-led participation. Conversational prayer is defined as prayer that unites people in conversation with each other and with the Lord Jesus Christ. It is simple, from the heart, and draws people together.[13]

Impart Vision (5-10 minutes)

The group's closing time reminds members of activities in between cell meetings. Specific faith goals and plans that God has given the cell group are reinforced. This also can be a time to pray for the Lord to increase friendships with the unchurched with whom members are in contact.

Vision building is a time to share plans for outreach, growth, ministry opportunities and multiplication of the entire church. The Lord's passion to reach the lost is the constant focus. Imparting vision reviews what God has done in the past and anticipates, by faith, what He wants to do in the future. Calendar adjustments and announcements can also be made during this time.

Dismiss

Ending on a positive note, dismissal is an upbeat statement or prayer that focuses on God's power and ability to work in Christians who are committed to a sense of community. People may want to leave or remain longer for further fellowship. For those who remain, this is often a time when even deeper Christian relationships are formed.

The cell group host/hostess takes charge of clean-up and restoring the room to its usual arrangement. This, too, is a relationship building time as strong friendships often form as people work together.

Cell group leaders will fill out a written report and give it to the cell group coordinator following each meeting. These reports allow the cell group coordinator to monitor the progress of various groups and work effectively with leaders in training.

Between Meetings

Contact with group members between meetings may be more important than the meetings. The cell group leader continues to facilitate the growth of cell group members by praying for them and staying in touch with them. Some people are cautious in a group but open up when sharing one-on-one. These personal contacts may provide additional opportunities for felt-needs ministry and spiritual growth.

Leaders infuse members of the cell group with the vision to reach out with God's love to people outside the group.

The cell group leader or the apprentice contacts members who have been absent. These calls express kinship and care without inflicting guilt about attendance. Also, prayer requests from cell group members ought to be followed up between the meetings.

Whenever possible, it's important to put cell group members in touch with each other outside the group. Every 8-10 weeks a cell group might plan a special fun activity together. This change of pace for the group furnishes additional opportunity for friendships to grow. Also, members of the cell group can bring new friends (potential new members) to these friendship-building events.

Some people will attend a cell group who might not come to a larger gathering, and vice-versa. Every three to four weeks the cell group can sponsor a newcomers night or join in a friendship - building event at the church. There, Type A unbelievers can be introduced to cell group participants and to other church members.

LENGTH AND LOCATION

Length

Cell group leaders need to watch the clock. The optimal length of a cell group meeting is about an hour and a half — no longer than two hours. Professionals and people with families are busy and depend on meetings being dismissed as scheduled. People may choose to linger longer, but those who must leave ought to be given the opportunity to do so.

Location

Choose a location that is comfortable and easily accessible to most members. Rotating between members' homes may prevent host burnout. This also encourages group members to view their homes as extensions of ministry.

SIZE, FREQUENCY AND EXTENT OF AUTHORITY

Size

A cell group starts with three to eight people and limits attendance to fifteen. When the group reaches this number another cell group is formed. Dynamics change in a group with more than fifteen members. A larger cell group becomes more leader-centered. Heart-to-heart fellowship, trust, transparency, intimacy and participation diminish as the group enlarges.

Frequency

Weekly meetings allows group members to bond much more quickly than less frequent meetings. In any case, cell groups should meet at least three times a month because they form the basic Christian community of the church. (Task groups may meet less frequently.)

Authority

It is essential that cell groups recognize that they are part of a greater vision and under the authority of a pastoral team. The church leadership team networks with and oversees all cell groups.

HOW DO YOU START A CELL GROUP?

Since multiplication is the goal, it is important for cell leaders and apprentices to know how to start a new group. When a new group is desired, the leader makes a prospect list of new people (drawn from celebration welcome cards or personal networks) and he or she outlines the where, when, who, etc., of the proposed group.

The next step focuses on building relationships. The leader plans a social event or meal together. At this time, the leader, assistant leader or host/hostess shares what the cell group experience has meant to him or her and presents the vision and parameters of the cell group.

Interested persons are invited to join the group on an introductory basis. If prospective new members are already familiar with and sold on the cell group ministry, an introductory period can be eliminated. When the focus of the proposed group is on outreach, be sure to involve people who have unchurched friends.

HOW DO YOU GROW A CELL GROUP?

The first principle in growing a cell group is for members to bring in new people. The group will naturally decline if members neglect to reach out to others.

On the average, one person will come to the cell group for every four people invited. Cell leaders should follow-up contacts made at church services. If new contacts are diligently pursued, cell groups will grow.

Church attenders, unchurched nominal Christians, and Type A non-Christians are all good candidates for cell groups. The leader infuses members of the cell group with the vision to reach out with God's love to persons outside the group. The cell group needs to be receptive to new people and create a warm, accepting atmosphere.

An important principle in multiplying cell groups is to set goals —

what the leader believes God wants for the group. Goals and objectives include: growth rate for the group, who will lead a new group (the apprentice for the group) and when the new group will begin.

CHECKLIST FOR A HEALTHY CELL GROUP

The following summary lists the common characteristics of healthy cell groups.

- ☐ A Christ-centered focus
- ☐ Caring relationships of members
- ☐ Encouraging, loving and edifying environment
- ☐ Ministry of members to one another
- ☐ Application of the Bible to daily life
- ☐ Assimilation, accountability and discipling
- ☐ Opportunities for meaningful tasks and roles
- ☐ Provision of one-to-one pastoral care
- ☐ Development and multiplication of leadership
- ☐ Non-threatening relational evangelism

Multiplying cell groups is fundamental to the high-impact church. It is the key to discipling, providing pastoral care for its members and penetrating the greater community. Cell groups allow the high-impact church to decentralize edification and pastoral care and are the primary environment for discipleship and nurture. This decentralization lays the foundation for unlimited growth potential. ▲

12

MULTIPLYING MINISTERS

We have taught the priesthood of all believers but we have not taught the ministry of all believers.
— Reiner Blanc

BURNOUT

As a seminary student, Robert tried to "do it all." He excelled in classes, was a guest preacher for small churches, and led a Friday night youth group.

Robert's unrealistic expectations followed him to his first church where he struggled to "super pastor" a growing congregation. He preached on Sunday morning, taught Bible on Wednesday nights, visited the sick and shut-in, and supervised the administration of the church. Committee meetings filled his calendar, squeezed in between weddings, funerals and counseling appointments.

A "faithful few" helped Robert, but he was reluctant to delegate. He hesitated to ask anyone else to share leadership tasks. Other people might be too busy, he thought, and besides, he feared that church members might not handle ministry correctly. Robert's wife knew firsthand the toll that being a "Lone Ranger" pastor had on her husband's health, and on their marriage and family life. Robert strived to be all things to all people. Even so, some members complained that certain things in the church were not getting done, or not done as they wished.

Robert was tired much of the time and so overwhelmed with immediate tasks that he did not take time to plan. Although he wanted the church to grow, it seemed to have more problems than promise. Unfortunately, Robert was blind to the hierarchical ministry structure he had unwittingly enforced.

MOBILIZE ALL BELIEVERS

For churches to recruit a work force capable of accomplishing the Great Commission, there must be a breakthrough in the way pastors view their role and the use of lay leadership. Carl George, church growth consultant, captured the main task of church leadership when he said,

> The number one task after hearing from God is to develop leaders for caring evangelistic cells, leaders to produce great congregational events, leaders to serve the whole church constituency, leaders to serve beyond the constituency, professional leaders who can develop other leaders. The central task of the church (leadership) is not preaching in a pulpit service but is to create obedient disciples of Jesus Christ. We cannot afford to pay for ministry, we can only afford to pay for those who create ministers.[1]

A hierarchical model of ministry has dominated the Western church for centuries. In this model, relatively few people at the top of the pyramid are ministers. Both Catholic and Protestant churches have perpetuated this structure that limits the decentralization of ministry.[2]

The modern Western church is like a football match with 22 people on the field in desperate need of rest and 50,000 people watching from the sidelines in desperate need of exercise. In many churches today, 10-20 percent of the people do 80-90 percent of the work. The hierarchical church model needs to be turned upside down.

Traditional Model of Ministry

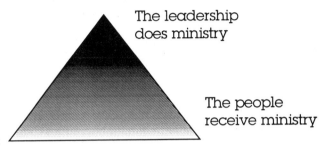

The leadership
does ministry

The people
receive ministry

High-Impact Model of Ministry

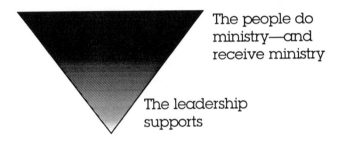

The people do
ministry—and
receive ministry

The leadership
supports

In contrast to the hierarchical model, the high-impact church encourages ministry opportunities for all believers. Programming and church leadership are evaluated on the basis of whether Christians are being discipled, mobilized, empowered, equipped and encouraged to use their God-given gifts.

Evangelism, discipleship and pastoral care need to be decentralized in order to help "church spectators" become active participants in ministry. God wants to use Christians to edify one another and to reach out to the unchurched. Cell groups decentralize ministry and provide maximum edification and pastoral care.

Pastors need to recruit, equip and mobilize people in the church to do ministry, instead of burning out by trying to do it all themselves. Paul made this clear in Ephesians where he said that God gave the church apostles, prophets, evangelists, pastors and teachers—to prepare God's people for works of service or ministry.[3]

It is not just pastors who have the responsibility to multiply ministers. Every person in leadership is responsible to recruit, train and deploy others in ministry. This should be part of the job description communicated to everyone in the church who takes on a leadership role.

Karen, a member of our church, knows that it is physically impossible for her to handle the responsibilities of running a children's ministry by herself. A professional musician and mother of two, Karen does not have much free time. Nonetheless, she oversees a thriving children's ministry of 100 children because she continues to rally others to help her.

"I really love this job. But I can't do it if it becomes too overwhelming. So I find other people to free me up," Karen said when asked about her success in recruiting and working with lay teachers.

ESTABLISH A SPIRITUAL GROWTH PATH

The most effective strategy for mobilizing lay people for ministry is to provide an effective path for spiritual growth and ministry involvement. This can be viewed as a series of concentric circles where the level of commitment and expectation increases as people move toward the center. Ministry programs are designed to encourage the movement from one level to the next.

The Community consists of Type A and Type B unbelievers and unchurched nominal Christians living in the targeted geographical area. The church's action item for the community is evangelism. The Crowd consists of newcomers who begin to attend the church's cells, services and events. The action item here is to clarify the crowd's commitment to Christ and assimilate them into the life of the church.

The Congregation is made up of those who are committed to Christ and

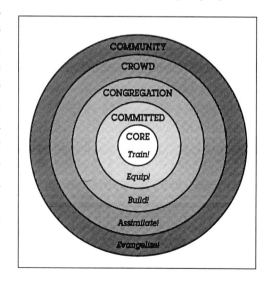

belong to the body. The action item here is to teach and lead them toward Christian maturity. The Committed are those who see themselves as ministers and are ministering in the church. The action item is to equip them for more effective service. The Core is made up of those who are leading and equipping others. The church's action item for the core is to train them to train others.

Spiritual maturity involves regular prayer, worship, intimate fellowship with the Holy Spirit and consistent application of biblical truths. Maturity also includes joyful and sacrificial giving, participation in ministry, and service in the world. A spiritual growth path builds these practices into the lives of church members through a well-planned grid of teaching, ministry involvement and apprenticeship training.

I asked a church leadership team about their church's vision. They wanted "to develop fully devoted followers of Christ." When asked how they planned to do this, they listed several good ideas. What was missing, however, was an integrated plan to connect the ministries of the church to their ultimate goal. They needed a pathway to lead people step-by-step from the point of initial contact with the church to spiritual maturity.

A spiritual growth path is necessary for a church to effectively multiply fully devoted, transformed, knowledgeable, ministering, witnessing, reproducing disciples of Christ. This "people flow" takes Christians through the steps of assimilation into the church, building faith, equipping for ministry and training to reproduce in the lives of others. These steps accommodate the crowd as newcomers, the congregation as learners, the committed as ministers and the core as equippers.

Step One—Assimilate

Healthy churches quickly assimilate newcomers into church life so they are less likely to drop out. They understand that responsibility for assimilation is with the church and not the visitor. They ask, *What will help newcomers become a part of this church?*

Assimilation of newcomers is easier when a person already has relatives or friends in the church. Encouraging members to network with unchurched friends, relatives, neighbors and associates is vital in incorporating people into the church and sustaining church growth.

Assimilation actually begins before a person decides to join a church. The more friends newcomers make, the more apt they are to become actively involved. People come to church for many reasons but primarily stay for two reasons—friendship and meaningful ministry involvement.[4]

Spiritual Growth Path

	Newcomer (Crowd)	Learner (Congregation)	Minister (Committed)	Equipper (Core)
GOAL	Welcome and assimilate into the church.	Teach basics of the faith; Mobilize for "Everybody Evangelism."	Equip to discover gifts and minister to others.	Train to equip others.
	1	2	3	4
ACTION	Attend church introduction; Connect with other believers.	Start discipleship series; Participate in cell group.	Take gift testing; Take up ministry role.	Equip Newcomers, Learners and Ministers; Advance to Apprentice level.

The larger the group, the more difficult it is to assimilate new people. Individuals who become part of a cell group—where there is meaningful, face-to-face interaction and ministry involvement—are the least likely to drop out of the church. Feeling wanted and belonging to a group are strong influences on a person's continued involvement.

Cell groups are the best place to build friendships and incorporate newcomers into the church. Thus, it is important to encourage existing cell groups to remain open to newcomers and to continually redivide to form new cell groups.

Some newcomers, however, will come to the church through other avenues, such as church services and special events. Consequently, it is important to provide friendship-building opportunities at celebration events. Well-trained greeters and ushers make newcomers feel welcome. They are key to reducing a newcomer's anxiety level, introducing them to others, and directing them to appropriate activities and locations.

Newcomers can leave their names and addresses at a hospitality table or write it on a communication card during the service. Within a week, a pastoral leader writes each newcomer a warm personal letter welcoming them to the church. The names are passed on to a cell leader or the friendliest person in the cell group who also makes personal contact and invites them to the cell meeting. If a special ministry interest is indicated, the person's name should be passed on to the appropriate ministry leader.

All newcomers should be invited to an introductory welcome and information session, presenting the church's vision and purpose. The atmosphere at this event is upbeat, informal and relational with a goal of connecting newcomers to other Christians, the church and its leadership.

Calvary Community Church of Westlake Village, California, has an effective monthly newcomer's event — called "Church Chat" — at the senior pastor's home. After refreshments (cookies, coffee, tea and juice), there's a "get acquainted time" when two questions are asked: "What led you to first attend this church?" and, "Why did you come back?" The answers help newcomers identify with each other as they highlight attractive features of the church.

Calvary's Pastor DeWitt gives a brief overview of the priorities and purposes of the church. He concludes the chat with a challenge for newcomers to commit themselves to the church and to join one of the church's cell groups or other ministries. Later in the week, a ministry or cell leader — who also attended the church chat — personally contacts each person.

The Crossroads International Church of Amsterdam hosts a monthly "Welcome to the Crossroads" immediately after the Sunday church service. A light lunch is served for all who come and food and childcare is provided for children so that parents will be free to stay.

Step Two — Build

The next step in the spiritual growth path is to establish newcomers in the basics of the faith and move them through the various stages of spiritual formation. The question to ask once newcomers have clarified a commitment to Christ and are incorporated into the church is, *What will help them mature in Christ?* The most crucial time in a new believer's life is the first six to eighteen months. Just as in a baby's life, when over 70 percent of his or her total neurological patterns are formed in the first 18 months, so the newborn Christian's spiritual life-style is shaped in the first few months of his or her new life.[5] Edification, encouragement and nurture are essential at this stage for proper development.

In addition to regular worship, biblical preaching and participation in a cell group, the new Christian can be discipled by assigning a more mature member of the church to him or her. Each newcomer is paired with a discipleship partner of the same sex (or with a couple if appropriate) who is a trained cell group member. The discipleship partner's responsibility is to guide a newcomer through spiritual formation material.

If the newcomer is a new believer, he or she is taught the basics of the Christian life and is given an overview of the Bible.[6] For several months, the newcomer meets with the discipleship partner before or after their cell group meeting to discuss the self study of the new believer of the discipleship materials.

Assurance of salvation, the character of God, the person of Jesus, the role of the Holy Spirit, the authority of the Bible and the importance of the church are some of the topics to cover with new Christians. Training sessions combine printed material, questions, feedback and hands-on ministry assignments.

Equally important, however, is to introduce newcomers to the foundational values and ministries of the church. In the high-impact church this includes the importance of the cell group ministry and evangelism (see following chapters). It is in this stage of development that new Christians are excited and want to tell others about their new found faith. This is one of the church's best sources of continued outreach and growth.

Some churches conduct a special class (or a special series) for newcomers led by the pastoral staff. Holy Trinity Brompton, an Anglican church in London, holds a ten-week "Alpha" course followed by a weekend retreat. The topics of the Alpha course include: assurance of salvation, uniqueness of Jesus, purpose of

Jesus' death, reliability of the Bible, how to pray, guidance, healing, the church, telling others, and spiritual warfare.[7] The Alpha weekend retreat also presents the person, work and transforming power of the Holy Spirit. Those attending Alpha courses are encouraged to join one of the ongoing pastoral cell groups led by laymen.

Newcomers tend to get lost once a special class for them concludes unless they become involved in cell groups. Small groups decentralize the pastoral responsibility of incorporating new members into the body and grounding them in the basics of the faith. Teaching and discipling in cell groups provide a smooth spiritual growth path, rather than keeping newcomers dependent only on church staff.

> **A newborn Christian's spiritual life-style is shaped in the first few months of his or her new life. Nurture is essential at this stage.**

Step Three—Equip

If the newcomer is already grounded as a Christian, he or she may be able to bypass some of the material in step two and move directly to the third stage of the spiritual growth path. This stage addresses the question, *How can Christians be mobilized to use their gifts in ministry?*

Here, the Christian is introduced to spiritual gifts and his or her role in the church. Through special classes and/or through cell group discipleship partners, Christians come to see who they really are in God's eyes. A combination of teaching, testing and counseling can help believers discover their blend of spiritual gifts, talents, passions, temperament and schedule. Once this is accomplished, they can be directed toward the ministry role that best utilizes that blend.[8] The goal of the equipping stage of the spiritual growth path is to engage Christians to use their spiritual gifts in ministry to others.

While teaching and testing are helpful in matching equipped ministers to ministry tasks, these are no substitute for hands-on experience. To develop in the use of spiritual gifts, Christians need to be exposed to occasions for ministry. The cell group—the basic arena for Christian community and edification—is the best place for believers to experience and use spiritual gifts.[9] (Spiritual gifts are more caught than taught!)

The equipping level also includes teaching about spiritual warfare. Lay ministers, now grounded in a relational approach to evangelism and cell ministry, are trained in how to handle spiritual opposition. The discipleship trainer takes new lay ministers on appointments to share the gospel with nominal or Type A unbelievers where such opposition may be encountered.

Step Four—Train

The final step in the spiritual growth path is to train those who have some ministry responsibility in the church. The question that this answers is, *How can the church train the maximum number of people?* Too often people are given a responsibility and left to figure out on their own what they are supposed to do. This results in frustration and failure. Skilled ministers do not just evolve, they are trained.

All members who have any ministry responsibilities should receive further training. It is the role of pastors to oversee the training of others who do the work of the ministry. In a small church, the pastor initially does most of the training. As the church grows, the pastor assigns someone else as a recruiter/trainer to work with ministry leaders. These ministry leaders then raise up others in their groups to train yet others.

Every significant job should have a person who is doing the job, an assistant who is training to do the job, and the person who is doing the training. Those who are involved in a specialized ministry are given specialized training. For example, cell group leaders need specialized training in cell groups, children's workers need specialized training in teaching children, etc. Before such specialized training, everyone who is in a ministry role should receive generalized training in the fundamental philosophy and vision of the church.

In order to decentralize evangelism, discipleship and pastoral care, and mobilize the maximum number of people for ministry, special equippers are needed. Some of these will serve as apprentice cell leaders and go on to lead cell groups. Others will not assist or lead but will play a strategic role as discipleship partners in cell groups or other ministries of the church.

Discipleship partners assist the cell group, felt-need or task-oriented group leader by helping to assimilate, build and equip newcomers and other group members. Discipleship partners have in-depth training in the philosophy and strategy of the church and are trained to reach Type B unbelievers.

VISIBILITY AND RECOGNITION

Recruiting is the life blood of any organization. This is especially true in the high-impact church. Churches that want to mobilize their members for ministry must continually recruit people to help assimilate, build, equip and train others. They also give visibility and recognition to those who are making these ministries happen, which makes the task of recruiting easier.

To mobilize its people for ministry, the high-impact church has a plan to move people from initial contact to incorporation, spiritual formation and ministry development. Not every Christian will become a leader, but every believer should have a sense of being a part of Christ's Body, be grounded in the basics of the faith, and become equipped and trained to minister to others. Leaders will then emerge from those who have completed the teaching and equipping courses of the spiritual growth path.

13

MULTIPLYING LAY LEADERS

And the things you have heard...
entrust to reliable men.
—1 Timothy 2:2

EQUIP LEADERS

When I asked Billy Riggs, pastor of the Crossroads Fellowship Church in Raleigh, North Carolina, what he would do differently if he were just starting his pastorate, he replied, "I would spend enormous energy training small group leaders."

Billy says that he made the mistake of thinking small groups would work on their own. He now understands that successful small group programs need someone to continually train leaders and to troubleshoot as problems arise.

The Raleigh Crossroads Church, which emphasizes both small groups and large celebrations, began as a ministry to singles and in five years grew to 1,500 in attendance. Fortunately, the church now has a leader who works directly with its cell groups so the church's strategy is catching up with its dynamic growth.

STRUCTURE FOR UNLIMITED GROWTH

In Amsterdam, the idea of multiplying cell groups was viewed skeptically by some people in the church, especially by those who resist change. But I believed that if we recruited and trained leaders with vision, the cell group ministry of the Crossroads would naturally flourish.

I asked Peter to assist me in leading a cell group at Crossroads. I had some reservations because Peter was new to the church—I worried the responsibility might be too overwhelming. But he agreed to help me by leading the worship part of our weekly meeting and the group responded positively to Peter's leadership.

Next, I encouraged Peter to lead the entire cell group session, under my supervision. I also asked him to contact members in-between meetings. Soon, the leadership team invited Peter to enroll in the church's leaders' training program. Eventually, Peter took full leadership of his small group, freeing me for other responsibilities.

As a leader, Peter recruited Nico, a faithful attender also interested in becoming a cell group leader. Peter trained Nico as he had been trained. After Nico completed the leader's training, he took over the cell group leadership so Peter could begin another group.

Now, Peter supervises three apprentice leaders. In fact, Peter and his wife Jane (along with another couple in the church), are leading the cell group ministry for the entire church.

Peter, Nico, Jane, and others like them, are all non-professional ministers helping the Crossroads International Church grow in size and depth. Because of their ministry, other potential leaders are nurtured through the loving, healthy environment of the church.

HOW TO ORGANIZE A CELL-STRUCTURED CHURCH

The high-impact church spreads the burden of ministry by mobilizing lay people and training them to lead cell groups and felt-need ministries. The biblical precedent for delegated ministry comes from Jethro's advice to Moses in Exodus, Chapter 18.

As a busy judge of Israel, Moses suffered from exhaustion. From morning to evening he settled disputes. His father-in-law, Jethro, saw that this burden was too great for one person. So, although

The Cell-Structured Church

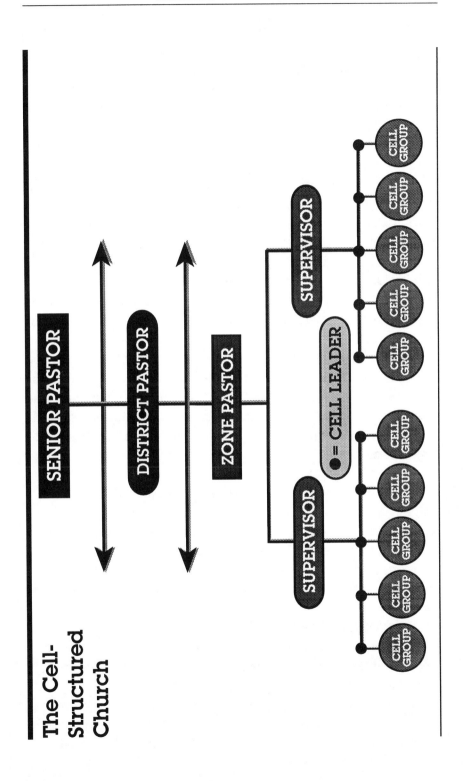

Jethro advised Moses to remain the teacher of the Israelites, he also suggested that Moses appoint other capable leaders as officials over "thousands, hundreds, fifties and tens."[1]

The basic ministry building block of a cell-structured church is groups of about ten people (3-5 families) led by a trained lay leader. As cell groups multiply, they are grouped into clusters. Every cell group leader is under the authority of a cluster supervisor who oversees up to five cell group leaders. This is a critical level of leadership missing in many churches that already have a small group ministry.

As the church grows, cell clusters are organized into zones (or divisions of ministry) overseen by trained zone or divisional pastors. A zone is a division of ministry marked off from others by particular activities, qualities or geographical location.[2] Zone pastors are responsible for two to five supervisors. Zone pastors are in turn responsible to the district or senior pastor (depending on the size of the church).

All ministries of the high-impact church—geographical, affinity (life-stage and interest), felt-need (special need groups) and task-oriented (drama, music, greeters, ushers, etc.)—benefit from this strategy. Each group emphasizes the church's overall goals of edification, leadership development, evangelism and multiplication of ministry.

RECRUIT POTENTIAL LEADERS

Leadership development is fundamental to the high-impact church. The best candidates for leaders are active members of cell groups who consistently give their time, energy and money to the church. Ministry opportunities are provided on three levels: helper, apprentice and leader.

At the "helper level" candidates may be inexperienced in ministry. Simple tasks are delegated to these helpers. Then, additional responsibilities are added as each person demonstrates faithfulness at the helper level.

The next level is the "apprentice level." Persons who have evidenced ability, responsibility and faithfulness at the helper level are asked to become apprentices. As apprentices, they are given further training and supervised in more significant responsibilities.

Apprentices who are active in ministry and committed to the vision, philosophy, style, goals and pastoral leadership of the church are the best "leader level" students. Two initial qualities to look for in selecting a potential leader are faithfulness to God and likability by others.

Teachability and the ability to teach, are two additional criteria for leadership. All true leaders are learners. Teachability means that a person is not a "know-it-all." The ability to teach first involves a natural modeling of the Word of God—incorporating scriptural truths into real-life situations; and second, the ability to communicate that effectively to others.

Potential leaders first prove their ability, responsibility and faithfulness at the worker level. After they complete training, they will serve as apprentice leaders in designated areas of ministry before being given full responsibility as pastoral lay leaders.

MULTIPLY CELL LEADERS

Quality leadership is the most crucial ingredient to keeping cell groups healthy and multiplying. It is the task of each cell leader to constantly recruit and train apprentices. Then, apprentices are assigned tasks and responsibilities for a cell group's operation until they take on leadership of another newly formed cell group.

This point cannot be emphasized strongly enough: A major responsibility of every cell leader and ministry leader in the church is to recruit apprentices and help them develop the skills needed to lead their own groups. Each cell or ministry leader is responsible not only for pastoring the members of his group, but also for equipping at least one apprentice leader.

The key to a successful cell group ministry is training, training, and more training! Apprentice leaders take an introductory cell leaders course and are given specific tasks within the weekly cell group. Cell leader training and team building should be provided at least every six weeks for both group leaders and apprentices. (The New Hope Community Church requires its leaders to attend training every week).

Midway through their training, apprentice leaders begin to lead a cell group while the senior leader observes. When the training concludes, apprentice leaders start a new group or take over an existing group.[4]

In a very receptive environment, cell groups can reproduce every six months. (Groups which resist reproducing can be left to run their course.) In the high-impact church, time and energy is focused on groups that are willing to reproduce and on training leaders who have a vision for reaching the unchurched.

Leadership Development Path

	Apprentice	Cell Leader	Supervisor	Zone Pastor
GOAL	Train to assist or lead cell group; Equip cell members.	Lead cell group; Recruit and train apprentices.	Supervise and train cell group leaders.	Train supervisors; Oversee ministry zones.
	5	**6**	**7**	**8**
ACTION	Complete entry level training.	Report to supervisor; Attend ongoing training sessions.	Report to zone pastor; Lead cell leaders training.	Report to senior pastor; Lead zone ministries.

DEVELOP SUPERVISORS

A major cause of cell group breakdown is failure to supervise leaders. Here's a story to show that demonstrates this crucial aspect of church growth:

A sizable church in Southern California needed more space on Sunday mornings. The leadership decided to try the small group structure and assigned everyone in the church to a regionally based group. Each group was to meet once a month on a Sunday morning. So, on any one Sunday, approximately one-fourth of the congregation would be meeting off campus.

People in the church were recruited to lead the groups and were briefly trained. But most of the small groups failed miserably; at least one-half didn't make it through their first year. One of the main reasons for this failure was the lack of experienced supervisors to oversee and encourage small group leaders and help them deal with difficulties that arose.

Because of the overall demands of ministry, the pastoral staff of a church does not have the time to supervise cell leaders. Lay supervisors, serving under the pastoral staff and providing oversight for cell leaders, are needed for a successful cell group ministry.

> **The key to a successful cell group ministry is training, training, and more training!!**

A lay supervisor's role is to pastor cell leaders. Supervisors are chosen from among cell group lay leaders who have been successful in developing new cell leaders. Supervisors do not, themselves, lead cell groups. Instead (on a rotating basis) they attend several cell group meetings providing training and counsel for cell leaders under their care.

The supervisorial ministry is one of caring and continual training. Supervisors have basic counseling and leadership skills. They lead a monthly cell leaders meeting for their cluster, in addition to attending all-church cell leaders meetings led by the senior pastor.[3]

DEVELOP ZONE/DIVISIONAL PASTORS

The training for zone pastors is more rigorous than for other levels of lay leadership. Zone apprentices receive classroom instruction in theological and pastoral subjects and supervised practical-ministry experience.

The primary responsibility of the zone pastor is to recruit, train, deploy, monitor and nurture supervisors and apprentice zone pastors. Zone pastors have responsibilities for congregation events and visibly participate in the celebrations and fellowship gatherings. Both zone pastors and zone apprentices are full-time, salaried ministers.

ESTABLISH EFFICIENT ADMINISTRATION

The cell structure of a successful high-impact church is well organized and coordinated. A cell group administrator (or administrative team) oversees leadership selection and training. The administrator is qualified to handle a cell-structured church and is a proven motivator, trainer and organizer. The cell group administrator or administrative team's oversight includes:

- Monitoring the status of all cell groups (attendance, content and quality of sessions).
- Preparing monthly summary reports for the senior pastor and elders.
- Providing curriculum materials and resource lists for cell leaders.
- Arranging entry level training seminars.
- Organizing ongoing training meetings.
- Advertising the cell ministry within the church.

PRIORITIZE TRAINING

For a church to grow, training must be provided at every level of spiritual growth and leadership development. Training includes learning to relate well in groups, absorbing information, and having supervised experience. Ministry skills are emphasized and are sharpened as leaders coach their apprentices. The training formula is:

Training = Relationship + Information + Doing

Within cell groups, three kinds of training are needed:

- *Everyone* should be trained in the use of spiritual gifts to edify one another.
- *Some* should be trained for specific roles such as worship leading and hosting.
- *One or two* persons should be trained as apprentice leaders.

PROVIDE ENTRY-LEVEL TRAINING

Entry level training for cell leaders and their apprentices includes development of skills related to personal evangelism and leadership. Examples of other areas for entry-level training include:

- **How to become a skilled listener**
  The cell leader learns to listen to what is said and what is *not* said, reading body-language. The leader affirms emotions without being driven by them. He helps maintain coherency and focus during the cell meeting by using natural breaks to restate and summarize discussion topics.

- **How to give appropriate feedback**
  The leader learns to wait before talking; he doesn't answer his own questions. When discussion lags, he rephrases his questions, though he is not intimidated by silence. He respects and accepts all comments by responding empathetically with such statements as, "It sounds like you're upset" or, "I can see from your expression that you're concerned."

- **How to keep a balance of discussion between members**
  The sensitive leader encourages new or quiet members to participate, and discourages over-talkative members from dominating meetings. The leader helps keep the group on the topic by discouraging irrelevant and other non-essential discussion.

- **How to handle controversy without squelching it**
  The development of intimacy in a cell group may necessitate going through several stages of group growth in learning to relate. These may include getting acquainted, conflict and resolution, developing community, and ministering to others. Expressions of conflict and controversy don't mean that the group is unhealthy. In fact, working through conflict often increases the commitment of members to one another.
  During debatable subjects, the leader's influence should be carefully measured. Too much input squelches participation and good group dynamics. Too little influence creates confusion.

- **How to facilitate edification in the cell group**

Trained leaders know how to connect people together in friendship and help them discover opportunities for ministry. Relationships and ministry involvement insure that cell group members will feel fulfilled and remain in the group.

PROVIDE ONGOING TRAINING

Although specialized training is available for specific areas of ministry in the high-impact church, leadership core training is the same for everyone. A "leadership community" unifies the church and prevents departmentalization (staff members becoming more concerned about the interests of their own department than the well-being of the church as a whole).

The leadership community includes everyone who has responsibility for any aspect of the church life. Apprentice cell leaders, cell leaders, apprentice supervisors, supervisors, apprentice zone pastors and zone pastors are all part of the leadership community which meets monthly for leadership training. The objectives of this training time are vision building, team building, encouragement, problem solving and skill training.

The leadership community meeting has three parts: (1) The senior pastor casts the vision; (2) small groups huddle together, based on cluster groupings or common ministries; and (3) skill training. Carl George of the Charles E. Fuller Institute labels this structure for training the leadership, "VHS": "V" for vision, "H" for huddle and "S" for skill training.

Leadership community meetings begin with the senior pastor's vision for the church. It is essential for every person in leadership to rally around the vision of the senior pastor. Vision casting may touch on spiritual foundations, purposes, values or other unique and motivating concepts. The goal of vision casting is to unify and empower leadership. The larger a church becomes, the more important it is to bond people together in a common vision.

The small group or "huddle" portion of the leadership community gathering facilitates the specific needs of leadership. Because leadership community is usually a large group, people need to be gathered in smaller units based on similar ministry responsibilities.

Supervisors meet with cell leaders for sharing, problem solving, prayer and encouragement. There is a spiritual dynamic to this cellular gathering akin to that of the cell groups themselves.

"Skill training" focuses on the basic skills needed for ministry responsibility. These are how-to sessions that pass on new skills and reinforce skills previously taught. Skill training increases the performance of leaders. This training can be offered to the entire leadership community or tailored to affinity groups.

PRACTICE THE "TRAINING LOOP"

As discussed above, the high-impact church recruits leaders who, in turn, develop other leaders. These leaders are not merely gaining a following—they are multiplying leaders. The scriptural foundation for this concept is 2 Timothy 2:2: "The things you have heard me say in the presence of many witnesses entrust to reliable men who will also be qualified to teach others."

High-impact leadership has a player-coach plan. The leader is a coach who role models ministries for onlookers. Then, he allows hands-on experience and supervises apprentice trainees (players) as they practice leadership skills. The leader-coach is a back up when difficulties arise and provides appropriate resources to the player(s) on a need-to-know basis.

The process of developing leaders is called a "training loop" or "discipleship loop." The sequence is:

1. *You do it, they watch!*
2. *They do it, you watch!*
3. *They do it, you support!*
4. *They get others to do it!*

A cell-multiplying organizational structure is fundamental to the high-impact church. To multiply cell groups, it is critical to reproduce trained cell leaders and provide ongoing supervision and training. The high-impact church multiplies cell groups, cell group leaders, supervisors and zone pastors so that it continues to grow as it provides high-quality pastoral care. ◢

14

EVERYBODY CAN DO IT!

You will be my witnesses....
—Acts 1:8

ANDREW AND ELIZABETH

My wife Sharon met Andrew and Elizabeth in a grocery store in Holland. Wanting to get better acquainted, Sharon invited this friendly couple home for coffee and Dutch pastries.

Andrew and Elizabeth, from South Africa, were finding it difficult to adjust to a new culture. We noticed a special sadness when they mentioned their daughter's name.

Several weeks later they returned our invitation and entertained us with a home video taken in Nelspruit, South Africa. They enjoyed showing us the pictures of their former home and the sons and grandchildren they had left behind.

When we asked why they had moved to Holland, Andrew told us how their 23-year-old daughter had mysteriously drowned. Their family suspected it had been murder, but could not prove it. Tearfully, Elizabeth said that remaining in South Africa was just too painful—they needed a change.

We listened and empathized with the sad story of these new friends. Then, Sharon and I explained that we had come to Amsterdam to start a church to encourage international English-speaking people, many of whom, like them, now lived far from family and friends.

Several Sundays later, Andrew and Elizabeth visited the Crossroads International Church. About half way through the praise songs, I noticed that Andrew was crying. He and Elizabeth departed quickly after the service, and although Sharon called them occasionally, they seemed reluctant to come again.

Two years elapsed. Then I had an unexpected telephone call from Andrew asking my advice about a personal problem. After encouraging Andrew to call on God's strength, I asked if I could pray for him and Elizabeth—and did so over the telephone.

Soon afterwards, this couple began coming to church often. As we renewed our friendship we were able to reassure them of God's love, help and guidance.

Andrew and Elizabeth could not have been reached by an aggressive or confrontational approach. Yet, even two years after our initial meeting, they felt free to call because of Sharon's graciousness. They were Type B unbelievers, but were receptive to the messengers. As they grew comfortable with us, and with others in the church family, they gradually opened to the gospel message.

The story about Andrew and Elizabeth illustrates the effectiveness of "Everybody Evangelism." Everybody can do what Sharon did. My wife does not consider herself an evangelist. She merely looks for opportunities to be friendly. All of us can start conversations. Even casual friendships lead people into close fellowship.

Developing relationships is an effective means of evangelism because it is natural, non-threatening, and everyone in the body can do it. When relationship-building is combined with seeker-sensitive programming, it leads to explosive church growth.

Everybody Evangelism breaks through the resistance that secular people have to the gospel. The key concepts to this approach are: Identify networks; build friendships; respond to felt needs; share sensitively; invite to seeker-friendly events; allow time for the process; and depend upon God's power.

BUILD FRIENDSHIPS

Strategies to evangelize urban people rely on networks. Research indicates that 75 to 90 percent of those who come to Christ do so through the influence of a friend or relative.[1] Kinship and friendships provide a natural network for sharing the Good News of God's redemptive love.

The average Christian, however, has few—if any —significant non-Christian friends. Christians are often too busy with church activities to join in community events. Sometimes Christians resist friendships outside the church because they're turned off by non-Christian attitudes and lifestyles. Or, they believe they should avoid non-Christians for fear of being influenced by them. Even if Christians have unchurched acquaintances, often they are not equipped to reach them with the gospel.

Non-Christian relationships are bridges that God provides over which the gospel can travel. The high-impact church encourages every believer to build bridges with non-Christians and provides fellowship opportunities for this to happen.

Instead of withdrawing from non-Christians, believers need to reach out to them. While new life in Christ makes the Christian different from the non-Christian, people can still discover common interests that spark friendship.

Christians should be trained to love and care for unchurched people, rather than avoid friendship with them. Christians are to be open, honest and vulnerable with the unchurched. The following four steps outline a plan that everybody can use in building friendships that lead to sharing the faith:

1. Reach out to people, caring about their needs, frustrations and problems—without reservation or thought of manipulation.
2. Establish a trust relationship where genuine two-way communication takes place.
3. Share what Christ has done in your own life and encourage a personal commitment to Him.
4. Continue communicating on a supportive and encouraging level until you free the other person from dependence on you to service for others.[2]

When building friendships, it is important to be non-judgmental. Often non-Christians will relate things that go against Christian values. Holding a response will open the door for further communication.

I met Joel, a basketball player, on a flight from Amsterdam to Atlanta. He had been visiting his girlfriend. When I asked him what she did he told me she worked in an erotic shop. I just smiled and kept the conversation going.

Later, I asked Joel if anyone had ever told him how he could have a personal relationship with Christ. He responded enthusiastically, "No, but I wish they would!" I did — and was amazed to see him open his life to Christ. I was glad I had not been judgmental.

FRIENDSHIP-BUILDING EVENTS

Seeker-friendly programming in the main celebration event (next chapter) and complimentary friendship-building events are essential to Everybody Evangelism. Visitor-friendly occasions — whether for the whole congregation or for a particular cell group — are designed specifically for the unchurched and set the stage for evangelism.

The primary purpose of a friendship-building event is to enable Christians to build relationships with non-Christians in a non-threatening, enjoyable environment. These events provide members with a tool for building relationships with unchurched networks. Events are scheduled well ahead and Christians are encouraged to bring unchurched friends.

Cell groups can regularly organize friendship-building events. In Amsterdam, our home fellowship group organized a Thanksgiving event, internationalized to include British and Dutch friends along with Americans. After all, the original Pilgrims, seeking religious freedom, left England for Holland and then sailed to the New World in North America. So we featured all three cultures in our Thanksgiving event.

Half of those attending our Thanksgiving frienship event were non-Christians. The response was so positive that it is now an annual event — and it opened the door for the Christians in our group to share further with the newcomers.

"Everybody Evangelism" Path

NETWORK	BEFRIEND	IDENTIFY	SHARE	INVITE	HARVEST
Goal: Make contact with unchurched.	**Goal:** Build trusting friendships.	**Goal:** Look for felt need.	**Goal:** Share your story.	**Goal:** Expose to gospel.	**Goal:** Encourage commitment to Christ. Assimilate into church.
Action: Establish visibility in community. Identify, pray for and contact personal and social networks.	**Action:** Build bridges socially. Show love and care. Look for divine appointments.	**Action:** Listen attentively. Identify whether person is Type A or Type B unbeliever, notional or nominal Christian. Show concern for felt needs.	**Action:** Look for receptivity. Sensitively share your story.	**Action:** Bring Type A unbeliever to celebration or cell group; bring Type B person to friendship-building event or share group.	**Action:** Persuade through presentation of gospel at celebration service or personal witness. Invite to church introductory session and cell group.

THE PROCESS OF EVANGELISM RECEPTIVITY SCALE (ENGELS)

NETWORK	BEFRIEND	IDENTIFY	SHARE	INVITE	HARVEST
-12 No contact with genuine Christians or vital church.	-11 No awareness or belief in God. -10 Awareness of supreme being but no knowledge of the gospel.	-9 Openness to message or messenger. -8 Recognition of felt need.	-7 Awareness of the gospel's influence in Christian's life. -6 Recognizes personal need for the gospel. -5 Positive attitude toward the gospel.	-4 Understands basics of the gospel. -3 Grasps the gospel's implications. -2 Belief in Christ and decision to act. -1 Repentance and faith in Christ.	0 New Creature—Discipleship/spiritual growth path begins. +1 Assurance and confirmation of what has taken place. +2 Assimilation into church.

Regular church-wide events also emphasize friendship building. Friendship-building events complement the relational Everybody Evangelism expected of church members. At these affairs, evangelism is low-key. The unchurched visitor is considered in the program, music, terminology, etc. They are not singled out, embarrassed or pressured. The atmosphere is neutral, non-threatening and enjoyable—ideal for prospective members to get acquainted with the church.[17]

Examples of fun, non-threatening pre-evangelism opportunities include picnics, ice cream socials, Valentine's Day banquets, square dances, sports events, special holiday musicals and/or dramas. High profile city-wide activities are excellent friendship-building opportunities. An example of a pre-evangelism community event is Calvary Community's annual Christmas musical attended by over 10,000 people in the Conejo Valley, an hour's drive north of sprawling Los Angeles.

The Crossroads Church in Amsterdam has frequent outings—barbecues, athletic events, Mexican fiestas, chili cook-offs, square dances, and boat cruises. This high-impact church also sponsors concerts ranging from classical to pop to reggae, appealing to Europeans' diverse musical tastes. Food and music are the key ingredients to successful friendship-building events.

Socially-oriented need-meeting programs such as crisis pregnancy and crisis hot-line ministries, special addiction and victim support groups, job training classes, counseling centers and daycare centers are additional examples of pre-evangelism and are vital expressions of God's love and care for people.

IDENTIFY FELT NEEDS

Once networks have been identified and relationships are being built, the next step is to look for felt needs. Outwardly, people may seem to have their lives together. Appearing successful and comfortable, they may deny a need for God or the saving work of Jesus Christ. Inwardly, however, most unchurched people have hurts and needs which can lead to an opening for the gospel message.

Pastor David Yonggi Cho teaches his church members to practice what he calls "holy eavesdropping." People are instructed to be on the lookout for those having difficulties in their lives. When needs are discovered, the Christian inwardly asks himself, *Is there some way I can witness to this person? Is there some way I can introduce him to Jesus, who can really solve his problems?*[3]

The psychologist Maslov lists a hierarchy of needs: physiological, safety and security, love and affection, esteem and self-actualization. According to Maslov, once a lower level need is met, people are then willing to seek ways to satisfy their needs at the next higher level.[4] Christians who understand

Outwardly, people seem to have their lives together... inwardly they have needs that can make them open to the gospel message.

this are better able to share their faith with those who are struggling with financial, relational, physical, emotional, psychological or spiritual problems.

Felt needs are often connected to transitions and changes in our lives. A "period of transition" is the time in which a person's (or family's) normal, everyday behavior pattern is disrupted by a stressful event or unfamiliar situation.[5] Transitions are windows of opportunity—when people are more receptive to the gospel.

"I have my life together okay," said Kirk, a non-Christian friend in Amsterdam. "I don't see a need for the church." Despite our different spiritual perceptions, my friendship with Kirk grew. One day, he knocked on my door and asked if we could talk. Kirk cried as he told how he had been out of work for some time and had been mistreating his wife.

Up to this time, Kirk had not been open to talking about his personal needs. In the stress of life's dilemmas, however, he was willing to speak his heart. Kirk's freedom to share hurts created an openness for me to share how Christ could help him mend his life.

The level of trust that had developed in our friendship allowed Kirk to be vulnerable and share his problems. Trust is necessary before most people will reveal their needs, hurts, frustrations, fears, joys, interests, and dreams. It is important for the believer to show

God's love and care by listening attentively and sensitively to a person's concerns.

SHARE SENSITIVELY

Christians who understand an unbeliever's way of thinking will be more apt to communicate effectively. The longer we are believers, the less we think like unbelievers. That's great for personal holiness—but unfortunate for personal evangelism. Christians use terms that are just not understood by non-Christians. Jesus commanded His disciples to be "fishers of men." The key to successful fishing is to understand fish.

Christians should be trained to compassionately share God's love with unbelievers. Timing is important. Believers have a better chance of sharing their faith after they have developed a friendship and a person feels comfortable expressing felt needs.

The manner of sharing is also important. Rather than sounding preachy, Christians can simply share what God has done in their life. Use easy-to-understand language and avoid Christian jargon. Show how Christ relates to everyday experiences and felt needs. And, when the door is open to do so, be prepared to give a concise explanation of the gospel.

A carefully thought-out presentation of the gospel is necessary for effective evangelism. Many people are ready to respond to the gospel if they hear it presented in a clear, logical way. Every Christian should be trained to make such a presentation and to relate how Christ has made a difference in their own life.

INVITE TO VISITOR-FRIENDLY EVENTS

The high-impact church schedules visitor-friendly programs to assist Christians in Everybody Evangelism. These winsome and sensitive events are opportunities for believers to bring their unchurched friends to a meeting where they can hear the gospel in a life-related way.

Andrew and Elizabeth, mentioned earlier, told us that at Crossroads they met people who were "friendly and showed love, joy and inner peace," and they liked the messages that had "modern day relevance" and "gave inner strength." This couple became active because they found an informative and reasonable approach to Christianity, rather than an indoctrinating and guilt-producing one.

The discovery of faith came in stages for Andrew and Elizabeth. First hesitantly, then through friendship-building events (Mexican fiesta, square dance, boat cruise), seeker-sensitive Sunday services, and conversations with Christians who gave reasons for their faith (but did not push), this couple began to believe that the Bible was relevant and that God cared for them.

ALLOW TIME TO PROCESS

The story of Andrew and Elizabeth proves the effectiveness of Everybody Evangelism. Christians do not need to be gifted evangelists. To evangelize, a person needs only to identify networks, build relationships, share how Christ has worked in his or her own life, and invite the unchurched to visitor-friendly events where the gospel is presented.

Andrew and Elizabeth's journey to faith demonstrates that evangelism is a process. Sociologist James Engel captures the process of evangelism in the Engel Scale.[6] Engel recognized that people are at different stages of belief. His scale delineates the necessity of discerning where a person is spiritually before sharing the gospel.

To determine where a person is on the path of faith, ask: *Does a person believe in a Supreme Being? Do they have some awareness of the gospel and understand its fundamentals and implications? Do they have personal needs and problems? What is their attitude — negative toward faith, or seeking repentance and acceptance?*

Evangelism is the process of moving a person from one stage of belief to the next. Some people experience sudden conversions, but most come to know Christ the same way they get acquainted with others—a step at a time. The ultimate goal is to lead a person to profess Christ and incorporate them into the church.

Christians do not fail when someone does not respond immediately to the love of Jesus. Be encouraged when people are simply in process and you can help them take the next step. A process-oriented evangelism allows unchurched persons time to analyze the gospel and its relevance to life.

HARVEST

The ultimate goal of Everybody Evangelism is for people to put their trust in Christ as Savior and follow Him as Lord. This decision can be made privately or at a church event.

God has specially gifted some believers as evangelists—those who find it easier than others to help a seeker make a commitment to Christ. But every believer is called to evangelize and needs to be trained on how to lead people to Christ. The entire church ought to be trained in Everybody Evangelism. Those with the special gift of evangelism should be used to train those without it.[7]

Dr. James Kennedy's "Evangelism Explosion,"[8] Campus Crusade for Christ's "Four Spiritual Laws," and "Knocking on Doors, Opening Hearts," by Dr. Ralph Neighbour[9] are useful tools for evangelism. Kennedy's approach to training laymen in personal evangelism is an especially effective church-based method when people are already seeking Christianity (Type A unbelievers).

The church service is one of the best places to harvest the fruit of the relationship-building efforts of members. Even when the pastor does not have a gift of evangelism, low key invitations to respond to the gospel can be given from the pulpit.

DEPEND UPON GOD

Everybody Evangelism depends on God's power. Seekers cannot enter the kingdom of God unless they are "born from above."[10] As church leader David Watson pointed out, the Holy Spirit empowers Christians to be effective witnesses:

> Only the Holy Spirit can bestow spiritual life, and if there is no life, there will be no powerful preaching of the gospel, and where there is no powerful preaching of the gospel, there will be no transmission of life to others. The only way out of this impasse is to look for, ask for, and receive the power of the Spirit. No exhortation to evangelize, no call to mission, no reminders of the Great Commission, can ever be a substitute for the revitalizing, energizing work of the Holy Spirit.[11]

An experienced Christian worker gave me good advice when Christian Associates International embarked on its church planting ministry in Europe: "Linus, I trust that you will see the need for 'power evangelism' in your work. Drugs, immorality and the occult are so rampant in Europe that a purely cerebral presentation of the gospel is inadequate."[12] (The same could be said about North America.)

Power evangelism happens when we depend upon God to break the evil forces which would otherwise prevent people from coming to saving faith. No harvester, however skilled, can be effective without the work of the Holy Spirit.

The high-impact church mobilizes, trains and supports a relational "Everybody Can Do It!" evangelism program. All believers are called to witness to networks of unchurched friends, neighbors, associates and relatives — bridges over which the gospel most easily travels.

The high-impact church decentralizes the ministry of evangelism. Lay people are the best means for fulfilling the Great Commission. They are the most effective witnesses to the fact that the gospel works in the lives of ordinary persons. When the church mobilizes and trains every Christian to be an "Everybody Can Do it" evangelist — and is structured to facilitate this — there will be explosive growth.

PART IV

THE EXTERIOR OF THE HIGH-IMPACT CHURCH

Centralized Leadership and Ministries

15

CELEBRATION EVANGELISM

They were highly regarded by the people.
—Acts 5: 13

THE MAGNETIC CHURCH

Dick and Martin, brothers, lived in a small apartment in east Amsterdam, Holland. Both were in their late twenties, unmarried, without steady jobs, and with little hope in the future.

One typical grey day, Martin was walking home from a temporary job, anxious to get out of the brisk Dutch wind. He hurried through the familiar, crowded downtown streets, past gilded buildings, and quaint coffee bars. Then, eastward along the canal, the city blended into high-rise apartments. Mothers with school children on the back of their bikes and other assorted bikers whizzed past as plentifully as cars.

At a pedestrian traffic light, Martin looked down at a fluorescent-orange flyer lying on the sidewalk. As it fluttered in a gust of wind, he stooped and picked up the small piece of paper. Reading as he walked along, Martin saw that the flyer from the Crossroads International Church communicated what he had always thought — "Church is Boring!"

But Crossroads promised people something fresh and exciting. *Well, it just might be worth a try,* Martin thought.

He persuaded Dick to go along, — but with much skepticism. "Sure, let's go see what's wrong with *this* church — they're all alike, aren't they?" Dick sneered.

Neither Dick nor Martin expected to find contemporary, upbeat live music playing as they entered the large auditorium. Several people warmly shook their hands, smiled and said "hello!" The brothers clapped to the music, sang along with the simple tunes and soon were glad they'd come. The rest of the service wasn't boring at all — the message was an interesting extension of a humorous drama. They were sorry to see it end — and quickly planned to return.

Indeed, this church *was* different! It was warm and relational — people seemed so friendly. At Crossroads, Dick and Martin found another friend, too — Jesus. In just a few short weeks, both gave their lives to Christ and were baptized.

CELEBRATION EVANGELISM

"Celebration Evangelism" is the impact that the gospel has on non-Christians as they come into a gathering of believers and sense the presence of God and the living reality of the Christian faith. Celebration Evangelism can take place in the cell group, but is more powerful in a large assembly. The joy of the music, inspiration of the message, and warm Christian fellowship combine to inspire visitors.

God reaches the world through both visualization and verbalization of the gospel. When believers gather together in loving celebration, the gospel is easily visible.[1] Jesus prayed that His disciples would have oneness, love, purity and joy. He said their love for one another would actually be *the evidence* that they *were* His disciples.[2] People respond to the beauty of redeemed people living, acting and relating in concert with God's will.[3]

Celebration Evangelism drew Martin and Dick back to the Crossroads Church and, ultimately, to Christ Himself. "I was moved by the music and the message. I didn't feel like an outsider — though I was," Martin recalls. But soon he and his brother were drawn into the loving fellowship.

Celebration Evangelism goes hand-in-hand with Everybody Evangelism and ministering through cell groups. It enhances the efforts of Christians who want to reach out to their unchurched friends.[4] When Celebration Evangelism combines with cell group evangelism and Everybody Evangelism, the result is explosive! Put mathematically:

Cell Group Evangelism (Decentralized)
\+   **Everybody Evangelism (Decentralized)**
\+   **Celebration Evangelism (Centralized)**

=   # EXPLOSIVE EVANGELISM!

Each of these dimensions contributed to the explosive spread of Christianity in the first century. The first Christians spread the gospel to their personal networks; evangelism was the responsibility of every Christian.[5] And the impact of the gospel was magnified when Christians gathered together in small groups and in dynamic celebrations.[6]

WHAT MAKES CELEBRATION EVANGELISM EFFECTIVE?

"I really liked the music. I got choked up as I listened to it."

"I felt like the pastor was speaking directly to me."

"I didn't realize they did drama in church—I thought it was great."

"I don't know what it was, but I felt something special in this place. I plan to make this my church from now on."

"The people were so friendly."

"This was not at all what I expected church to be."

These are comments from people who were visiting the Crossroads Church for the first time—even those who didn't think they would enjoy going to church, but through the influence of a friend, gave it one more try.

The quality of the corporate gathering in the local church is the most important factor in Celebration Evangelism.[7] The following are essential elements in attracting seekers to church.

Friendliness

Unchurched people are attracted to warm and friendly churches. Although many churches consider themselves friendly, surveys show that unchurched people perceive church to be an unfriendly place for outsiders. The discrepancy lies in the fact that members are generally more friendly to those who already belong, than they are toward newcomers.

Churches may seem to be friendly as *members* relate to one another. However, as a visitor, I have walked through clusters of church members after a service to find out how they would respond to a visitor. I'm disappointed to report that in nine out of ten churches not a single person introduces themselves.

If newcomers are to feel welcome, it is imperative to give a high priority to friendliness in church gatherings. Outgoing members should be trained and assigned the responsibility of looking for newcomers, introducing themselves, and making sure that visitors meet other people. One church appropriately labels their newcomer-hospitality program "tying shoelaces." This is made easier when the newcomer is brought by a friend or relative who is a member of the church—and easier still if they have already joined a cell group.

The primary questions newcomers ask when they come to church are not theological, but sociological. Questions like, *Are these people like me? Is their life situation similar to mine? Can I can relate to them...can they relate to me?* Very few unchurched people ask, *What denomination is this?* or, *What is the doctrinal position of this church?*

Formal welcomes from the pulpit and visitor packets are good, but informal welcomes impress people the most and influence their decision to come again. When visitors are welcomed and followed up by individual church members, newcomers feel they have found a friendly church.

Positive Emphasis of Grace

Unfortunately, some churches—even whole denominations—emphasize rules and regulations and cause people to be racked with a sense of failure and inadequacy. Others are full of fear, guilt ridden, angry, frustrated and, worst of all, self-righteous.

Too many churches emphasize rule keeping and try to motivate people out of guilt. The result is that many churched and unchurched people alike misunderstand the purpose of the Ten Commandments. They believe that the Ten Commandments are the way to get to God, but the opposite is true. The Ten Commandments show people that they cannot reach God by their own righteousness.[8]

The New Testament message is that Christ has freed believers from the Old Testament law and placed them under the Holy Spirit.[9] The overall emphasis in the New Testament is positive (the grace of Christ) rather than negative (how people fail to fulfill God's laws). Christians actually fulfill the law of God as they are filled with the Spirit and manifest spiritual fruit in their lives.[10]

When people comprehend God's grace, they are healed of feelings of guilt, shame, failure and inadequacy. The direction of their lives becomes positive, rather than negative; productive rather than destructive. Their focus turns to Christ—His love, grace and mercy toward those who believe in Him.

Unchurched people generally have a stereotype concept of the church as a dull, negative place—filled with critical, condemning people. They perceive Christianity as a fear-motivated human attempt to live up to God's standards where God is "making a list, checking it twice, going to find out whose naughty and nice." Many Christians even focus on problems and human merit instead of divine resources. For them the glass is always half empty.

This contradicts the Good News of the New Testament that Jesus' sacrifice makes it possible for us to know God the Father in a loving, intimate way—and to experience His glorious inheritance and incomparably great power in our lives.[11] Christians are acceptable to God through *faith* – not because of human merit. The Body of Christ, therefore, should present the positive message of grace. The message of grace not only ministers to unchurched people, but also helps believers to grow.

Good preaching can communicate God's grace. Pastors who speak out against sin by promoting a positive alternative motivate people to serve the Lord out of thankfulness, not guilt. Redeemed people can be grateful for God's power and the abundant resources He gives His people.

Love, Acceptance and Forgiveness

Christians are called to bring the world not only a message but an attitude. When the atmosphere of a church is one of love, acceptance and forgiveness, unchurched people are drawn to Christ. This environment occurs as believers are encouraged to see each other as being in process and to love and forgive each other.

Unchurched people tend to look at the church either as a place filled with hypocrites or as a place for people who don't have problems. There's the impression that if outsiders attend church they will be criticized and condemned. Because of this they tend to write off the church.

> **Christians are called to bring the world not only a message but an attitude.**

In contrast, Jesus surprised His disciples and offended the Pharisees with ready acceptance of people from various ethnic backgrounds and viewpoints.[1] He taught His followers to love one another as He had loved them.[2] The apostle Paul, reinforced this openness in Romans 15:7: "Accept one another, then, just as Christ has accepted you, in order to bring praise to God."

Church leaders that are vulnerable and transparent and emphasize God's love, acceptance and forgiveness, and members that are caring and loving, will help dispel negative misconceptions. This climate not only attracts the unchurched but has a healing impact on believers. Christians live with tension between the biblical call to strive to "be perfect," (as our Father in heaven is perfect), and the reality that (on this earth) the church we will never achieve perfection. Despite this ambiguity, believers find peace when they keep focused on God's love, acceptance and forgiveness.

Expectancy and Hope

Another ingredient that makes Celebration Evangelism effective is expectancy and hope. Christians are called to accept people where they are in their spiritual pilgrimages, while at the same time offering hope for growth through God's power. This hope becomes a reality as the Holy Spirit uses the Word of God to change people's lives. The emphasis on hope in a high-impact church causes people to expect God to bless and mold them.

I was in Russia trying to put together a leadership team for a church filled with new Russian Christians. These people had lived all their lives under communism and belonged to the Russian intelligentsia. They were as enthusiastic about their new faith as they had formerly been about communism—but they were spiritually immature.

Bill, an American living and working in Moscow volunteered to teach a Bible study for this new church. Although Bill knew the Bible well and was a skillful teacher, his narrow background caused him to look at spiritual issues in only absolute right or wrong terms.

The new believers of this Russian church *did* have many problems. But Bill saw only their faults. In his frustration, he began to confront people. He wanted to discipline or kick out those who didn't measure up to his biased standards. Wisely, the church leaders replaced him with a more understanding Bible teacher.

The church leaders counseled with some trouble-makers, handling problems in a loving pastoral way, not dogmatically. Other problems dissipated in time—as the Holy Spirit worked in people's lives. These new followers of the faith were just beginning to understand the principles of Scripture. Leadership needed to be patient and not address every problem with confrontational demands. Through biblical training, growing Christians learn to regard others in love. The love and grace of Christ and our oneness in Him eradicates selfish attitudes.

Faith in the Word of God and in the power of the Holy Spirit keeps Christians forbearing with everyone in the body of believers. Even when things are going badly, Christians believe the scriptural promise: "Greater is He who is in you than He who is in the world."[14]

It is not enough, however, for the church to just teach and preach words of encouragement. The fruit of the Spirit must be evident as Christians deal with one another. The gift of the Spirit is the ointment that makes us whole—the Holy Spirit heals wounds and assures us that God is at work in and through us.

212   PART IV • THE EXTERIOR OF THE HIGH-IMPACT CHURCH

Credibility

To reach the most people, the gospel must be regarded as spiritually, ethically, intellectually, and socially credible:

• *Ethical Credibility* — A common stereotype is that the church is filled with hypocrites. To be attractive and credible, the church needs to model ethical integrity. The Apostle Paul noted his honor among the Thessalonians and urged Christians — especially leaders — to do likewise.[15]

A church is devastated when its leaders lack integrity in the areas of money, sex and power. Unbelievers who are favorable toward the church become disillusioned with Christianity when they discover an underlying hypocrisy.

Leaders may develop impressive ministry skills and still be immature in personal ethics. The church needs leaders with proven character. Christians who are saddled with unresolved personal problems or dysfunctional home lives make poor leaders. Unresolved minor infractions become magnified under the pressure and scrutiny of leadership. Weak leaders may resist dealing with spiritual difficulties, trying to "save face" as their popularity increases.

Not only church leadership, but all Christians need to have a credible witness. When pleasing others (colleagues, friends, spouses) is put ahead of pleasing God, relationships are infected with pretence. To be credible, Christians must face the pain of conflict resolution and live honest lives.

• *Intellectual Credibility* — A serious misconception is that Christianity is a blind leap of faith. Instead, the gospel is intellectually credible. Paul presented the gospel with rational evidence and Peter admonished believers to be able to give a reason for the hope within them.

The reasonable and historical credibility of Christianity (apologetics) is a high priority in preaching and evangelism. As the evidence of Christianity is presented, timely issues are discussed and comparisons are made between Christianity and other religions, the persuasive truth of Christianity is evidenced.

Christianity is unique in that it is logically consistent, historically verifiable and experientially relevant. However, people do not come to Christ on the basis of reason alone. Most people become Christians through loving relationships, not just persuasive arguments.

• *Social Credibility*—Generosity, mercy and compassion for the needy and sacrifice for others are some of the ways Christians demonstrate social credibility. Even evangelism has a social benefit as the lives of those who embrace the gospel are lifted. "Redemption and lift" is a historical phenomenon where the social and economic conditions of entire people groups improve when they embrace Christianity.

Contemporary and Winsome Style

Although some unchurched people can be reached through traditional expressions of Christianity, most cannot. Formal church services are predictable, therefore boring. The liturgy, preaching and music are impersonal, therefore irrelevant to life.

A contemporary and winsome ministry style draws back those who have given up on the church.

Commitment to Excellence

A high standard is needed to reach secular people—particularly business and professional people. Excellence in worship is consistent with the majestic and glorious nature of God. The high-impact church strives for overall quality—including facilities, programs and leadership.[16]

The saying, "You never get a second chance to make a first impression!" is true. Newcomers size up a church in their first impressions. The campus ought to be attractive—the buildings and grounds well maintained. Excellence in music, drama and preaching mark the celebration services of a high-impact church.

Friendly greeters and ushers, experienced children's workers and other group leaders impress newcomers, as does an appealing gathering place. All aspects of quality celebrations are carefully planned and show creativity. During services, there should be few distractions or uncomfortable pauses.

Excellence is a priority for quality ministry. The church's ministry is routinely evaluated by the leadership team. All leaders are accountable for high standards.

HOW TO HARVEST

The ultimate goal of all visitor-friendly and friendship-building events is to introduce non-Christians to Christ. Harvesting may take place on a personal level but often occurs in the celebration service or event where visitors are encouraged to make a commitment to Christ.

Testimonies of new believers are powerful factors in harvesting. Nothing is more effective in persuading a non-believer to come to faith than the witness of a peer whose life has been changed by Jesus Christ. Usually baptisms follow the confessional formula where the pastor asks, "Do you believe that Jesus is the Son of God, died for your sins and do you promise to follow Him with the best of your ability?"

In a variation of this style, Pastor Larry DeWitt of Calvary Community Church, interviews those being baptized asking, "How did you come to the point of placing your trust in Christ?" Immediately afterward, in a winsome way, DeWitt invites non-Christians who identify with the life situation of the person being baptized, to make their own commitment to Christ. Typically, 10-20 people come to Christ in this way each month.

Calvary Community Church, also has an annual "Apple Sunday" when new believers share how they came to Christ and tell about those who most influenced them in their decision. This sharing time demonstrates the success of relation-focused evangelism and inspires church members to continue to reach out to others. Apple Sundays are also harvesting events — verbal invitations are given to seekers to profess their commitment to Christ.

Effective evangelism is tri-dimensional with Everybody Evangelism, cell group outreach and Celebration Evangelism. Together, they result in a ripening harvest. Relation-focused evangelism — believers reaching out to networks of relatives and friends coupled with the proliferation of cells penetrating the city and visitor-friendly celebration services and events — provide a steady flow of spiritually responsive people. These seekers need to be challenged to commit their lives to Christ; they need to be harvested.

The visitor-sensitive celebration is an effective harvesting event. When the gospel is presented in a "user friendly" way, non-Christians become receptive. High-impact churches provide regular low-key invitations to make commitments to Christ in their celebration services.

16

SEEKER-FRIENDLY PROGRAMMING

*For the Son of Man came to seek
and to save what was lost.*
—Luke 19:10

GOD LOVES ROCK 'N' ROLLERS

Willow Creek Community Church, Barrington, Illinois, is a culturally attractive church that understands the importance of Celebration Evangelism. At a conference in Paris, sponsored by Willow Creek, a contemporary musical presentation set the tone for a seeker-sensitive service led by Pastor Bill Hybels.

I felt nostalgic and moved as I listened to the soft-rock music with a Christian message. As a young man, I played the guitar and sang in a rock 'n' roll band called "The Pendletons," named for our matching western-style jackets. This was the music of choice for my generation. It culturally bound my peer group.

There was a different style of music, however, in the churches I attended after I became a Christian. Most did not tolerate the contemporary rock-style music I had grown up with.

That morning in Paris, as I listened to the muted music and

pondered its Christian message, I thought of my unchurched friends and the cultural gaps that separate them from Christ and the church. I am grateful that high-impact churches understand God's desire to communicate the gospel through contemporary music.

WILLOW CREEK'S SEEKER-DRIVEN STRATEGY

Churches can effectively use cultural avenues to attract unchurched people to Christ. When planning a celebration service, the leadership team needs to consider whether the target audience will be mostly believers or unbelievers. They should ask, *Who are we trying to reach? Will the emphasis be believer-oriented teaching and worship, or seeker-sensitive?* The target audience determines the approach.

Traditionally, churches program almost exclusively for believers. Willow Creek, on the other hand, has pioneered a *seeker-driven* celebration service that targets the non-churched, non-Christian.

Few churches have the resources of Willow Creek. But even small churches can adapt the underlying principles....

Before launching Willow Creek, Bill Hybels surveyed the local community to learn why people were not attending church. People felt that church services were predictable and boring. Non-Christians were not able to relate to church music or to messages filled with unfamiliar terminology. Going to church made them feel guilty.

So, Willow Creek designed seeker-driven Sunday morning and Saturday evening services. Hybels believes that God seeks lost men and women until they are found — this is why the church exists. And Hybels knows that people who are accustomed to quality performances will not enjoy a substandard performance. Willow Creek's services aim to honor Jesus Christ, who is excellent in all His ways.

Hybels believes that in today's secular world, the needs of the unchurched are radically different than those of Christians. The Willow Creek celebration services therefore consider the needs, vocabulary and interests of seekers. Hybels recognizes that the unchurched need to hear the gospel in words they can understand.

Seeker-driven services assist Willow Creek's members to evangelize their unchurched friends, neighbors and associates. The services appeal to those who might not be attracted to a church that offers a traditional, preacher-to-audience message. Non-threatening programs ease people through stages of analyzing faith until they understand the meaning of personal commitment to Christ.

At Willow Creek, seekers feel free to think about spiritual things without being pressured to "sing anything, sign anything, say anything or give anything."[1] Seekers appreciate time to evaluate the implications of Christianity before committing to its life-changing message.

Few churches are a match for the talented members and abundant resources of Willow Creek. But even new, small cell-structured churches can adapt the underlying principles for a more effective ministry to reach the unchurched. Start with mobilizing members for an Everybody Evangelism and cell group ministry until the needed critical mass of people is gathered to start a winsome celebration.

WILLOW CREEK SEEKER-SERVICE CREED

Willow Creek's seekers service creed sums up the sensitive philosophy of this high-impact church:

1. A belief in the biblical mandate to evangelize the world, beginning with our own community.
2. The desire to never bore anyone out of the kingdom of God; therefore, a commitment to being contemporary and creative.
3. A deep respect for the anonymity of the seeker.
4. An understanding of the seeker's need for time in decision making; therefore, an emphasis on the process not the event.
5. The recognition of the need for excellence in everything we do, especially with those things that communicate the very character and nature of God.
6. An understanding that people will desire to support the cause with their time, talents and treasures since the cause is handled

with excellence, integrity and honesty, and leads to results.
7. Commitment to providing a relevant connection between Christianity and the seeker's daily life.[2]

SADDLEBACK VALLEY SEEKER-SENSITIVE SERVICE

Saddleback Valley Community Church of Mission Viejo, California also targets the unchurched in their Sunday services. The *seeker-sensitive* Saddleback strategy, however, is somewhat different than the *seeker-driven* strategy of Willow Creek.

Saddleback's Pastor Rick Warren, like Hybels, surveyed the specific attitudes, needs and interests of the surrounding community before pioneering Saddleback Valley Community Church. Warren asked four questions:

- *What do you feel is the greatest need in this community?*
- *Why do you think most people do not attend church?*
- *If you were looking for a church what would you look for?*
- *What advice can you give me?*

Warren found that people were negative toward the church because they felt that sermons were generally boring and that members were not particularly friendly toward visitors. Also mentioned was a concern for quality child-care and the perception that the church was more interested in money than in people. Warren concluded that most unchurched people are not atheists, they are simply dubious about the church. He was convinced that these unchurched people could be reached if the church responded to their hurts, needs and interests.

Like Hybels, Warren designed the Saddleback Valley Community Church in response to survey findings. Sunday morning celebrations focus on the felt needs of the unchurched since more unbelievers are likely to attend then.

SEEKER DRIVEN VERSUS SEEKER SENSITIVE

Although each church is programmed from different perspectives — seeker driven vs. seeker sensitive — both Willow Creek Community and Saddleback Valley Community have experienced explosive growth and effectively reached the unchurched.

In Willow Creek's seeker-driven celebrations, Hybels avoids anything (other than the message, perhaps) that might make seekers feel uncomfortable. Hybels believes that the unchurched should not be pressured to participate in singing songs about God, whom they do not yet know. The service is performance oriented and congregational participation is minimized. (Willow Creek has services for believers on a different day.)

Saddleback's celebrations target both believers and seekers. Warren feels that the needs of the unchurched are

> **Warren concluded that most unchurched people are not athiests, they are simply dubious about the church.**

similar to those of the churched—both desire celebration. Saddleback's Sunday services reach seekers and, at the same time, build and nurture believers. For example, Warren is convinced that the dynamic of congregational singing has a positive impact on the unchurched. Even if people don't care to sing, they do like to listen to music and corporate singing.

A difference between a seeker-driven and a seeker-sensitive strategy is also evident in the preaching styles of Willow Creek and Saddleback churches. The pastors at both churches preach practical, topical sermons relevant to the felt needs of unbelievers. Hybels, however, begins by focusing on things that might interest seekers and then shows how Christianity relates to these issues. Using logic and appealing to listeners' experience, Hybels affirms the credibility of Scripture.

Warren, like Hybels, teaches on topics that interest the unchurched, but, in contrast to Hybels, he uses more Scripture and provides an outline of his message with biblical texts. Warren is convinced of the positive value of integrating Scripture into his seeker-sensitive presentations. Warren's seeker-sensitive approach is advisable if trying to transition an established congregation to be more seeker oriented.

WHO DO YOU PRIORITIZE?

A seeker celebration format may compete with a church's emphasis on worship and teaching. Worship, prayer and teaching are
essential to revitalize the spiritual life of the believer. Unless these
emphases are properly maintained with a resulting sense of the
presence and empowerment of the Holy Spirit, the ministry of a
church becomes mechanical and dry. It is easy to slip into a mode in
trying to reach secular people where we act as if the spiritual world
does not exist.

The Church of Christ the King in Brighton, England, resolves this
tension by maintaining a Sunday morning emphasis on worship and
teaching targeting believers. The format of this service is a sustained
times of praise music (designed to lead Christians into intimacy with
God), teaching and openness to the Holy Spirit's intervention.

More recently, The Church of Christ the King holds a monthly
seeker's service with 10-15 minutes of high energy praise, contemporary music and low threat, high interest, well illustrated, succinct
preaching targeting seekers. Those who are interested are plugged
into a "Just Looking" group.[3]

Fellowship Bible Church of Park Cities compliments its Sunday
morning seeker-sensitive service with in-depth Bible teaching on
Wednesday nights, a Sunday morning adult education program,
monthly leadership training, an every other month concert of praise —
as well as its home fellowship groups.

Where the goal of the celebration service includes reaching Type
B unbelievers, a seeker-driven format is necessary. Services which
target Type A unbelievers, as well as believers, can use a seeker-
sensitive or friendly approach but include substantive teaching and
worship, and even offer special prayer for felt-needs following the
service. In this way, believers are targeted with newcomers in view.

The seeker-driven approach above will necessitate complimentary believer services while a seeker-friendly approach may not.[4]
Visitors relax when they are given permission to "just to watch if you
are a newcomer to our church and do not know the songs." In a large
group there is less pressure to sing and visitors are often taken aback
as they observe others around them praising God and sense God at
work in their midst.

SEEKER-SENSITIVE PROGRAMMING

Only contemporary, attractive, seeker-friendly programming will appeal to the masses of unchurched people living in Western urban settings today. City people are infected with entertainment overload and turn away from a dull, highly cerebral, dogmatic or confessional approach to Christianity. They respond more readily to talented performers, inspiring music, quality drama and life-related preaching.

High-impact church services energize, empower and attract newcomers. The following elements are critical to seeker-sensitive programming.

Careful Planning

Carefully planned, streamlined and meaningful services in a high-impact church most effectively communicate the Good News to modern business and professional people. This format should be planned with enough structure to be efficient without stifling.

Planning sheets allow the leadership team to coordinate the various elements of each service. Minute-by-minute planning keeps services moving along, interesting and on schedule.

Convenient Services and Location

Some people prefer early morning services; others like a later service that allows a leisurely Sunday pace. And some people like Friday or Saturday evening meetings, leaving the weekend free. Offering multiple, conveniently scheduled services makes it possible for as many people to attend as possible. (The Bible doesn't specify worship at 11:00 a.m. on Sunday morning!)

The safety and ambiance of the neighborhood where the church is located also influences attendance. People like to locate the church easily—and to find a parking space and seat inside. If they are delayed, they may turn around and go home. The unchurched (who come out to church alone) are easily discouraged.

A directional map is advisable in church advertisements. I've been lost at least five times trying to locate one church in a warehouse in an industrial park. Twice I gave up and went home; other times I was a quarter to one-half hour late. I've wondered how many other people have tried to find a "hidden" church and just gave up.

Favorable First Impressions

People form perceptions of a church by drive-by appearance, what others say about it, and their first visit. Available parking (friendly parking attendants) and cordial church-door greeters make good first impressions.

An attractive campus communicates that the church is seeker friendly and cares about the facility. A well-equipped, clean, safe nursery assures young families that their children will be well cared for. (A Tennessee church proudly boasts that it changes 1000 diapers each Sunday. The sign over the creche reads, "We shall not all sleep, but we shall all be changed!)

> **Newcomers may forget the sermon but long remember an unkept washroom.**

Visuals today are more than decor—they send an important message. Banners and attractive backgrounds add ambiance and eye appeal. A printed bulletin that is bright and cheery (with few typing errors) is more apt to be read.

Lighting also affects moods, as does sound. Good lighting allows people to read easily and well-controlled sound with no loud or soft spots lessens distractions. People with hearing problems should be given amplifiers. Seating space varies from culture to culture. For example, Americans prefer more personal space than do Dutch, who expect tighter quarters.

The distance from the pulpit to the audience communicates a level of relationship. The smaller the group, the closer the speakers stand. In traditional protestant churches, the pastor often spoke from an elevated pulpit indicating that the Word of God is over and above. Modern Westerners, however, are more comfortable having the speaker on their same level.

Clean rest rooms are also a witness to guests. Newcomers may forget the sermon but long remember an unkept wash room.

Appropriate Dress

Although styles vary from country to country and location to location, the seeker-sensitive church allows for informality yet requires its staff to wear appropriate attire. In high-impact churches leadership teams maintain an agreed upon standard of dress for all large gatherings.

Positive Programming

The service's emotional tone reflects the enthusiasm of the worship leader, the manner of announcements and the relevance of the pastor's message. In a high-impact church, it is important for a celebration to begin positive, stay positive and end positive. Unchurched people are not inclined to return to a negative, guilt-producing environment. Visitors are likely struggling with a sense of failure and searching for something *hopeful* to relieve their burdens.

Clearly communicated instructions help newcomers know when to stand or sit, so they don't feel self-conscious. People want to participate without being noticed. And a joyful, alive service is more apt to appeal to unchurched visitors than a staid, dead one.

Following each church event the leadership team of a high-impact church should come together to evaluate the event: *Was it emotionally refreshing, or did it feel heavy and oppressive? Did the message give a lift or was it a letdown? Did it help prepare people for the responsibilities and pressures they face in the world?* An inspiring, encouraging and motivating service is more readily received by visitors.

Relevant Announcements

Announcements are an integral part of a celebration service. Future events can be printed in a weekly bulletin, but verbal reminders — presented creatively and enthusiastically — are effective in stressing particular occasions. The larger a church becomes, however, the more programs there are. Only a minimum of carefully chosen announcements can be highlighted during a service.

A church of two hundred or more needs an efficient communications plan to match the church's vision. Only events that apply to everyone (and especially to visitors) are announced from the platform. "Churchy" terminology should be avoided, along with appeals for helpers for these activities.

Appealing Music

Music is a major communicator of values in modern society — it impacts people as the spoken word cannot. In the high-impact church, music is not just a preliminary activity for the message but in itself is a form of communication that penetrates the heart. It is both a form of evangelism and worship — communicating God's care and truth.

One example of the impact music has is the response of a visitor at the Crossroads Church in Geneva who responded to the warm, lively, engaging and upbeat worship style commenting, "We feel we can 'dance' to what you're offering. Other churches are somber. We need something to encourage us as we struggle to survive in a culture with so much tension."

Commonly, people today enjoy music with a beat and do not identify with music written before 1950.

The selection of songs in a seeker-friendly celebration is done with newcomers in mind. Gatherings for believers who want to praise in greater depth for longer periods can occur at other times. Cell groups, special praise and worship meetings or Sunday evening worship services can supplement the seeker-friendly celebration.

Western musical tastes vary, ranging from classical (a small percentage in North America; a larger percentage in Europe) to jazz, pop, folk and rock. It is a mistake, however, to try to be eclectic, offering a little bit for everyone. A high-impact church decides on a target group and then chooses music to match that cultural taste.

Commonly, people today enjoy music with a beat and do not identify with music written before 1950. To rock 'n' rollers, classical music means Elvis Presley! Modern rock music has been more universally accepted around the world than any other style. Author Russell Chandler writes, "Close to one out of two households (in the United States) is headed by a person born between 1946 and 1964. He or she is media oriented and likes rock music."[5]

Electronic bands, live accompaniment, vocalists, small ensembles, electronic keyboards, and soloists make for variety. Musical packages — praise songs, new arrangements of older hymns, songs written with personal statements and short participatory songs—all appeal to the Westerner. Organs, canned musical tracks, large choirs and long, drawn-out hymns are usually ineffective in reaching the unchurched. Professional musicians playing with a modern beat and style work best with unchurched audiences. High-quality musical performances with life-related messages are a contextualized expression of pre-evangelism.

Guidelines for Programming

- Replace the organ with a band.
- Keep music moving! Don't let it drag.
- Keep music upbeat! Avoid minor keys.
- Don't sing too much—or too little.
- Demand well-performed music.
- Minimize hymn singing or recast in contemporary style.
- Don't introduce lots of new songs at once.
- Be sensitive to the message in the words.
- Screen and minimize talking of musicians between songs.
- Smile! Musicians also communicate with body language.
- Preview all music—make sure there are no surprises!
- Keep creativity flowing with a variety of songs and performers.

Engaging Drama

Jesus used parables to illustrate theological truths. Drama is still a powerful communications tool. Visual sketches that touch the heart or bring humor to current issues can carry a service.

Good drama is related to life, fast moving and always relates to the sermon theme. A rule of thumb: no drama is better than poorly presented drama. When amateur players see the effectiveness of good drama their performances usually improve.

Drama and multi-media presentations hold an audience's interest and aid in understanding the Good News. Values, information and principles are retained much longer through drama than by a sermon. Author Paul Hiebert writes, "When sight and sound are used together, we remember more than six times as much as we would have remembered if we had only heard the information."[7]

Inspirational Preaching

Pastor Rick Warren of Saddleback Community Church advocates the following questions in order to "preach to produce growth:"

1. Does the message begin with needs, hurts and interests?
2. Is the message good news?
3. Does it offer practical help?
4. Does it build faith and hope?
5. What is the most positive way to say it?
6. What is the simplest way to put it?
7. How can it be said to make the strongest impact?
8. What is the most interesting way of saying it?[6]

Since peoples' attention span is about 15-30 minutes, sermons should be short and succinct. Warm, caring messages with a touch of humor are appreciated. (Preaching will be discussed more fully in the following chapter.)

Modern Translation

Scripture should be read from popular translations, not versions that seem archaic and difficult to understand. Remember, Koine Greek – the language of the New Testament – was the most popular language of the first century, A.D.

Program diversity

Reaching modern audiences calls for program diversity. This is especially critical with younger generations. Dan Reeves, founder of the Church Consultants Group, observes, "This *virtual reality* generation has been brought up on MTV, video games, and instant access to information. It has little interest in the past, and a short attention span when it comes to the future."[8]

A shorter attention span demands tighter, quicker-paced, highly visual segments. Communicating with the TV generation is enhanced by multi-media, drama, special music and highly illustrated messages.

Continual Evaluation

Strive for excellence in programming! Honestly evaluate church services and congregational events. Ask, *Did each part of the service fit together as a whole? What things worked? What didn't?* Privately ask participants and select members of the audience for feedback.

It is important to immediately praise the positive elements of a service or event. Good leaders remember to sincerely thank participants. Periodic personal notes are also appreciated. Evaluations should be prayerfully considered. In group evaluations, positive affirmations always precede negative critique.

Evaluations can bruise egos, but people are more receptive if objective criteria (presented above) are used in routine debriefing sessions. There is an important distinction between excellence vs. perfectionism, and process vs. product. Critiques are product-centered, not person-directed. This minimizes the emotional impact on the personality of a performer. The common goal is to effectively communicate to a target audience.

During evaluations, it is important to create a safe environment and spirit of free exchange among team members. Participants are carefully selected according to their role in church services or their area of expertise – they need to be sensitive and godly servants. The key in evaluation is mutual respect for one another.

A "First Impression Card" is a good way to get visitor feedback. What did newcomers like most? Least? People do not sign these cards, they only indicate an age group. Most negative comments will come from persons outside of the church's target group.

Summary Profile of a Seeker-Sensitive Service:

1. **Overall Atmosphere of Warmth and Acceptance**
    a. Have greeters make the atmosphere warm and friendly.
    b. Make sure facilities are clean, bright and attractive.
    c. Play taped music in the background during the pre-service.
2. **Instrumental Prelude and Greeting** (3-5 minutes)
    a. Use a variety of instruments and styles.
    b. Have the worship leader give a warm welcome.
3. **Upbeat Music or a Special Vocal** (2-5 minutes)
    a. Set the tone for the service with music or a vocal.

    b. Help the audience focus their attention with this.

    c. One to three songs to prepare the audience for worship.

4. **Announcements/Offering/Prayer** (2-6 minutes)

    a. Greet and announce only events that pertain to everyone.

    b. Explain the Communication Card.

    c. Explain the offering with disclaimer that guests need not feel obligated to give.

    c. Collect Communication Cards and Offering Envelopes.

5. **Congregational Singing** (6-10 minutes)

    a. Use simple melodies with words of integrity.

    b. Format style of music to your target group.

    c. Strive for celebrative and vibrant singing.

    d. Leader must be "real," not distant from audience.

    e. Invite people to greet those around them before sitting.

6. **Optional Scripture Reading/Story Telling** (3-5 minutes)

    a. Verbally introduce the service topic.

    b. Use current events as illustrations.

7. **Drama** (4-10 minutes)

    a. Illustrate the problem.

    b. Don't preach or provide solution!

    c. Vary the style. Interchange humorous and serious dramas.

8. **Special Song** (2-4 minutes)

    a. Tie-in with drama.

    b. Relate to the message theme.

9. **Message** (30 minutes) (See next chapter.)

10. **Closing application and commitment** (2 minutes)

11. **Special music** (2-4 minutes)

    Relate to application of the message.

12. **Closing Congregational Song** (2-6 minutes)

13. **Benediction** (1 minute)

    a. Teacher/preacher closes with prayer and/or challenge.

    b. Taped music begins immediately following the dismissal.

The high-impact church programs celebrative events that appeal to seekers. Non-believers are attracted to occasions that offer a relevant message in a winsome setting. Believers are more apt to bring their unchurched friends to attractive visitor-friendly services. ◪

17

TRANSFORMING PREACHING

Our gospel came to you not simply
with words, but with power.
                              —1 Thessalonians 1:4

WHY PREACH IN A VISITOR-FRIENDLY WAY?

Two years after we started the Crossroads International Church of Amsterdam, our leaders decided to try a more seeker-sensitive format. First, we identified three categories: un-churched practicing Christians (not regularly attending any church), unchurched professing Christians (who consider them-selves Christian, but haven't made a personal life-commitment to Christ) and unchurched pre-Christians (those not yet ready to believe).

Because a founding goal of the Crossroads was to see unchurched people become fully devoted followers of Christ, it was already somewhat successful in attracting people from all three groups. But overall, the ministry style was too believer oriented to be effective in reaching the unchurched.

We asked, *When would our members most likely bring a non-Christian friend to church?* The answer was, *Sunday morning.* We asked, *When are the most unchurched people likely to attend church on their own?* Again, the answer, *Sunday morning.* We needed a guest-sensitive format on Sunday morning not only for visitors themselves, but also to help our members build relationships with their unchurched friends.

But we were met with resistance. Several members argued that Sunday morning services were for believers. If the church targeted seekers, these Christians were afraid that their needs would be neglected. They looked forward to worship as a time of recuperation from fatigue due to ministry and service outside of the church.

These objections needed to be considered, but dissenters were assuaged as they were willing to sacrifice their comfort for the sake of winning the unchurched. It is difficult to make the transition from a believer-oriented ministry to a seeker-oriented ministry without some initial misunderstanding and conflict. In the case of the Crossroads, we were successful in switching to a visitor-friendly Sunday service so that we could minister to both believers and unbelievers.

HOW DO YOU PREACH TO SEEKERS?

A transition to a seeker-sensitive format influences the style of preaching. To appeal to visitors (Chapter 16), guest-sensitive life-transforming preaching is essential. The qualities of seeker-oriented communication are:

Scripturally Sound

Good preaching communicates God's Word in a way that impacts lives. The fundamental building block of faith is God's Word. Teaching and preaching, therefore must be faithful to Scripture.

An experienced preacher understands the difference between *drawing out* the meaning of Scripture (exegesis) and *reading meaning into* Scripture (isogesis). Good exegesis illuminates the meaning of scriptural texts. Sound preaching necessitates an interpretation of the Bible based on a historical, grammatical and exegetical approach to Scripture.

To impact people's lives, however, more than interpretation is needed. Preaching that transforms involves biblical information, contemporary illustrations and personal application.

Relevant to the audience

Effective evangelistic preaching uses subjects that concern non-Christians. Speaking to the secular mind means communicating with compassion.[1] Listeners ask, *What does this mean to me?* Sermons geared to the interest of the unchurched facilitate church growth.

> **When preparing a sermon, the teacher should consider, "Who am I preaching to?" not "What should I preach on?"**

The traditional approach to preaching assumes that listeners have a Christian worldview and some biblical knowledge. In contrast, seeker-oriented preaching communicates the Good News by applying it to life. This modern preaching style speaks to the needs, hurts and interests of a target audience. It offers practical, life-changing messages.

When preparing a sermon, the teacher considers, *Who am I preaching to?* not *What should I preach on?* The listener is the focus. Scriptural texts should be chosen that show how spiritual principles relate to both seekers and believers. Jesus Himself used this approach as He addressed the needs, pain and interests of those who came to hear Him teach.

Interesting

The dictionary defines "entertainment" as holding a person's attention and interest. This is a challenging aspect of preaching! Speakers must counteract the myth that all sermons are boring.

Good communication is more important than good oratory. Personal illustrations are meant to identify with the audience rather than create awe. Former U.S. President Ronald Reagan has been called "The Great Communicator" because he spoke to audiences the same way he talked to individuals. He told touching stories and aimed a lot of humor at himself. He seldom laughed at others.[2]

Humor is probably the most lasting way to make a point because it relaxes people and makes them receptive to new ideas. And word pictures make ideas interesting and entertaining. Jesus used both humor (about common things) and word pictures (parables) in his teaching.

A short series is an effective way to develop a theme. Announcements for upcoming series should be advertised to the congregation several weeks ahead – enough lead time for the word to spread. A church newsletter might highlight how the Sunday series for the month of August will address the problem of fear, for example.

Outlines printed in the church bulletin help people track the content of a message. Since most unchurched people are unfamiliar with the topography of the Bible, printed scriptural references reduce embarrassment and lost time. Obviously, this requires advanced preparation. Pastors and worship leaders who have thrown together "Saturday night specials" need to schedule planning sessions well in advance of celebrations.

Edifying

When preparing a sermon, a preacher should ask himself: *Do these ideas encourage and build faith and hope. Or do they discourage and tear people down?* The primary goal of preaching is to lead people to Christ and transform them to His likeness.

Exhorting listeners to examine whether or not they measure up to some command of the Bible leaves people with a sense of guilt, failure and heaviness. Although this may be necessary on occasions, a steady diet of admonishment falls on closed ears.

Both Christians and non-Christians are looking for something that refreshes, renews and recharges. People look for relief from the stresses of life they encounter all week in fast-paced modern culture.

What is the most encouraging way to communicate God's truth to people? Scripture gives a ready answer. Romans 15:4 says, "For everything that was written in the past was written to teach us, so that through endurance and the encouragement of the Scriptures we might have hope."

Practical

The purpose of Scripture is transformation, not information. An effective pastor/teacher emphasizes the application of biblical principles to real life. A practical message uses colorful, contemporary illustrations to make major points come alive and avoids the dogmatic, cerebral and theoretical.

Here's the sequence in the application approach to preaching: Identify a felt need, choose a text that relates to that need, draw out relevant spiritual principles and then decide on the application. Then the applied principles become the main points of the outline.

Simple

Effective sermons have only one main point. People tend to forget 95 percent of what they hear within 48 hours of hearing it. Therefore, a sermon topic that can be expressed in one sentence helps people understand and retain the specific emphases.

No more than five sub-points (preferably just two or three) should support the theme. People get lost or

A simple sermon does not have to be a shallow one.

tune out when too many ideas are presented in one message. Unfamiliar religious terms (that a speaker feels are necessary) need to be explained in common terms. Technical jargon and Christian clichés cause newcomers to feel like outsiders.

But a simple sermon is not a shallow one. The renowned scientist Albert Einstein said, "You don't really understand something until you can explain it in a simple way."

Before the legendary Methodist pastor John Wesley preached a sermon he read it to their 15-year-old household servant. "Stop me if you hear something you don't understand," he told her. When she looked puzzled, he would reword his point. Wesley's preaching shook England for Christ because his messages were simple and understandable, yet true to the gospel.[3]

Precise

A sermon should not be long and drawn-out since the average attention span is between 15-30 minutes. One of the hardest things to teach leaders about seeker-sensitive services is to keep their sermons *short*.

I still struggle with this. My teaching skills were developed in the classroom where a lesson lasted about 50 minutes. I developed an internal, psychological "teaching clock," that was difficult to change. This, combined with an inclination to be thorough, meant that I tried to cover too much material when I preached.

When I realized that I was over-communicating, I worked at changing my style. I now understand why God gave men wives. They are sure to tell you when you "went on too long – again." Through Sharon's feedback (sometimes just a look would do), I've been able to cut down on sermon time.

Visual

Every applied point should have a word-picture or example. Illustrations are like windows that let in light, they illuminate the minds of listeners. Most people remember stories and vignettes long after they have forgotten the title of a message.

Jesus – our model for teaching about faith – used word pictures. He talked about sowing seeds and reaping harvests to farmers; He spoke of "fishing for men" to fishermen; He invited a thirsty woman to a well that would never run dry; He spoke of being born again to a scholarly rabbi.

Visual illustrations are also important in our media-oriented Western culture. People are accustomed to taking in sights, sounds, emotional moods and information at the same time.[4] A mini-interview with a person who has successfully applied a principle to their life is an emotionally moving visual. There is hardly anything that motivates an audience more than a true story by the person who experienced it. Remember, much of the Bible is stories about how God deals with people.

Other ways to make a message visual include drama, multimedia and special props and backdrops. I still remember a message on the power of faith because I was given a mustard seed at the beginning of the church service.

Personal

The traditional approach to preaching disassociates the message from the pastor's personal life. Perhaps this stems from the idea that it is unspiritual to have problems. Many pastors are therefore guarded in sharing about themselves (often with some justification).

The best illustrations help the listener identify with the speaker, rather than create awe and separation. Although some discretion must be used about what is shared, preaching from personal experience is powerful. A pastor's life is his greatest message — he is a fellow traveller in applying Christ's Word. People learn best from role models of faith. As I share honestly about my own struggles and doubts (provided that I am not bogged down with them), people are persuaded to rely on God's power in their own troubles.

Positive

Positive, inspiring messages that motivate people out of love and hope dispel negative impressions of Christianity. The goal of the high-impact church is to attract — not repel — the unchurched. People need to hear the Good News that God sent His son to save, not condemn.

Teaching-preaching deals with negatives by presenting positive alternatives. For example, instead of preaching against adultery, preach about faithfulness. Pastor Rick Warren says that the key to encouraging people to change is: "Don't tell it like it is; tell it like it *could be.*"[5] The significance is showing the benefits of change, not the penalty of failure.

Negative sermons fill a church with negative members. When a Scripture with a negative slant is used, preach with a humble attitude and a broken heart. Even delicate moral issues and a call to holiness can be done in a positive way — one that communicates hope from a compassionate, forgiving and loving God.

Generally speaking, upbeat and how-to sermons appeal to people much more than sermons that condemn and deride. Instead of emphasizing being saved from the fires of hell ("turn or burn !"), emphasize being saved from meaninglessness and aimlessness in this life.[6]

Motivational

Good teaching and preaching is not only *sound*, but *motivational*. Both believers and unbelievers want to hear messages that encourage and motivate them to be better people.

As I search the Scripture, I pray to be open to the Holy Spirit in my own life. I listen and I ask, *What is the Holy Spirit saying to me through this passage? What quickens my own heart? What does He want to say to others in the contemporary situation? How can others best be helped to discover what the Holy Spirit wants do in their lives?*

The goal of preaching is for people to be doers of the Word, not just hearers. Fruitful preaching inspires listeners to make a decision or take action. In order to communicate that people are to *do* something, use a verb in the application statement.

> **Both believers and unbelievers want to hear messages that encourage and motivate.**

Motivational preaching leads unbelievers to make a commitment to Christ. Bill Hybels advocates two principles in asking non-Christians for a decision. First, they must have freedom of choice. (Western society guards personal choice and bristles at violations of this "right.") Second, Hybels says that the non-Christian needs *time* to make a decision. (Westerners are conditioned to approach issues analytically and critically.) The bigger the decision, the more thoughtful the person may be.[7]

Although individual non-Christians need time to process the gospel, frequent invitations—perhaps weekly—give them ample opportunities to receive Christ. In any audience people are at different spiritual stages. Only the Holy Spirit knows who is ready for the harvest. Charles Spurgeon expected people to be saved every time he preached—and so they were.

Rather than ask people to come forward to indicate their commitment (a practice instituted by 19th-century revivalist Charles G. Finney, 150 years ago), simply raising their hand or noting their decision on a feedback card is effective. Willow Creek encourages decision makers to turn to the person who invited them to the service and share their new commitment.

OLD STYLE OR NEW STYLE?

Leith Anderson contrasts yesterday's style with today's style in preaching. He notes that the preaching of yesteryear was characterized by sin-naming and condemnation. Today's preachers recognize that the modern generation is discouraged, depressed, tired, lonely and guilt ridden. They need to hear about hope.[8]

Yesterday's style of preaching was oratorical – formal, loud, polished and intense. This method used historical illustrations to prove points and bluntly told people what to do. Oratorical preaching puts the spotlight on the communicator. We need to swing the spotlight so that it highlights the ministry of others.[9]

Today's style is conversational, like the monologue of a talk show host. Words like "ought" or "should" punctuated the older style of preaching. According to Anderson, "the new style explains the issues, presents the alternatives, and seeks to persuade – but clearly leaves the decision up to the listener."[10]

Yesterday's style was deductive, starting with a premise and then elaborating on it. Today's style is inductive, beginning with explanations, followed by certain conclusions. Anderson reasons that the deductive approach works best with those who are already convinced, while the inductive approach is better for the undecided and hostile.[11]

CAN YOU PREACH TO CHRISTIANS AND SEEKERS AT THE SAME TIME?

After I spoke on the importance of "the person, power and purpose of Christ" at the Fellowship Bible Church in Park Cities, Texas, 29-year-old Sobrina called the office to ask what the preacher meant when he referred to "a personal relationship with Jesus Christ." She hadn't been in church since she was a pre-teen and now wanted to understand who God is.

My message had been targetted to believers, but I knew that there are always people in the audience who are new to church. I chose my words and stories so that I could connect with unbelievers as well as Christians. Sobrina related to the contemporary-style service and the seeker-friendly preaching. She had caught a glimmer of the truth – that knowing Christ is the key to life. Soon a staff person counseled with her and she became a follower of Jesus.

These principles apply in preaching to both believers and to nonbelievers. Christians and seekers alike respond to teaching and preaching that is sound, relevant, edifying, visual, simple, interesting, positive, practical, inspiring, personal and precise. That's a real challenge for today's modern preachers!

TOPICAL OR VERSE-BY-VERSE?

Some evangelical traditions are critical of topical preaching because they believe that it does not communicate the "whole counsel" of God. They advocate, instead, a verse-by-verse Scripture-expository approach. Preachers in the New Testament knew Scripture (Old Testament) and faithfully communicated the whole counsel of God. But Scripture does not dictate that the verse-by-verse method held is the only — or even the most effective — means of communicating to either believers or unbelievers.

I believe that God can use a variety of traditions and methods. I am also convinced that it is possible to communicate in a seeker-sensitive way using an expository verse-by-verse approach.

My friend, Bill Counts, is the pastor of the Fellowship Bible Church (mentioned earlier) — a contemporary, seeker-sensitive church that has experienced significant growth and impacted many lives with the gospel. Each Sunday he preaches with a low key, exegetical, reasoned style on sequential passages of the Bible.

Counts begins his messages with an observation or story that identifies with the interests, hurts and needs of his audience. He then relates his theme to a principle from the Bible and teaches from a particular, relevant scripture. Counts explains each verse in a simple way that his audience can comprehend. His messages, given in the verse-by-verse expository style, are grace-oriented, encouraging, practical and seeker-sensitive. Counts has found that a lot of folks who were formerly turned off by church oratory enjoy this simplistic style of comprehending the Word.

WITHOUT LOVE...

Finally, more than the right method is needed for lives to be transformed by the gospel. Whatever the principles or style of preaching, the preacher must be motivated by love for God and for people — or his words will not ring true. The Apostle Paul, an effective communicator to both believers and non-believers, said it eloquently in 1

Corinthians 13:1, "If I speak in the tongues of men and of angels, but have not love, I am only a resounding gong or a clanging cymbal." The high-impact preacher is motivated by the love of Christ and empowered by the Holy Spirit.

18

IDENTIFYING PLATEAUS

Do not put out the Spirit's fire....
—1 Thessalonians 5:19

THE NEED FOR PLATEAU-BREAKING CHURCHES

I asked a long-term Christian worker in France, "What does God want to do in this country?"

"We need more churches of four hundred or more people!" he answered. "French people do not notice the church because it is small and insignificant. We need regional churches that will impact a whole city."[1]

Most French reformed and evangelical churches are small, having reached a plateau at between 50-60 members, or less. They meet in garages, store fronts or small buildings—causing people to view them as ineffectual and anemic. Small churches contrast with the grandeur of French culture. To impact France for Christ, churches are needed that will break through these plateaus and begin to grow.

The need for high-impact churches extends beyond France to all of the Western world. In Western and Northern Europe, there are very few large churches.[2] The 1989 English Church Census indicates that over half the people who attend church find themselves in a congregation of 70 or fewer people, and eight out of ten worshippers are in a church with under 120 people.[3] The average size Protestant congregation on a typical Sunday morning in North America is fewer than forty people.[3] Of the 350,000 churches in the United States, four-fifths are at a plateau, or declining.[4]

To reverse static or declining churches, leaders need a vision and strategy to reach and incorporate new people. There are only three kinds of churches: *growing, plateaued,* and *declining.* Most of the plateaus and declines reflect lack of vision and/or lack of an appropriate strategy for growth.

To grow, a church must develop its organizational structure. Many growth plateaus are organizational rather than spiritual in nature, although the two are often related. Organizational development does not guarantee growth, but without it, growth is stifled.

SMALL CHURCHES—ADVANTAGES AND DISADVANTAGES

There are advantages to being small. A small and medium-size church has the sense of being a family. Everyone in the church knows everyone else; people are missed when they're absent.

There are more opportunities to be involved in a small church. Members can have a close relationship with those in leadership, and usually, there are more things to do than people to do them—every person counts.

A third advantage of a small church is that it can make decisions quickly. The number of people influenced by decisions is relatively small, so it's not difficult to obtain a consensus.

There are, however, disadvantages to the small church. It is encumbered with expensive facilities that take a disproportionate percentage of the budget. Routine maintenance tasks and administration take just as long for a small church as for a large one.[6]

The proportion of church members needed to make any activity visible, is higher than a large church. And, the fewer people in the small church results in limited cash and manpower for expansion. Many smaller churches are forced to operate without a pastor and struggle for survival.[7]

There has been a tendency to overly idealize small churches. The notion that small churches are friendlier than large churches is a misconception. Members of small churches are friendly to other members, but often resist outsiders.

Although some argue that small churches are better able to reach out, many have little vision to do so. Most small congregations tend to stay plateaued, year after year, decade after decade.[8]

THE VALUE OF LARGE REGIONAL CHURCHES

God wants lost people to be found and incorporated into Christ's body. The church that is serious about this task reaches out with the gospel and organizes itself with the expectation that God is going to bring growth.

A large regional church has a larger staff, organization, facilities, budget, vision, and outreach ministries. Thus it can reach and disciple more people because it can respond to a broader range of needs and is better

> **Although the majority of churches in North America are small, statistics show that the vast majority of church members belong to larger congregations.**

able to cope with change. The more variety of choices, the more entry points and growth opportunities for new people.[9] The regional church also has the advantage of drawing from a greater geographical radius than a small, neighborhood church.

Although the majority of churches in North America are small, statistics show that the vast majority of church members belong to larger congregations. According to church growth expert Lyle Schaller, 15 percent of the largest churches in North America are home for 50 percent of the total church membership, while 50 percent of the smallest churches are home to only 15 percent of the members.[10]

The shortage of large, vital, regional churches in Europe may account for the overall low church attendance there.[11] In England, only eight percent of churches have congregations with more than 150 people. Although the number of churches with small congregations is relatively large, the number of people cumulatively attending those churches is actually small.

According to research done by MARC Europe,[12] only 24 percent of all the people who go to church go to the over 50 percent of churches with less than 50 people attending on a Sunday. Nearly half of all those who go to church on a Sunday attend the 31 percent of churches with between 51 and 150 people. The remaining 25 percent attend the eight percent of churches of more than 150.[13]

The ability of large churches to preserve intimacy and a sense of belonging is often underestimated. Although large churches are sometimes perceived as being more impersonal than smaller churches, members in large congregations are frequently friendlier because their focus is on the vision and task of the organization as a whole.[14] A large church also has the capacity to preserve intimacy and care for people through the decentralization of pastoral care in multiple cell groups.[15]

To reach the unchurched, God's norm is that churches should grow. More high-impact churches are needed in our modern, urban world. This requires breaking through the small-church mentality of most Western congregations.

GROWTH MENTALITY OF HIGH-IMPACT CHURCHES

The focus of the high-impact church is not on size, but on reaching the lost and making more and better disciples. The primary characteristic of the high-impact church is not its size, but its mentality — its vision for growth. God can work through any size church when leaders and members are committed to God's will. A church can be small and growing, or large and plateaued. On the other hand, the reverse may be true. The late Donald A. McGavran, founder of the Fuller School of World Mission and Institute of Church Growth, comments:

> Everything starts small. We must not say smallness is a sign of failure.... To some He has given one talent, and to some He has given ten.... It is not helpful to think of

bigness as a mark of success, and smallness as a mark of failure. We must also look at the situation....[13]

To reach cities for Christ, small, medium and large high-impact churches are needed that have a mentality of reaching the lost. An analogy that may capture this is a shopping mall with small, medium and large "anchor" stores. The one thing that they all have in common is that they are in business to make a profit. The profit envisioned for the church is not monetary but making more and better disciples.

The high-impact church may start out small but it is committed to growing and eventually becoming a regional church. From the beginning, evangelism and pastoral care is decentralized while maintaining a centralized programming and leadership structure. The loyalty of people in a regional church is directed toward the decentralized ministries, whereas loyalty in a small church is directed toward the pastor.

> **The focus of the high-impact church is not on size but on reaching the lost and making more and better disciples.**

The key ingredient to growing a church, whether it is large or small, is a desire to make disciples for Christ. Once a discipleship plan is in place, corresponding leadership skills must be developed to facilitate the expected growth. Knowledge of organizational plateaus and dynamics will help keep a growing church on the move.

UNDERSTANDING ORGANIZATIONAL PLATEAUS

Plateaus are discernible levels of numerical size that require different forms of organization. The following describes typical church plateaus.

Plateau #1. The House Church (Size: 10-25)

The church of 10-25 people is a home group or "house church" typically meeting only once a week. They stand alone and do not recognize any structure beyond themselves. (In contrast, the cell-structured church recognizes a centralized leadership structure with the cells clustered under a common leader and ministry team.)[17]

Most house churches grow slowly and have little or no effective evangelistic outreach because they lack a vision and strategy for reaching the unchurched.

Plateau #2. The Single Cell Church (Size: 25-85)

The church of 25-85 people is a "single cell"[18] or "clan"[19] church. The single cell church is like a family where all the members know each other very well. Family members have regular places to sit and an "insider's humor" not understood by outsiders.

Single cell churches usually don't grow beyond 80-100 people because they resist change. In North America, 50 percent of churches fit into the single-cell church category with fewer than 75 active members.[20] According to MARC Europe, 61 percent of English churches have fewer than 50 people in attendance, including morning and evening services.[21]

People are attracted to a single cell or clan church because of close-bonded relationships. However, when the church reaches 50-60 people, intimacy is diffused and the church stops growing. Without skilled leaders who can subdivide the church and regain the intimacy factor, it's hard for the church to grow beyond 65-75 people. Single cell churches usually cannot support a pastor and are often led by persons who have other full-time jobs.

Plateau #3. The Small Church (Size: 85-150)

A "small church" has 85-100 members. It usually has a single pastor and operates with lay organizations and volunteer leaders for Christian education, music, and women and youth ministries. If a small church "thinks small" it never seems to marshal the resources, vision or know-how to move beyond its smallness.

Smaller churches are not just miniature larger churches. They have a different character altogether. The primary focus of a small church tends to be on the comfort and well being of each individual. (This contrasts with the large church which focuses on the well being of the congregation as a whole and on institutional health.)

There are no strangers in small churches. The social circle is predictable and comfortable. Preserving familiarity becomes a high priority for these church members as they hold on to the status quo — an obstacle to growth. The intimacy in small (and even medium-size churches) is no accident, it is part of its nature.[22]

Plateau #4. The Mid-Size Church (Size: 150-250)

The "mid-size church" is made up of about 150-250 people and faces the formidable "200 barrier." Approximately 99 percent of churches have fewer than 200 people in attendance.[23]

Like the small church, mid-size churches usually have a single pastor with multiple lay organizations staffed by volunteers or part-time personnel. Mid-size churches make it to 200 and find that further growth is stifled by lack of staffing. Overworked lay leaders also experience burn-out at this level.[24]

Plateau #5. The Large Church (Size: 250-750)

The church of 250-750 people is a "large church." Fewer than 1 percent of churches grow to this size. These churches are multi-staffed, with pastors in charge of one or more aspects of church life. Each pastor ministers in much the same manner as a pastor in the one-pastor church.[25]

The large-size church has specialist-supported lay organizations such as a choir, Christian education, women's and youth ministries. People usually come because the programming is attractive, the preaching is good, and the services are culturally relevant.

One of the greatest problems in the large church is the assimilation of new people. They may be attracted to the church, but drop out if they do not get involved on a small-group level. Unfortunately, one-half of new members in large churches become inactive within a year.[26]

Plateau #6. The Very Large Church (Size: 750-2,000)

A church averaging 750-2,000 people is a "very large church." Only 0.4 percent of churches have more than 1,000 people in Sunday attendance. The church that hits the 1,000 mark has usually been successful in responding and programming according to the interests of the larger body.

The very large church has a divisionalized ministry and generalized staff. These generalists lead age-related or life-stage ministries (camps, special seminars, etc.) and supervise lay-volunteer run sub-organizations. More corporate management is needed to manage the programs of a very large church.[27]

Plateau #7. The Mega Church (Size: 2,000-10,000).

The "mega church" has 2,000-10,000 people attending Sunday services. These are matrix-organized churches led by teams of generalists, supported by specialized staffs.

Generalists give pastoral and organizational oversight to age-graded or need-meeting ministries. Specialists lead a variety of programs including music, Christian education, evangelism training and outreach. Many laymen act like staff and each adult group operates like a satellite church. Adequate facilities, leadership and opportunities for incorporation are critical issues for continued growth.

Plateau #8. The Meta Church (Size: 10,000 and up)

Carl George, Director of the Charles E. Fuller Institute for Evangelism and Church Growth, Pasadena, California, has coined the church of more than 10,000 the "meta church." The meta church is a model for unlimited growth while simultaneously maintaining high-quality, individualized care.

The organizational structure of the meta church is a multi-staff congregation committed to nurturing the maximum number of believers. These trained leaders discover and use their God-given gifts to oversee lay ministries throughout the church.

According to George, there are six kinds of meetings in a meta church:

1. The high presentation event—a service designed for guests and seekers.
2. The celebration or worship event—the people of God coming into the presence of God. This central worship event can sometimes be combined with seeker friendliness.
3. The leadership cultivation and supervision meeting—for reports, problem solving, and planning.
4. The rehearsal—the ministry team prepares for leading ser-

vices; this assures a cultivated event.

5. The serving meeting—workers are organized for tasks.

6. The cell—mutual ministry where people cared for one another in a small group setting.[28]

Other features of the meta church include frequent opportunities for fellowship in a variety of ways, continual teaching of concepts and skills and regular opportunities for service. This church gives consistent support to lay-led ministries and maintains an over-abiding spiritual dimension through prayer.[29]

ARTIFICIAL LIMITS TO GROWTH

A healthy church grows as it pursues the spiritual growth of its members and the evangelization of its community. Most limits to a church's effectiveness and growth are self imposed. The factors that artificially limit growth are lack of visionary leadership, members unwilling to risk new ideas, and an inadequate organizational structure. The church that breaks through these faith obstacles is on its way to becoming a high-impact church.

19

BREAKING PLATEAUS

*Forgetting what is behind and straining toward
what is ahead, I press on toward the goal to win
the prize for which God has called me....*
—Philippians 3:13-14

STEPS TO GROW THROUGH PLATEAUS

Most Western churches are either plateaued or declining. If a church has a healthy spiritual core and a vision to impact its community, it probably needs new organizational dynamics in order to begin growing again. High-impact churches anticipate and — in advance — plan for structural changes needed to break through the various plateaus.

Plateau #1. Growing the House Church (Size: 10-25)
To break through the 10-25 person plateau, the house church (or home group) must first decide that it *wants* to grow. Once this decision is made, it is essential for this church to develop a strategy to reach the surrounding unchurched community. In a new church plant, the planting pastor should set aside at least 50 percent of his time for making new contacts. Core members are also trained how to make new contacts. Evangelism becomes the responsibility of

every member.

The house church can build on the strength of its small group experience by dividing into cell groups, then multiplying. New people and new resources will keep the growth going.

A visionary leader who is trusted and esteemed by the group might come from the present group, or be called in to serve. The leader's primary responsibility is—under the guidance of the Holy Spirit—to be a catalyst for growth.[1]

Buckhead Community Church of Atlanta, Georgia, began as a home group. Four families had a vision to reach the unchurched of their city for Christ. They recruited an enthusiastic pastor whose vision matched theirs—a Scottish evangelist, Peter Grant. (Grant had been praying that God would send him to lead a seeker-sensitive church.)

The church has grown primarily though a seeker-driven celebration and an emphasis on network evangelism. Five years later, the church averages 350 people on Sunday morning and 100 in their Sunday evening believers service. With 130 people in cell groups, the church now emphasizes the role of cell groups in evangelism and discipleship.

Plateau #2. Growing the Single-Cell Church (Size: 25-85)

To break the 25-85 person plateau, it helps to understand what sociologists call a primary group—people who share a significant and prolonged common history. The single-cell church is a primary group so tightly bound together that it shuts out those who do not share in its traditions—or sometimes even those who do not have a "blood tie." The group is an end in itself—exclusive rather than inclusive.[2]

The single cell shields itself from the surrounding culture. Members draw their identity from the past. They perpetuate their heritage and protect their territory. Single-cell churches are resilient, but difficult to grow because their primary goal is survival and maintaining the status quo. Single-cell church members mistakenly believe that a large church means an impersonal church.

The best of both worlds is being part of a small group in a large church. New relationships develop as cells are formed on the basis of reaching out, instead of keeping out. A church can grow while preserving the intimacy afforded by a small group. There is a growth consciousness—two to ten people added by each new cell group. Meanwhile, the church gathers all the groups together for times of celebration.

To break through the single-cell plateau, a single-cell church first identifies a reachable target group and establishes outreach events that match the felt needs of that group (Chapters 10, 11 and 15). Generally, people are searching for friendship, love and belonging.

> **It may take a crisis for a church to break through the single-cell structure.**

To succeed, a single-cell church needs a visionary leader who can mobilize people for ministry. Then church members themselves must "own" and share the pastor's vision and dream for the church. Lay leaders need training to establish new cell and task groups such as Sunday school classes, women's activities, music ensembles, bands, clubs for kids and other groups that fit targeted needs.

Calvary Community Church of Westlake Village, California, broke through the 25-85 plateau because Pastor Larry DeWitt was committed to church growth and had a vision to reach the rapidly growing community. His first-year goal was for the fifteen families who shared his dream to create a new, exciting, contemporary environment that encouraged conversions. At first, some church members were uncomfortable with growth because the church changed in style.

A significant change came when they moved from a small obscure building to a visible, seeker-friendly restaurant. DeWitt challenged his congregation, "What if each of you developed a friendship with one or two unchurched people and invited them to come and enjoy our fellowship?" As people responded to DeWitt's suggestion, the church experienced explosive growth.

It may take a crisis for a church to break through the single-cell structure. The threat of extinction became a catalyst for Calvary Community. However, the best motivation for moving beyond the single cell is a compassion for the lost. From this vision, the church can train its members and organize itself for effective evangelism and cell multiplication.

Plateau #3. Growing the Small Church (Size: 85-150)

Members of small churches may spend time and energy lamenting their weaknesses, shortcomings and limitations. Their vision is limited to survival—a "fortress mentality." They are oblivious to harvesting opportunities.

The way members view a church—their level of congregational self-esteem—determines the growth potential of a small church. Negativism hinders growth.[3] To break through the 85-150 plateau of a small church it is necessary to identify, affirm and build on strengths.[4] In most growing churches, members are enthusiastic about their faith, congregation and pastor.

Replacing negative attitudes in a small church with a "possibility mentality" leads to an increased awareness of the church's strengths and call to reach its community. The small church with a faith perspective seeks answers to questions like, *What people are being overlooked by other churches in our community? What needs do they have?* and, *Which needs could we respond to?* The most effective new-member recruitment strategies draw upon the strengths of the congregation to respond to the unmet needs of the unchurched.[5]

Good leadership is critical in breaking through the small church plateau. Long pastorates do not in-and-of-themselves produce numerically growing churches, but it is rare to find sustained growth without the benefit of a long pastorate.[6]

An effective pastor will gather church members into a corporate identity and vision. He also motivates members to wholeheartedly embrace their goals. The church's vision is kept in the forefront, especially as newcomers are added.

To continue growing, leaders increasingly depend on lay persons for ministry tasks associated with adding new cells and need-meeting ministries. The overall leader will then function as a "rancher" who shepherds the body through cell units and the centralized ministries of the church—goal-setting, recruiting, training, delegating, monitoring, nurturing and motivating lay leadership.

As the church grows, events are scheduled at least a year ahead—preferably, two to three-years. Programs should reinforce the evangelistic outreach of the church. Associated hands-on training programs equip members for outreach, cell groups and cell-cluster leadership.[7]

To grow beyond a small-church level, every facet of church life must improve—beginning with better-quality preaching.[8] An improvement in the quality of preaching usually requires better planning and delegating on the pastor's part. One cause of poorly prepared sermons ("Saturday night specials") is lack of time for preparation.

An overall approved appearance of the church and an emphasis on friendliness is critical to attract newcomers. Also, the style of music for gatherings may need to be upgraded. It is easier to improve the quality of celebration services as the church grows and new resources are added. (There is a breakthrough point where the church achieves the "critical mass" necessary for quality programming.)

With 85-150 people in attendance, a rented facility will suffice for weekly gatherings. Most meetings can still be held in homes. Home offices are sufficient and keep overhead down, freeing resources for outreach and quality programming. The church should, however, make long-range plans for larger facilities and a centralized office.

> To grow beyond a small-church level, every facet of church life must improve.

Plateau #4. Growing the Mid-Size Church (Size: 150-250)

The mid-size church faces the formidable "200 barrier." Leaders and members must decide if they really want their church to grow. To break through this barrier, the organizational dynamics of the church must change. This may result in conflict when those in control do not want to make room for new leaders to emerge.

A church can make it to mid size by good pastoral skills, but to grow larger than this, leadership and managerial skills are needed. The pastor can no longer function as the one who does most of the ministry. Instead, he must delegate ministry to others.

Church growth increases proportionately to the amount of ministry that shifts from the pastor to the congregation.[9] Members that have looked to their pastor as "the" minister become hands-on ministers and see their pastor as a leader-supporter. The congregation gives more authority to the pastor as primary leader and equipper of lay people for various ministries.

As a mid-size church grows, the network of care must be expanded to counteract an impersonal image. A continual emphasis on multiplying cells is the key. Church growth is proportionate to the number of people who have meaningful relationships and/or ministry involvement.

Growth goals coupled with big events help mid-size churches to grow.

To break the mid-size church plateau, new staff is needed. As cells multiply and new units of ministry are added, more oversight and training is expected. Statistics in North America show that one staff person is needed for every 150 people over age 13. This ratio may be less in the cell-structured church where trained supervisors are in place.

New staff are selected on the basis of their ability to complement the pastor and contribute to the growth, outreach, assimilation and/or administration of the church. Normally, the salary for additional staff will come from giving units attracted within the first 12-18 months of the new staff person's tenure.

Saddleback Valley Community Church in Southern California, began with a co-pastorate—two leaders who were both generalists and had essentially the same roles. The church grew to 300 people and then plateaued. Not until the church designated Rick Warren as senior pastor and Glen Kreun was brought on board as administrative executive assistant, did the church begin to grow again.

Growth goals coupled with big events help mid-size churches to grow. Special holiday programs for Christmas and Easter and Mother's Day can attract nominal Christians who do not usually come to church. A quality event—and a well planned follow-up—is a key to breaking through mid-size plateaus.

The larger the church becomes, the more important it is to focus on a corporate identity and keep the church's vision strong. A sense of excitement is created by realistic goals, building positive expectations, sharing stories of God at work in people's lives, celebrating victories and successes, planning outstanding programs, featuring special guests, developing inspiring worship and meeting the needs of people.[10]

Keep energy and resources focused on fruitful activities (even if there are only a few), and not on non-productive ones. Activities that succeed are simple enough to be understood and enjoyed by a broad range of people. These times are conveniently scheduled to fit people's busy lives. Quality programs will result in qualitative and quantitative growth.

As the church grows, new, expanded facilities will be needed.[11] Sociological strangulation and growth retardation occurs when a facility reaches 80 percent capacity. It is important to anticipate restrictive growth problems and replace them quickly. The longer a church is plateaued, the more difficult it is to get it going again.

Plateau #5. Growing the Large Church (Size: 250-750)

The aspects discussed above are also important to break through a large church plateau. The key to growth is equipping and involving laity in ministry so they bring in new people.

A more sophisticated organizational structure is needed as new units and leaders multiply. Effective ministry roles are based on individual strengths, interests, passions, and gifts. Detailed job descriptions for leaders provide direction.[12]

To grow beyond the 250-750 level, additional trained administrative staff is vital. Some new positions to consider if not already in place: full-time minister of music, minister of education (children and/or cell group ministry), administrative assistant, part-time pianist/keyboard player and custodian.[13] Staff selection is based on past ministry track-records and compatibility with the church's style and philosophy.

Staff orientation will change from *providing* ministry to *arranging* ministry.[14] Managerial and rancher skills are not only important for the senior pastor, but for other staff leaders as well. Management training in skills such as management by objective (MBO) — where people, services and programs are pointed toward specific goals —

are beneficial.

It is imperative to keep improving the quality of the celebration service and multiplying cell groups. The ministries of the church will shift from a minority-target group to multiple-target groups. New programs that match the surveyed felt needs of the unchurched community determines the nature of these groups. For future blessing, growth goals are inspired by God and motivated by love, obedience and Christian service.[15]

Plateau #6. Growing the Very Large Church (Size: 750-2,000)

The strategy to grow a very large church is — you guessed it — gathering people and multiplying cells. Special groups to meet felt needs are a key to attracting new people. For example, extensive age-graded ministries (youth, singles, young married without children, couples with children, single parents, seniors) and support groups where people can find acceptance and hope (divorcees, single parents, substance abusers, victims, and newcomers). New pastors, for example, a minister of education and a part-time age-division minister, direct these ventures.

> # The strategy to grow a very large church is —you guessed it— gathering people and multiplying cells.

Sunday school classes can supplement the cell structure but may compete with cell groups for church resources. A better plan is to develop a training structure for the various levels of leaders (cell leaders, supervisors, zone pastors). Cell groups are the most conducive way to provide pastoral care, meet individual felt needs and incorporate newcomers into a church.

It takes exciting, culturally attractive and appealing programming to draw people to church and create openness to the gospel. Charismatic festivals and seeker-sensitive services have both effectively reached the unchurched in Western countries. These programs have quality music and a strong pulpit ministry.

Organizationally, it may be necessary to divisionalize the church — to subdivide leadership and ministries based on the church's sub-purposes. In the cell-structured church, divisions are made on the basis of geographical or special ministry zones.

In a very large church, the senior pastor is a managerial leader who delegates ministry appropriately to divisional pastors. Ministry fatigue can only be avoided if leadership shifts from a sheepherder to a rancher mentality (Chapter 20). Delegation and accurate assessment are critical senior-pastor skills since it is impossible to be available to everyone and attend every event.

The role of the laity also changes as a very large church grows. Instead of being *provided for*, the laity become *providers of* ministry within the organizational structure.

Staff roles change, too. Staffs do less hands-on ministry; they do more training, planning and coordinating of laity. Greater administrative skills are needed as the senior pastor and staff move from shepherd-style to rancher-style ministry.[16]

Plateau #7. Growing the Mega Church (Size: 2,000-10,000)

By the time the church nears mega-church size, a structure for multiply cells and training cell leaders is operating smoothly. Now, specialist ministers (associates, education, music, business administration, evangelism and outreach and family life) are added. Support staff (administrative assistants and custodians) work cooperatively with leadership staff.[17]

Expanded facilities and multiple services are needed in the growing mega church, perhaps requiring another location. An alternative to increasing facilities is to plant daughter churches by sending out large groups of people. However, each daughter church needs qualified church-planting leadership.

In growth, it is critical not to lose the spiritual essence of the church. Fuller Seminary's C. Peter Wagner observed that in charismatic churches with 2,000 or more people in attendance, spiritual dynamics undergirded numerical growth.[18]

Plateau #8. Growing the Meta Church (Size: Beyond 10,000)

The meta church is a decentralized/centralized model quite different from the traditional Western way of approaching ministry. The meta church draws heavily upon the cell-church model of the Yoido Full Gospel Church of Seoul, Korea.

This church has proved that the ability of a church to meet the needs and expectations of its people is not related to size, but to organizational structure. The cell-structured church has unlimited ability to grow, yet can continue to meet the pastoral needs of its people.

New Hope Community Church of Portland, Oregon, is not yet an example of the meta church in terms of its size but is organized according to the Meta model. New Hope confirms that the cell-structured church is not limited to the oriental culture or an oriental mind-set. Both Yoido Full Gospel Church and New Hope Community Church demonstrate that church growth is a function of leadership, vision, faith and organizational structure. (Review Chapter 12.)

Whether house church or meta church, breaking plateaus requires prayer and the empowering of the Holy Spirit. The steps to grow a church are too complex and demanding to be undertaken by human strength alone.

SUPERNATURAL STRENGTH AND STRATEGIC STEPS

The high-impact church recognizes that skilled leadership, strategic steps and supernatural strength all go together. Through God's guidance and power and man's prayer and careful planning, church plateaus can be broken and the kingdom of God advanced.

Breaking through plateaus and growing a church requires new skills. Leaders experience the full gamut of a learning curve — including times when the leader may feel inadequate and tempted to give up. But proficiency develops as pastors, staff and lay leaders persevere. The new ministry style then becomes a rewarding and fulfilling adventure!

20

HIGH-IMPACT LEADERSHIP

Behind every great achievement
is a dreamer of great dreams.
—Robert Greenleaf

RECOGNIZE YOUR LIMITATIONS

Michael Shaw, a gifted pastor committed to reaching the unchurched, found it increasingly difficult to manage his staff and the administrative responsibilities of his church. The church, having grown to 2,000 people, started to plateau.

Pastor Shaw had several strengths—life-related preaching, a vision for the church and community, and an ability to inspire his congregation with vision. But the church staff (about 20 full- and part-time persons) suffered from his inability to build a team.

Fortunately, Shaw recognized the organizational strain and hired an executive assistant. He chose a man with experience in business and the ability to organize people and delegate responsibility. The new executive's gift was administration, not preaching.

As Pastor Shaw learned to trust his new assistant, the quality of his own leadership improved. He felt less stress. And the spirit of the staff improved immeasurably.

Pastors are tempted to hang on to ministries and responsibilities that they should delegate as their church grows. Perhaps they feel that only "doing" proves their worth. But the true mark of a good leader is the ability to trust others who complement and contribute to the church's overall vision.

WHAT SHOULD PASTORS DO?

The greatest difficulty facing pastoral leadership is defining the role. Is the pastor to be a prophet, teacher, resource person, enabler, religious expert, preacher, counselor, therapist, CEO, facilitator, leader, equipper, administrator, shepherd, social activist—or, all of the above? Pastors are often expected to be omnicompetent and omnipresent.

In *A Church for the 21st Century*, Leith Anderson notes that social and cultural expectations make the present day a tough time to be a pastor. "Pastors are expected to be strong leaders at a time when all leadership is suspect, expected to communicate with the skill of Jay Leno [comedian, talk-show host], be as socially informed as George Gallup [U.S. pollster], and as effective managers as the best Harvard M.B.A.'s."[1] These expectations are often hopelessly unreasonable!

Pastors burn out, tune out, or drop out from unclear or unrealistic expectations—whether self-imposed or imposed by others. The pastoral role needs to be clearly understood. What are the primary functions of the leader of a high-impact church?

SPIRITUAL DIRECTOR

The first priority is the leader's own relationship with God. The pastor is a minister to God, of God and through God. The healthy pastor focuses on prayer, meditation on God's Word and fellowship with the Holy Spirit. Only when the pastor receives direction and strength from God can he effectively lead others.

The principle function of the pastor is to be the spiritual director of the church. Effective leaders realize that it is Christ who draws the world to Himself. He is the author of salvation and He transforms followers into His image. A strong leader, therefore, abides in Christ while pointing others to the Savior and the life that He gives.

Leaders without a close relationship with Christ and accountability in the church are more prone to the sins of the flesh, the influence of the world and attacks of spiritual forces. The carnal leader with motivational and management skills is easily manipulative. Authentic leadership is fundamentally spiritual and flows from a walk with God in community with other like-minded church leaders.

> **Pastors burn out, tune out or drop out from unclear or unrealistic expectations.**

The primary struggle of the church is spiritual. Competent leaders give priority to their own spiritual walk and nurturing and inspiring spiritual life in others. Christians are engaged in spiritual warfare and must be alert to Satan's schemes to distort, disrupt, deceive and devour. Careful spiritual leadership keeps close watch!

VISION CASTER

Assuming a healthy spiritual walk with God, the leader's next responsibility is to generate, communicate and sustain a common purpose and vision within the body.[2] Pastor and author Dale Galloway states that the three qualities of a successful leader are love for God, love for people, and vision.[3] The authority to impart vision and to mobilize a congregation to implement that vision is a God-given gift to destined leaders.

In his book, 44 *Steps Up Off the Plateau,* Lyle Schaller notes the importance of the visionary leader's role. He says that the primary source of leading a congregation up off a plateau is a pastor who brings "a combination of transformational leadership skills, pastoral competence, persuasive communication abilities and productive work habits. He has an emphasis on excellence, contagious enthusiasm, attention to detail, and—most important of all—a positive vision of what God has in mind for His congregation."[4]

The high-impact leader must guide the church into the future. He is a possibility thinker whose dynamic leadership catalyzes the church into action and growth.[5] A pastor who focuses solely on the present, lacks continuity and direction. Visionary leaders understand where God wants their church to go.

Every person in every church needs vision. Vision gives life meaning, helps us survive and thrive. It determines our future, and in the church, it unifies the body. The visionary leader discerns Christ's purpose for the church and casts that vision in personal conversations, in the celebration service, in the leadership team gatherings and staff meetings.[6]

The visionary leader is an agent of change. Change is frightening and discomforting to most people, so he anticipates emotional struggles within the staff and congregation. The leader is an enabler through analyzing, organizing and climatizing (e.g., providing information and comfort during times of change).

An agent of change creates a non-threatening environment that allows people to reveal their fears. He then encourages change by casting vision—celebrating past visionary decisions, telling faith inspiring stories and pointing to the fruit that fulfillment of the vision will bring.[7] The wise leader identifies opinion makers and elicits their support before introducing changes in a church's vision.

But it is not enough to simply impart vision. The vision casting leader must help implement it. This requires long-range planning.

TEAM BUILDER

The high-impact church leader acts as a senior partner of a leadership team. He is committed to accomplishing the mission of the church, building and maintaining team spirit, and promoting the well-being of each individual.[8] All of these characteristics are related to each other creating an effective whole. The mission, team and individual continually interact and each must be seen in relation to the other two. High-impact leaders are continually aware of all three.

High-impact leadership values team ministry. Teamwork does not detract from strong pastoral leadership—it enhances it. A fruitful leader builds a team through gift-based programming—structuring the church around gifted people that God raises up. He places team members in the area of their special gifts and gathers the right mix of people to accomplish various visionary tasks.

The high-impact leader invests time in building ministry leaders and administrative staff. This core leadership team functions like a cell group with team members committed to loving, encouraging and being accountable to the task and to one another. Relationship-building activities and celebrating corporate achievements are essential in developing a team.

The Team Builder

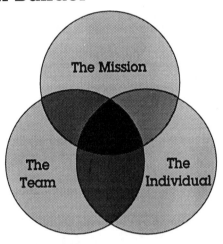

The larger the organization, the more important it is to coordinate the team members' relationship to the organization. This is enhanced by clearly delineating responsibilities, procedures and policies. Effective procedures and policies are purpose-based, reflecting not only the well-being of the organization but individuals.

An effective working team contributes ideas, gives opinions and tests the feasibility of potential decisions. Trust, creativity, challenge, recognition and job satisfaction are all important in creating a visionary team-building environment. The leader values each team member's needs and encourages healthy interaction.

CHARISMATIC LEADER

A charismatic leader is gifted by God and sensitive to the Holy Spirit. God uses high-impact leaders to provide inspiration and give direction. Charismatic leadership crystallizes and kindles collective vision and inspires the body to action. The church recognizes those whom God has gifted and raised up for leadership by sensing their God-given vision, direction and authority.

The most important spiritual gifts needed by a high-impact pastor are leadership, pastor-teaching and evangelism. Leadership is the special ability God gives to set goals in accordance with His purposes, and to communicate those goals to others in such a way that they voluntarily and harmoniously work together to accomplish the goals for the glory of God.[9]

The high-impact church pastor is the number-one leader of a congregation. Gifted leadership is crucial for the church to grow, solidify members toward the church's vision and goals and impact the community.[10]

The pastor-teaching gift builds up the body to maturity. This God-given gift allows a leader to make a long-term personal commitment to the spiritual welfare of a body of believers. As he serves, he communicates relevant information for the health and ministry of the body.[11]

The gift of evangelism is important because a major focus of the high-impact church is to reach the unchurched. Evangelism is the special ability to share the gospel with unbelievers so that they become disciples and responsible members of the church.[12]

Although important, leadership, pastor-teacher and evangelism is not a complete the list of the gifts needed to lead a high-impact church. Apostolic and prophetic gifts are mentioned by the Apostle Paul as critical in equipping and building up the body of Christ. The gift of administration, or "helmsman," is another gift needed by the leader of a high-impact church. If the pastor does not have some of these gifts they can be added by complementary associate leaders.

C.E.O.

The high-impact church requires the integration of charismatic and executive leadership. To develop a high-impact church, more than charismatic leadership is needed. Executive or management skills are essential.

Good management principles and strategy include planning,

goal setting, discerning priorities and delegating tasks. Monitoring the performance of team members keeps quality high. In addition, an executive leader must build consensus and goal-ownership, listen to opinions, deal with objections, identify resources and remove growth restrictive problems.

The executive pastor is responsible for initiatives that carry out the purposes of the church. He acts as a liaison between the elders and the staff, participating in the mutual accountability of the leadership counsel.

Executive leadership is purpose-directed and sets measurable and realistic goals that clarify individual and corporate responsibilities. Goals are faith statements reached through God's grace and strength. They move Christians from where they are spiritually to where they believe God wants them to be.

Goals are faith statements reached through God's grace and strength.

Executive leadership evaluates the progress of the church and strives for excellence.[13] High-impact churches have leaders that recognize and develop potential gifts within the body. They motivate people to assume responsibility by encouraging individual initiative and risk-taking.

The concept of a pastor as a CEO (Chief Executive Officer) of the church is more common in North America than in Europe. In North America, pastors are apt to be hired from job descriptions and specific criteria.[14]

In both North America and Europe, the church is in competition with secular and non-Christian forces for the hearts and minds of people. This pressure necessitates that leaders be more effective in organizing and managing resources in order to accomplish Christ's objectives. The senior pastor is a chief executive officer (CEO) who knows how to direct people toward goals. (The greatest test of leadership is whether the body is following the church's vision and strategy.)

Although there are some fundamental differences between the business world and the church — and not everything from the corporate world is applicable—important management skills can be gleaned. Executive leadership, according to organizational consultant Peter Drucker, is characterized by five practices or habits of the mind. Effective executives:

1. Know where their time goes and manage the little bit of time that is under their control.
2. Gear efforts to expected results, rather than the work to be done.
3. Build on strengths and not weaknesses—on what they can do, not what they cannot do.
4. Set priorities and concentrate on the few major areas where superior performance will produce outstanding results.
5. After seeking "dissenting opinions" effective executives make decisions based on the right steps in the right sequence, rather than on consensus."[15]

The larger the church, the more essential a centralized executive structure. This structure complements and supports the decentralized cell structure of the church. The executive leader is a catalyst who motivates, inspires and unifies the church's centralized and decentralized ministries.

RANCHER EQUIPPER

Both the centralized and decentralized dimensions of the high-impact church call for pastors to act as equippers. One of the functions of the pastor is to feed the flock. This involves an ability to stand up before an audience and teach God's word in such a way that people understand its meaning and are motivated to apply it to their lives. Effective preachers know how to vary their rate, rhythm, volume, and emotional intensity to hold the attention of an audience and keep them alert. But preaching performance is not enough to pastor a church.

An equipper doesn't rely solely on preaching—or even try to do all the pastoring—but sees that all the pastoring gets done. Equipping involves a "rancher" perspective that shifts from *providing* care for the sheep to *arranging* care for them.[16] The rancher leads others to do the shepherding.

The role of the equipper is to recruit, train, deploy, lead, inspire, monitor and nurture members of Christ's body as lay ministers. If there is no one trained and available to lead a strategic ministry, the rancher may model what he wants done until someone else is recruited and prepared to take over. Strategic deployment and goal setting become the focus.

SERVANT LEADER

A competent pastor is a servant leader, able to balance authority and responsibility with humility and service. The function of a servant leader is to discern what is important, guide the church into the future and keep the church on track.[17]

To fulfill this mission, a servant leader uses his or her gifts, abilities, authority, expertise and position to pursue God's purpose for the church while at the same time seeking the well-being of others.[18] The servant-motivated leader helps fellow believers achieve their God-given potential and structures the church to involve the maximum number of people. Such leaders know where the church is going, what it takes to get there, and how to motivate and inspire others to join in the quest.

The authority of a servant leader is earned through manifesting spiritual gifts, displaying moral and spiritual integrity, and evidencing a genuine desire to serve Christ and others. Jesus did not force or coerce His disciples to follow or obey him. Neither should the leader use God-given authority to dominate or manipulate—but to serve.

At the same time, the servant leader is not "tentative," catering to the wishes and desires of people. Jesus did not defer His God-given authority to the whims of His disciples or other followers.[19] The servant leader has a sense of what is right for the times, the organization and the people of the church.

A servant leader will receive not only love but anger. Many church members become angry with the person who proposes change. But a confident leader knows that Christians grow when stretched beyond their comfort level. He is strong enough to help people journey through change without taking their criticisms personally and without trying to please everyone.

HOW DO YOU GET FROM HERE TO THERE?

At a recent breakfast, Steve, a pastor friend of mine, asked my advice about a list of opportunities he was considering. His dilemma was which of the following he should choose: a summer study emphasizing the leader's devotional life and role as shepherd, a Doctor of Ministry program developing leadership skills, a seminar presenting a contemporary approach of ministry, a management skills course training him in an area where he felt weak, or a mission trip that would stretch his ministry horizons and involve him in intense evangelism.

My advice was that he pursue all of these — but spread them over several years. I believe that all of the items he mentioned would contribute to his and his church's long term development. The tendency is to major in one area and neglect others.

Complex skills are needed to pastor a high-impact church. To the novice, or the pastor of a small congregation, the pathway to obtain the skills and roles described above may appear too mountainous to climb. But, the old Chinese proverb applies: "The way to begin a journey of a thousand miles is to take the first step." The pathway to leading a high-impact church involves a journey.[20]

The ideal way to develop high-impact leadership skills is through an apprenticeship in a high-impact church. The leader-to-be takes on increased responsibility as he exhibits proven character, spiritual gifts and effective ministry. Potential leaders who have not been apprentices in a healthy, growing church or who have been enculturated in an ineffective church model, will find it more difficult (though not impossible) to acquire the needed skills.

Good resources are available to help the aspiring high-impact church pastor to develop. Church growth and renewal books and tapes, functional workshops, practical courses, and interaction with pastors and leaders from thriving high-impact churches provide much-needed training. Even in a growing church, the pastor-leader must continue to develop new skills needed for the next anticipated levels of church growth.[21]

Developing any new skill involves a learning curve. Initially a lack of training and experience results in frustration, awkwardness and a sense of inadequacy.

Some pastors balk at attempting to become more proficient in new areas because of fear of failure or unwillingness to go through the discomfort of leadership development. They prefer to specialize only where they are already competent. The pastor aspiring to lead a high-impact church will face the challenge of learning new skills.

The effectiveness of a church is directly related to its leadership. Building a high-impact church calls for spiritual sensitivity and giftedness and technical proficiency. The leader must be a spiritually sensitive, strategic thinking, teachable person. To be successful, he needs to provide spiritual and organizational direction to the multiple ministry systems of a growing church.

21

MULTIPLE MINISTRY SYSTEMS

The body is a unit.
—1 Corinthians 12:12

BODY SYSTEMS

A high-impact church must be carefully organized. The Apostle Paul compared the Body of Christ to a human body made up of many different parts: eyes, ears, hands, feet, and so on. Each member of the body is dependent up the other members. No part can exist independently from the other parts. The eye cannot say to the hand, "I have no need of you."[1] Likewise, each member of Christ's Body is dependent upon all members of His church.

There is another way to consider Paul's analogy. The Body of Christ (and its counterpart, the human body) is made up of a number of different "systems." A system is a combination of the body's individual parts which operate and function together.

The human body's systems include the respiratory system, cardiovascular system, circulatory system, and so on. Each system is vital to the whole body and intricately related. Survival itself depends on the healthy functioning of all systems.

Just as the human body depends upon the existence of certain criticial systems, so the high-impact church depends upon its systems. God intends each member of the church to fit together with other believers to make up the vital systems of the local church.

Intercessory System

The most critical system in a high-impact church is intercessory prayer. Through prayer Christians tune into the spiritual dimensions of the universe and grasp the connecting links between the natural and the supernatural. Prayer alerts Christians to God's will and releases His power. Every church needs an intercessory system.

> **Just as the human body depends upon certain critical systems, so the high-impact church depends upon its systems.**

The world's largest church, the Yoido Full Gospel Church of Seoul, Korea, has an effective intercessory prayer system. The pastor, David Yonggi Cho, prays for two to three hours a day. He dedicates this time to fellowshiping with God, breaking the power of Satan, and infilling of the Holy Spirit. The Yoido Church is known for its "prayer mountain" where thousands of church members gather every day to fast and pray. Friday night prayer meetings attract 50,000 or more participants.

There is a connection between Cho's emphasis on prayer and the impact that the Yoido church has in Seoul — and throughout Korea. The conversion rate in Korea (a predominantly Buddhist country a century ago), is three times its birth rate. Korea is approaching the 50 percent-Christian mark. There are other contributing factors to this church growth, but prayer is undoubtedly the most important.

In the high-impact church, intercessory prayer is emphasized in several ways. Congregational prayer times are regularly scheduled. Private prayer is important for every leader and member of the church. In addition, especially gifted intercessors are commissioned and called on for special prayer needs.

Outreach System

The high-impact church needs an outreach system for its evangelistic mandate to attract and persuade the unchurched. At the heart of this system is a leadership team with a compassion for the lost.

A desire to reach out is imbedded into the philosophy of the high-impact church. The following "4-T" action steps will create a passion for evangelism. Leadership:

1. *Talks about* the need for outreach.
2. *Typically models* an outreach life-style.
3. *Takes along* others in outreach ministry.
4. *Trains persons* to lead outreach.

If Christians are consumed with believer-centered activities, outreach will be only minimal. An effective church mobilizes for outreach.

First, leaders impart an outreach mentality to the congregation and to cell groups. Cell leaders are trained to help members reach out and gather new people into their groups.

Friendship-building activities facilitate relationships in urban settings where people feel distant or alienated from the church. Target group ministries, pre-evangelism and harvesting events all contribute to a productive outreach system.

Another important part of the outreach system is a missions focus. (In mega and meta churches this may be a sub-system.) Missions motivate people to become "World Christians." The high-impact church's vision is to reach the unchurched both near and far and should permeate the church. The church therefore needs a structure for sending gifted members to evangelize, disciple, and plant churches.

People-Flow System

A commitment to reach the unchurched inevitably leads to numerical growth. This, in turn, demands a new system of assimilation and spiritual growth. In order for people to mature as Christians and become ministers, they must be guided in spiritual formation and given opportunities for effective service.

Cell groups constitute the primary entry point into the church.

When people come to an introductory event they are soon intro-duced to the pastors, purposes and ministries of the church. Inter-ested persons are then invited to attend a cell group. As stressed throughout this book, cell groups encourage decentralization of ministry and thereby increase the number of people who can be comfortably assimilated into a church.

The goal of assimilation — or people flow — is to help new church members realize their potential as ministers. Through teaching and role-modeling, gifts are discovered. As many ministry roles as possible are identified so that the maximum number of people can be involved. On-the-job apprenticeship is the best way to train people.

Nurture System

A nurture system is closely related to people flow. The primary place of nurture in the high-impact church is the cell group structure. However, other avenues also nurture believers.

Preaching and teaching are vital ingredients for building matu-rity in believers. If the Sunday celebration is seeker driven, it is important to also have a believers' service with greater depth of teaching and worship.

Baptism and communion are essential to the Christian commu-nity and to the growth of believers. Baptism is not only an act of obedience to God but can be a powerful witness to seekers. A brief interview before a baptism draws out the testimony of how Christ has impacted a person's life. Seekers are greatly influenced by testimonial stories from peers who have made a commitment to Christ.

Communion is also an important part of the believer's walk of faith. Communion is for believers, so the seeker-sensitive service may not be the best place to observe communion. A seeker may feel pressured to participate or feel self-conscious not taking part. The best place to celebrate communion is in meetings targeting believers, including cell group meetings. The early church celebrated com-munion in the privacy of homes.

Instruction in basic beliefs and principles of Christian living is part of the assimilation and growth system. These lessons are covered in the cell groups or in a new believers' class. Other classes to consider doctrine, discuss social issues, and study helpful books are offered, but do not compete with or replace cell groups as the basic place for edification.

Celebration System

Celebration is the central worship or gathering event for the high-impact church. Quality components are needed for an attractive celebration system. Some of the most important of these: Engaging music, inspiring message, a future challenge, and an awe-inspiring experience.[2]

The celebration event provides a unique inspirational experience. It is important, however, not to look at the celebration system as the main system of the church. The larger gathering event *complements* the other ministry systems and the overall strategy of the church.

Ichthus Christian Fellowship, based in London, England, uses the celebration event to rally and inspire its cell and congregational groups. Willow Creek Community Church of South Barrington, Illinois, sees its Sunday celebration as an outreach tool to help members evangelize their unchurched friends.

The celebration event is an opportunity to involve many people in ministry. It utilizes many interrelated specialized ministries and gift-based talents.

The critical roles in a highly developed celebration include pastor-teacher, music and worship leader, program director, drama leader, media coordinator and a children's ministry director. Other roles are musicians, teachers, technical support, set-up, greeters, parking attendants, ushers and secretarial support.

The celebration system of a new church will be less sophisticated and depend on available resources. From the beginning, however, it is wise to strive for a celebration system that builds believers and attracts the unchurched. As a church grows it will be able to plan more engaging and dynamic services.

Leadership System

Leadership is the church's most important resource. A high-impact church needs an effective leadership team — pastors, elders, division supervisors, special ministry and cell group leaders.

A healthy leadership system is united in vision and purpose. The leadership team's responsibility is to impart that vision to the rest of the body. This vision is the glue that unifies and gives the church its identity and direction. Every person in the church needs to know why the church exists and where it is headed.

For the leadership team to work together effectively, each team member must know his or her role, and how it relates to the overall purpose of the church. Job profiles clarify individual leadership expectations, and an organizational chart shows the relationship of these roles.

Leadership is the church's most important resource.

Good leaders reproduce themselves by continually training apprentices. Both entry-level and specific leadership training is provided. The leadership system in a growing church is dynamic — always increasing the number of able leaders.

Management System

Closely akin to the leadership system is the management system. A competent executive management system includes vision building, goal setting, and strategic planning.

A good management system starts with vision. Vision flows out of the purpose that God has for His church. Visionary leadership asks, *What does God want done that is not presently happening?* The answer reflects the contemporary situation of that city, addressing both practical and spiritual needs and societal problems.[3]

God gives His people vision through impressions, burdens, and passions that need to be confirmed through Scripture, the counsel of other godly Christians and good research. To translate this vision into action, broad objectives or thrusts are needed which are simply stated and broken down into short- and long-range goals that are specific, measurable and time related. Once goals are clarified and prioritized, specific steps can be taken.

Good planning begins with research and information gathering. It considers where you are, where you want to be and how you can get there. Research allows leaders to convincingly present a vision, set reasonable goals and plan appropriately. Brainstorming with team members to unearth all possible means of reaching goals is part of early planning and research. Each brainstorming idea has value. By comparing and weighing merits, leaders choose one or more ideas for action.[4]

Evaluation is an integral part of a good management system. Evaluation helps determine the effectiveness of plans – if strategies are accomplishing the set goals. It also brings to light growth-restrictive problems so leaders can make adjustments to keep the church moving toward its goals.

A good management system maximizes the use of time and people. This requires attention to proper delegation, clarification of roles, encouragement of team leaders, and conflict resolution and reconciliation.

Communication System

The larger a church grows, the more critical it is to have a good communication system. Small organizations can function well passing verbal information, face-to-face. Decisions are made by consensus and easily reported to members. As an organization grows, a more formal means of communication is needed to prevent confusion and inefficiency.

Media support is important in a growing church. A media department handles bulletins, announcements, flyers, letters, brochures, banners, advertising, newsletters, the church magazine and possibly, even a newspaper. Multi-media presentations are also a powerful modern communicating tool.

The larger a church becomes, the greater its need for advanced planning, scheduling and communication. Written articles take time and energy to outline, write and publish. A professional approach meets deadlines and keeps the church's information flow on track.

Stewardship giving depends on a convincing communications system. In various ways, people are helped to understand how their financial giving is used to change lives and impact society. When this happens, they want to give more.

Administrative and Finance System

Inadequate administrative support slows – even prevents – the church from reaching its goals. When the pastoral team is overloaded with administrative detail it ceases to be effective. A sound administrative and financial system is crucial. Without this, bad decisions are made and good decisions are poorly administrated. The administration system of the church often makes the difference between pastoral effectiveness and ineffectiveness.[5]

A well-designed administrative system includes: staff, secretarial support, accounting procedures, financial and property management (procurement, preparation and maintenance) and capital equipment. As the church grows, there is an increased need for people trained to handle these specialized tasks and roles.

The high-impact church has many inter-related ministries and utilizes a "systems approach" to coordinate them. Competent leadership implements and develops these systems as the church grows. Pastors visualize the church with interconnected systems and delegate for various ministries. God then raises up competent men and women to fill the ever-expanding ministry roles.

22

VISION FOR THE FUTURE

Salvation and glory and power
belong to our God.
—Revelation 19:1

THE CHURCH IS THE KEY

The early Christian church had a high impact on the known world of their day. New Testament Christians enthusiastically proclaimed their faith everywhere they went. They were convinced that they had found God in Christ. Their dynamic personal and corporate witness attracted multitudes to the gospel and changed the course of history.

Similarly, today, multitudes can be won to Christ as that same Good News impacts society. To accomplish this, the Western church must wake up from slumber and counteract the present spiritual and moral vacuum caused by the rise of modern secularism and nominality. While Western societies have become culturally fragmented and morally paralyzed, Western Christianity has become anemic and no longer attractive in its traditional form.

The seriousness of the situation is exaggerated by urbanization and the growing world population. It is conservatively estimated that two billion of the world's five billion people have never heard the gospel. By the year 2000, the world's population will reach 6.259 billion. Unfortunately, traditional Western Christianity hasn't even preserved the status quo, let alone actively won the cities of the world for Christ.

In order to carry out its God-directed mission, the church must change. The church needs to recommit itself to recapture Europe and her cultural offshoots. Around the world, as Christians pray and plan strategically, existing congregations can grow and new churches can be started.

THE SECOND HALF OF THE REFORMATION

The second half of the Reformation waits on the horizon. The Protestant Reformation was one of the greatest awakenings in the history of Christianity, reaching about one-half of the Western world (primarily Northern Europe). This significant theological era produced remarkable leaders whose works are still acclaimed.

The key theological tenets of the Protestant Reformation were: justification by faith alone (*sola fide*); salvation based only on God's grace (*sola gratia*); and scripture as the sole authority of faith and practice (*sola scriptura*). Reformer Martin Luther believed that God's righteous demands were perfectly met by faith in Jesus Christ. When accompanied by supernatural power, preaching the Word regenerates dead sinners and calls them to righteousness. The Christian life is lived out in gratitude, not in trying to earn salvation.

The Reformation, however, did not go far enough. First of all, it lacked missionary zeal. The spread of the gospel was limited to those who lived in reformation countries. Fortunately, the modern missionary movement was birthed several hundred years after the Reformation and is maturing and marching steadily toward the goal of fulfilling the Great Commission.

The Reformation failed on another count: It did not mobilize church members for ministry. Although Luther wanted to reform the church and he taught the priesthood of all believers, he and other reformers maintained the medieval structure and practices of the church still in place today. Traditionally, a professional priest or pastor does the work of ministry. Because of this, ministry has been limited to relatively few ordained professionals.

Fortunately, the final chapter of the history of Western Christendom has not been written. Changes are astir as increasing numbers of churches wake up and Christians are mobilized. There is an emergence of new forms of church life. New churches are being birthed and existing churches are being revitalized with a passion to evangelize and disciple the Western world.

THE EPHESIANS FOUR REFORMATION

Visionary leaders are making a difference as they invest themselves in equipping and mobilizing the saints for the work of the ministry and the task of fulfilling the Great Commission. These leaders understand their role according to Ephesians Four: preparing others for works of ministry. But much more remains to be done—new churches birthed and existing churches awakened.

There is a need for *more* churches. An exciting shift that is occurring today is from saturation evangelism to saturation church planting. A notable example of this is the DAWN 2000[1] strategy which advocates fulfilling the global mandate of Christ through planting an additional seven million churches worldwide. There is evidence that more and more churches and Christian organizations are catching a vision for reaching the lost through the multiplication of new churches and are working cooperatively toward that end.

There is also a need for *better* churches. This calls for new paradigms and breakthrough thinking. Spiritual renewal is hindered by inflexible attitudes and restrictive ways of organizing the church. The majority of churches are plateaued or declining and vast numbers of people are unchurched. To reverse this requires renewing the vision of the church, rekindling the fire of the Holy Spirit and mobilizing an army of lay people for ministry.

THE HIGH-IMPACT CHURCH REFORMATION

Still more, there is a need for *high-impact* churches. Only fresh styles of ministry can reach each new generation. Modern, creative forms encourage the unchurched to come in, and eventually lead them to Jesus Christ. High-impact churches that are biblically based, spiritually dynamic, culturally relevant, growing and reproducing are needed throughout the world, particularly in urban centers.

High-impact churches, like apples, grow from the inside out. The first step in developing a new church, or transforming an existing one into a high-impact church, is to attend to the spiritual life of the church. The life and soul of the high-impact church is its spiritual core. The high-impact church manifests a vital relationship with Jesus Christ, draws upon the power of the Holy Spirit, and builds believers into a loving, caring, edifying, worshipping, ministering community.

When a core of believers has been established in the basics of the Christian faith and is spiritually healthy and vibrant, the church is ready to proceed to second step—mobilizing its members for ministry, especially the ministries of evangelism and edification. High-impact churches equip every believer to reach out to their webs of relationships and implement a cell group structure as the primary means of edification and pastoral care.

The real substance of the high-impact church is this decentralized approach to evangelism, assimilation, edification, pastoral care and discipleship. It is the primary ministry emphasis of the high-impact church. Without this emphasis, centralized ministry events and programs consume and ultimately stagnate a church.

When spiritually vital believers are using their spiritual gifts in the ministries of evangelism and edification, the church is ready for the third step—the centralized stage of ministry. This is the most visible and labor intensive dimension of the church. The high-impact church incorporates seeker-sensitive celebration events and other multiple ministry systems required for a growing church.

Centralized leadership, organization and events unify people and enhance the decentralized ministry of the laity. The attractive large gatherings complement the cell group ministry and evangelism of church members and unites them around the vision of the church.

Once a church has successfully incorporated its core, decentralized and centralized components, it will continue to grow by developing from the inside out. Some churches have attractive programs and are well attended but neglect the spiritual dynamics originally motivating the church. Others may maintain a spiritual vitality but fail to mobilize their members to use their gifts in ministry. In both cases, far less will be accomplished for the kingdom of God than the church is capable of.

The high-impact church has a spiritually dynamic core, mobilized members, attractive events, effective organization and visionary leadership. The following is a checklist of cross-cultural principles that make up the high-impact church:

- Holds a biblically-based evangelical theology
- Promotes spiritual vitality and dynamic work of the Holy Spirit
- Clarifies and keeps central its purpose, priorities and vision
- Targets and designs ministry to reach the unchurched
- Mobilizes and empowers every Christian to minister
- Instills a "Great Commission vision" in its members
- Trains believers to reach networks of relationships
- Provides a spiritual growth path for members
- Penetrates the community through a proliferation of cell groups
- Makes cell groups the primary provider of pastoral care
- Structures for an expanding network of cells groups
- Multiplies lay leaders
- Holds seeker-sensitive services and events
- Preaches in a positive, practical, inspiring way
- Emphasizes God's grace and mercy
- Creates an atmosphere of love, acceptance and forgiveness
- Utilizes creative, contemporary, culturally relevant worship style
- Has visionary leadership that equips others to minister
- Organizes to break through growth-restrictive barriers
- Reproduces other high-impact churches

These principles cannot be implemented all at once, but they can serve as a guide to the long range planning of a church. In order for a church to emerge into a high-impact church, it keeps the end in view and then works systematically toward that end.

These principles can be classified under the three categories of the core, the substance or the exterior of the church. A plan can then be devised to implement them from the inside out. As each element is sufficiently in place and resources emerge, the church can move from one level to the next, trusting God at every point to establish His church and give growth.

WE'RE NOT THERE YET!

I recently overheard a conversation upon arrival at the Minneapolis International Airport where a four-year-old boy exclaimed, "We're going to Minnesota!" His six-year-old brother objected, "We're already there!" The four year old countered, "No we're not, we're in the airport!"

My hope is that this book will help new and existing churches get out of the airport to the destination that God has for His church. I believe that this destination is high-impact churches — with spiritually vital cores, well mobilized and ministering members and attractive and culturally relevant ministries.

The overarching goal of this book is to present an attractive and dynamic high-impact model of the church that will extend the kingdom of God in our generation. The multiplication of high-impact churches is the most viable way for modern Christians to carry out the missionary mandate given by Christ.

High-impact churches are emerging in cities all over the world — from Seoul to London, from Amsterdam to Portland. Thousands more are needed to recapture the unchurched in modern urban culture and usher in a great spiritual harvest.

NOTES

CHAPTER ONE

1. Lesslie Newbigin, *Foolishness to the Greeks* (Grand Rapids: William B. Eerdmans, 1986), pp. 2-3.
2. Lausanne Committee for World Evangelism, *Thailand Report: Christian Witness to Secularized People* (Wheaton: LCWE, 1980), p. 6.
3. Ibid., p. 26. Modern science and technology provide the unifying influence of Western culture. Science and reason, rather than revelation, became the new headmaster of thinking people. Science works by observation and is coupled with reason and analysis to provide an understanding and mastery of the universe. Reason is the autonomous authority in Western society's search for reality.
4. Kalevi Lehtinen and the European Leadership Team, "Campus Crusade for Christ, European plan to the year 2000" (4th draft, 20 April, 1985), pp. 3-4.
5. Eddie Gibbs, "Contextual Considerations in Responding to Nominality" in *The Word Among Us: Contextualizing Theology For Mission Today*, by Dean S. Gilliland, editor (Dallas, Tx.: Word, 1989), p. 252.
6. Phillipa King, editor., "Information to Steer By," *LandMARC* (London: MARC Europe, Easter, 1991), p. 1. One example of this is England where on an average Sunday, 10% of England's adult population choose to be in church according to the "most thorough and comprehensive survey ever done of English churchgoing." The English Church Consensus was carried out on October 15, 1989, a normal Sunday, avoiding festivals or holiday seasons which swell or reduce attendance. By comparing the results with the last Census from 1979 the number of adults attending church in England declined 8% in the decade.
7. Peter Brierley, *Where is the Church is Going?*, MARC Monograph Number 5 (Bromley, Kent: MARC Europe, January, 1986), p. 20. Note: MARC Europe is now called Christian Research Association.
8. Gibbs, Op. Cit, p. 8. This process of secularization has roots in what is called "the Enlightenment." Around the middle of the 18th century, there was a profound and widely-shared feeling among thinking people in Western Europe that a new age had come and that its essential nature was "enlightenment." Prior to the Enlightenment, the nature of the universe and reality was seen in terms of a divine purpose, the revelation of which had been given in Scripture and the church's creed.

   The effect of the Enlightenment replaced this explanatory framework with the view that the real world was not governed by divine purpose but by natural laws of cause and effect. There was no longer a need to explain things in terms of purpose or design; there was no longer a place for the miraculous or divine intervention; Nature became the sum total of what exists.
9. Monica Hill, "The Secular World Bridging the Gap," paper presented to The European Church Growth Conference, DeBron, Holland, March 31, 1990.

10. Ibid.
11. Peter Brierley, MARC Europe consultation, the Netherlands, March 5, 1990, quoted from *Theological News*, 1989.
12. *World Christian News*, October 1990 (issue #11), from an article in *The International Herald Tribune*, October 30, 1989.
13. Peter Brierley, *Change in Europe, MARC Monograph 36* (Bromley, Kent: MARC Europe, September, 1991), p. 13.
14. Monica Hill, Op. Cit., p. 4.
15. Russell Chandler, *Racing Toward 2001* (Grand Rapids: Zondervan Publishing House, 1992), p. 189-190.
16. Ibid., p. 188.
17. Ruth Tucker, "Nonorthodox Sects Report Global Membership Gains" in *Christianity Today*, June 13, 1986.
18. Douglas Groothuis, *Unmasking the New Age* (Downers Grove: Inter-Varsity Press, 1986). New Age thinking covers a variety of psycho-spiritual ideas and agendas grouped into the same heading. Six core ideas characterize New Age thinking: all is One; all is God; humanity is God; all religions are one; the need for a change in consciousness; and a cosmic evolutionary optimism.
19. Monica Hill, Op. Cit.
20. Marc R. Spindler, "Europe's Neo-Paganism: A Perverse Inculturation" from *International Bulletin of Missionary Research*, Vol. 11, No. 1, January 1987, p. 8. Spindler says that Neo-Paganism is a result of the contemporary crisis of European culture which includes de-Christianization and an inability to find meaning through the secularism, atheistic philosophies and Marxism-Leninism of this century.
21. W. A. Visser 't Hooft, "Evangelism among Europe's Neo-Pagans" *International Review of Mission*, vol. LXVI, No. 264, October 1977, pp. 349-360. Neo-paganism drinks from both the wells of paganism and Christianity. Many who consider themselves Christians are outside the church and are therefore dominated by sub or non-Christian ideas. It is among these people that we find 'new' or 'neo-pagans'. T' Hooft notes that it is striking that paganism reduced to submission a nation of thinkers, scientists, poets and technicians, and that its defeat had to come from the outside.
22. W. A. Visser 't Hooft, Op. Cit. The atomic threat, pollution and lack of meaningful perspective that the technocratic civilization brought, have led to the growth of a new nationalism drawing elements of the earlier period. Nietzche, D. H. Lawrence and Hermann Hesse are more widely read than ever before.
23. Peter Brierley, *Christianity in Europe, MARC Monograph Number 22* (Bromley, Kent: MARC Europe, March, 1989), p. 4. In England, for example, two and one-half million abortions have been performed since 1967 (population fifty-five million). In Eastern Europe it is estimated that 50% of conceptions are aborted. The percentages in France and Finland are 15-24%. Norway and Sweden run between 25-34%.

    According to MARC Europe: "Illegitimacy is growing. Every other child born in Sweden is illegitimate. The incidence of AIDS and other sexually transmitted diseases is high. The amount of abuse is high - in some countries one fifteen year old girl in ten will be abused by the time she is twenty."

24. Carol Sarler, "Get that ridiculous family out of here!" (London: *The Sunday Times*, January 26, 1992).

25. Peter Brierley, ed., "Information to Steer By," *LandMARC* (Bromley, Kent: MARC Europe, New Year 1991), p. 1. In the 20-24 age group, 45% of Danes and 44% of Swedes cohabit. This is up from a mere 4-5% in 1966. While some of these couples will eventually marry when they are older, they are less likely to do so than previous generations. The number of single persons is also increasing, estimated at between 20-35% of the population in Northern and Western European countries.

26. Peter Brierley, *Where is the Church Going?*, p. 13. For example in 1966 in Denmark there were six divorces for every one thousand marriages; fifteen years later the proportion had almost doubled. Four out of seven marriages in Sweden fail, one of the highest divorce rates in the Western world. In England and Wales there were fewer than four divorces per one thousand marriages in 1966. There were twelve per one thousand in 1980. In some countries divorce is four to five times higher than twenty years ago.

CHAPTER TWO

1. *PRRC Emerging Trends* (Princeton Religion Research Center), Vol. 15, No. 3, March, 1993, p. 1.

2. Leith Anderson, *Dying For Change* (Minneapolis: Bethany House Publishers, 1990). In the *Pastor's Manual for Effective Ministry* (Monrovia: Church Growth, 1988), p. 11, Win Arn of the American Institute of Church Growth in Pasadena states that of the approximately 350,000 churches in America, four out of the five are either at a plateau or dying.

3. Andy Pollak, "Expanded role for laity seen as antidote to fall in numbers of priests and religious" (Dublin: *The Irish Times*, Friday, July 23, 1993), p. 12. This is especially true among the young. According to "The Church in Ireland: Youthful Society Loses The Faith of its Fathers" (*International Herald Tribune*, Thursday, May 13, 1982), "the bedrock of Irish Catholicism is being buffeted by the storms of the modern world, and the church and its teachings seem to many to be less and less relevant, particularly for the young."

   Ireland is now the youngest nation in Europe; half of its people are under 25. As in other Western countries, the young have become urbanized. The last official figures, for 1973-74, show that only 68% of the young urban dwellers attended Mass regularly, compared with 95% of married women over 50. According to Joe Duffy of the Union of Students in Ireland in the above International *Herald Tribune* article, "the institution of the church is not progressive, whereas young people are."

4. Eddie Gibbs, "Contextual Considerations in Responding to Nominality" in *The Word Among Us*, Edited by Dean S. Gilliland (Dallas, Tex.: Word, 1989), pp. 5-6.

5. Ibid., p. 240.

6. Russell Chandler, *Racing Toward 2001* (Grand Rapids: Zondervan Publishing House, 1992), p. 153.

7. Lausanne Committee for World Evangelism, *Thailand Report: Christian Witness to Secularized People* (Wheaton: LCWE, 1980), p. 6.

8. Ruth March, *Europe Reborn* (Bromley: OM Publishing, 1992) p. 19.

9. Paul Filides, ed., *World Christian News* (Amsterdam: 7/89) quoted from *Spektrum*, 7/89. The Republic of Ireland is the one exception as 80% of the population attend church regularly. Throughout the rest of Europe, however, the numbers are significantly lower. In Italy, Spain and Northern Ireland, approximately 40% attend church regularly. In Belgium and Luxembourg, it is among 20 and 30%. Although 81% of the Swiss population believes in God or an other-worldly spiritual being, only 17% attend church regularly.

    In France, this number is between 11-15%. In England, more than half of the Roman Catholics in the country do not attend mass on a regular basis. The same is true of those belonging to the Church of England and the Church of Scotland. Source: Peter Brierley, *Where is the Church Going? MARC Monograph Number 5* (Bromley, Kent: MARC Europe, January, 1986), p. 19.

    In Germany, 92% are church members, but only 11% claim regular church attendance. In Norway, 96% are church members through baptism but only 3% attend regularly. In Sweden, 98% belong and 3% attend. In Denmark, 99.6% belong and 5% actively attend (Paul Filides, Op. Cit., p. 5.)

    The Lausanne Committee for World Evangelism lists 67-68% of the fourteen million Dutch as Christians but only 8% as practicing (Zeist: LCWE, July 1989, pp. 6, 8). In a more recent study conducted for DAWN Europe, 51% of the Dutch now have no affiliation with any church (Joris Storms, "DAWN Dutch Country Report," Flavohof, Holland, March 21, 1991).

10. Peter Brierley, *Towards 2000: Current Trends in European Church Life*, *MARC Monograph Number 1* (Bromley, Kent: MARC Europe, May, 1984), pp. 10-11. Peter Brierley defines active Christians as those involved as active participants in the institutional or organized life of the churches they are affiliated to, or who are regarded by their churches as practicing members because they fulfill their churches minimum annual attendance obligations or other membership requirements, or who in some way take a recognized part in the church's ongoing practice of Christianity.

    The Lausanne Movement in its Thailand Report, "Christian Witness to Nominal Christians among Protestant Christians," defines a nominal Protestant Christian as:

    > One who, within the Protestant tradition, would call himself a Christian or be so regarded by others, but who has no authentic commitment to Christ based on personal faith. Such commitment involves a transforming personal relationship with Christ, characterized by such qualities as love, joy, peace, a desire to study the Bible, prayer, fellowship with other Christians, a determination to witness faithfully, a deep concern for God's will to be done on earth, and a living hope of heaven to come.

11. Kalevi Lehtinen and the European Leadership Team, "Campus Crusade for

Christ, European plan to the year 2000" (4th draft, 20 April, 1985), pp. 3-4. In an article in the "Third Way" (July 1984), sociologist David Lyon tried to answer the question as to why there are so many nominal Christians. His reasons include:

- The sense of the uniqueness of Christianity has been muted. There has been an increasing growth of relativism and other religious options.
- There has been a loss of intellectual confidence, essentially stemming from Darwinism, not just an intellectual framework, but a social and cultural framework, too.
- Many have lost their religion and see the world as losing its religion too. Max Weber, for example, lives in a world of rationalization, intellectualization and disenchantment and assumes everyone else does.
- Christianity has become marginal to many people's lives. There is a growth in double standard and role split lives.
- Christianity is a private middle class occupation, "Your hobby is going to church, as it were...."
- The church swings from bureaucracy to "destructured spontaneity."

12. Peter Brierley, *Where is the Church Going?*, p. 20. Another change taking place that is a cause of concern can be illustrated by the situation in Great Britain. Figures show that nearly half the population of Great Britain are 'notional' Christians. These people see themselves as belonging to the Christian community but do not attend church on a regular basis nor belong to a particular congregation. They are neither Christians, non-Christians nor nominal Christians. They are notional Christians.

According to Peter Brierley of MARC Europe, 3% of those living in Great Britain are active churchgoers who attend church but who do not belong. A mere 8% are active church members. Nine percent are church members who do not attend (these are nominal Christians). Forty-seven percent are notional Christians who consider themselves Christians but do not belong or go to church.

Active church goers tend to join the church. Active members of churches tend to stop going. Nominal Christians tend to stop being members. Notional Christians tend to stop thinking of themselves as Christians.

13. EKD nationwide survey entitled "Was Wird Aus Der Kirche?" from Hans Wilhelm, "The Problem of Nominality and Church Renewal in Germany" in *Interpretive Essays: The Church in Western Europe* (Pasadena: Fuller Theological Seminary, 1987), p. 247.

Dr. Reiner Blanc, Director of the Institute for Parish Renewal of the United Lutheran Churches in Germany, estimates that 1300 people a day or almost 500,000 people a year are leaving the church in Germany Reference: European Church Growth Conference, London, England, March 24, 1992..

14. Rev. E. Gunn, "In Darkest England," from *World Christian News*, May 1990, Issue #10, p. 6.
15. *PRRC Emerging Trends*, Op. Cit., p. 1.
16. George Barna and William Paul McKay, *Vital Signs* (Westchester: Crossway Books, 1984), p. 105. See also: *PRRC Emerging Trends*, Op. Cit., p. 2.

17. Win Arn, *The Win Arn Growth Report, Number 15* (Pasadena: Institute for Church Growth, 1986).
18. George Barna, *The Barna Report* (Ventura, Ca.: Regal Books, 1992), p. 90.
19. Lyle Schaller, *44 Questions for Church Planters* (Nashville: Abingdom, 1991), p. 78.
20. Win Arn, *The Pastor's Manual for Effective Ministry* (Monrovia, Ca.: Church Growth, 1988), p. 16.
21. Gallup, Jr., George H., and Bezilla, Robert, Gallup Poll , "Religion Influence Down?" (*Religious News Service*, May 5,1993).
22. George Barna, *The Frog in the Kettle* (Ventura: Regal Books, 1990), pp. 117-8.
23. Dean Kelly, *Why Conservative Churches are Growing* (New York: Harper and Row, 1972), pp. VIII-IX.
24. Ibid.
25. Herbert J. Betz, "Evangelism and Advertising - The Role of Advertising and Church Growth" in an "Inter-disciplinary Study" for the Betriebswirtschaftliches Institut, p. 136.
26. George Barna, The *Barna Report*, Op. Cit., p. 64.
27. John Dart "Mainline Church Strength Shrinks" (*Los Angeles Times*, April 6, 1985), Part I-A, pp. 5-6.
28. Peter Brierley notes that young people are leaving the church most rapidly. In 1979, 13% of England's young people attended church; by 1989, only 9% did so. Reference: "A Changing Vision" (a paper presented to the European Church Growth Conference in London England, March 1992), p. 15.
29. "Vineyard Questionnaire" (Tuscon: The Vineyard, 625 N. 2nd Ave., n.d.).
30. George Barna, *The Frog in the Kettle*, Op. Cit., p. 205.
31. Eddie Gibbs, "The European Scene" from notes taken at meeting with Christian Associates International staff (Thousand Oaks, Ca., Monday, June 1, 1987).
32. Jacques Ellul, "The Situation in Europe" from *Man's Disorder and God's Design: The Amsterdam Series* (New York: Harper and Brothers, 1949), vol. III, p. 51. The underlying reason for this can be found in Ellul's words: "The Church has left to others the responsibility for the spiritual life of the peoples. The Church has become introspective and has forgotten that the Gospel must be present in the midst of the people, and that this can only be achieved by great movements of evangelization which, even if they do not lead to the conversion of all, do draw the spiritual life of the nation towards the Gospel"
33. Herbert J. Betz, Op. Cit., p. 92.
34. Ibid.
35. According to "Church Scores over Soccer" (*LandMARC, Information to Steer By*, Easter, 1991), p. 3, around 65% of the population in Great Britain would say they believe in Christianity . An amazing 82% in a 1984 American Gallup poll said that growing into a deeper relationship with God was important to them. Source: Russell Chandler, *Racing Toward 2001*, Op. Cit, p. 1993.
36. Heb 1:1; 2 Cor 5:19.
37. "Church Scores over Soccer," Op. Cit., p. 1, notes that in the decade from 1979 in England, Roman Catholic church attendance declined 14%, Anglican 9%,

Methodist 11%, and United Reformed 18%. At the same time independent churches grew by 42%, including a 144% increase in attendance at the so-called house churches and 46% at the Fellowship of Independent Evangelical Churches. Attendance at charismatic evangelical churches rose 7% between 1985 and 1989 .

C. Peter Wagner estimates that there are 160 million Pentecostals world-wide. Source: *Spiritual Power and Church Growth* (Altamonte Springs: Strang Communications, 1986), p. 11.

38. C. Peter Wagner, "New Church Planting" from *Advanced Church Planting Syllabus* (Pasadena: Charles E. Fuller Institute, 1985), p. 7.

39. George Barna, *The Frog in the Kettle* , p. 140.

CHAPTER THREE

1. Peter Brierley, *Where is the Church Going?*, MARC Monograph Number 5 (Bromley, Kent: MARC Europe, January, 1986), p. 3.

2. Peter Brierley, ed., *Christianity in Europe, MARC Monograph Number 22* (Bromley, Kent: MARC Europe, March, 1989), p. 12.

3. Ibid.

4. Gordon Aeschliman, *Global Trends* (Downers Grove, Il.: InterVarsity Press, 1990), p. 69.

5. Paul G. Hiebert, "Social Structure and Church Growth" in *Perspectives on the World Christian Movement: A Reader*, Edited by Ralph D. Winter and Steven C. Hawthorne (Pasadena, Ca.: William Carey Library, 1981), p. 381. In 1880, 5% of the world lived in cities; in 1980 it had increased to 35%. The growth has been phenomenal: approximately two billion of the more than five billion people in the world today live in cities. There are another 27 million people a year moving from the countryside to towns and cities.

6. Frank R. Tillapaugh, *The Church Unleashed* (Ventura, Ca.: Regal Books, 1982), pp. 26-27. The magnitude of this change can be seen in the observation that 100 years ago, most Americans lived on farms. Fifty years ago most Americans lived in small towns. Today most Americans live in cities.

7. Raymond Bakke, *The Urban Christian* (MARC Europe, Bromley Kent England, 1987), p. 28. In 1800, there were no cities in the world with a population of a million or more.

8. Raymond Bakke, "The City and the Scriptures," found in *Christianity Today* June 15, 1984, p. 17.

9. Raymond Bakke, *The Urban Christian*, Op. Cit., p. 28.

10. Ibid.

11. "Urban Explosion and the Mission Challenge" from *City Watch*, Vol. 2, No. 1, February 1987, p. 3.

12. "The Mother of All Challenges" in *World Christian News* , June 1991, Issue #13, p. 1.

13. Frank R. Tillapaugh, Op. Cit., pp. 31-34.

14. Stephen T. Franklin, "Theology of Evangelizing World-Class Cities" (Chicago: *Trinary Consultation: A Consultation on Evangelizing World-Class Cities,*

March 14-17, 1986), pp. 3-4.

15. Leith Anderson, *Dying for Change* (Minneapolis, Bethany House Publishers, 1990), p. 52

16. Ibid., p. 10.

17. Ibid., p. 116.

18. Barbara R. Thompson, "Evangelicals' Subtle Infection," an interview with Senate Chaplain Richard Halverson in *Christianity Today*, November 12, 1982.

19. Dr. Sunand Sumithra, ed., *Theological News*, April-June, 1989, p. 3.

20. Charles Swindoll, *The Grace Awakening* (Dallas: Word, 1990), p. xv.

CHAPTER FOUR

1. Jack Hayford, *The Church on the Way* (Lincoln, VA: Chosen Books, 1982), p. 13.

2. Justin Martyr, (from memory, source unknown).

3. J. B. Phillips, *Letters to Young Churches* (New York: MacMillan Co), p. xiv.

4. Acts 4:8-13; 18:20; 4:33; 7:56.

5. 1 Cor 15:3-5.

6. 1 Cor 15:14-16.

7. Acts 1:3.

8. 1 Cor 4:20; 1 Cor 4:17; 1 Tim 3:14-15; Eph 3:7; Col 4:11.

9. Matt 24:14; 2 Tim 4:1-2.

10. Acts 2:36; Rev 19:16; Phil 2:11.

11. Matt 28:19.

12. Rom 6:17.

13. Acts 1:14; 2:42; Eph 6:18; Phil 4:6; Col 4:2.

14. Note: Paul Yonggi Cho recently changed his name to David Yonggi Cho.

15. Col 1:9; 1 John 3:21.

16. John 15:14.

17. Acts 1:4-5; 2:1-2.

18. Eph 5:18; 1 Thes 5:19

19. Acts 2:4.

20. 1 Cor 12:7-11; 13:1-13; Eph 4:11-13.

21. Acts 1:23-26.

22. Acts 6:3; 4:36; 9:10; 9:22.

23. Rom 16: 1 ff.

24. Acts 2:11; 1:8.

25. Acts 17:4; 27:28-29; 1 Thes 1:5; Rom 1:16; 2 Cor 5:11.

26. John 14:12 ff; Acts 1:4-8; Acts 1:22; 3:6 f; 4:31 ff; etc.

27. R. Daniel Reeves and Donald Jenson, *Always Advancing: Modern Strategies for Church Growth* (San Bernardino: Here's Life Publishers, 1985) p. 61.

28. Acts 2:41, 47; 4:5.

29. Acts 5:14; 9:31; 12:24; 8:1; 9:10,19; 8:40; 10:1; 11:19; 13:1.

30. John 15: 20, 26; 16:12-15.

31. Acts 2:42; Matt 16:17 ff; John 21:17 ff.

32. Acts 2:43; 2 Pet 1:21; 2 Tim 3:16.

33. Acts 6:2; 2 Tim 2:15; 1 Tim 4:13,16; 2 Tim 2:2.

34. Acts 2:42; 1 John 1:3; 2 Cor 13:14; Phil 1:2.
35. Acts 2:44-46; 2:42; 4:35; 5:4.
36. Heb 10:24-35; Acts 2:46.
37. Rom 5:8; 1 John 4:17.
38. Acts 2:46-47; 2:46; 22:9-12.
39. Eph 5:18-20; Col 3:16.
40. 1 Thes 5:16; Phil 4:4-8; Phil 3:3.
41. Acts 2:41; 1 Cor 9:23; Matt 28:17; Rom 6; 1 Cor 12:13; 2 Cor 1:22; Eph 1:13; Tit 3:5; 2 Cor 8:4; Acts 2:38; 9:17-18; 10:47; Rom 9:1 ff.
42. 1 Cor 10:16-17; 11:17-34.
43. Acts 2:46; 1 Cor 11:18 ff; Luke 22:10 ff.
44. Phil 2:13-14.

CHAPTER FIVE

1. Matt 6:33.
2. Eddie Gibbs, *I Believe in Church Growth* (London: Hodder Stoughton, 1981), p. 76.; John 3:1-8.
3. Mark 10:14,17-25.
4. John 1:12-13; Mark 1:15.
5. Rom 10:9; Acts 16:31; John 20:31.
6. Eddie Gibbs, Op. Cit., p. 75; Matt 7:21.
7. Matt 21:43; John 15:7.
8. George Eldon Ladd, *The Gospel of the Kingdom* (Grand Rapids: Wm. B. Eerdmans, 1978), p. 85.
9. Heb 13:15; Col 1:6; Eph 5:9; Gal 5:22.
10. George Eldon Ladd, Op. Cit., p. 97; Phil 1:11; Rom 8:1-8; 15:5,9; 15:7.
11. John 15:11-12; Gal 5:22.
12. Donald B. Kraybill, *The Upside-Down Kingdom* (Scottsdale, Penn.: Herald Press, 1978), p. 77.
13. John 6:35; Matt 6:19 ff; John 7:37-39; Matt 11:30; Luke 9:57-62; Matt 6:24; 10:34-37; Matt 7:14; Luke 9:23.
14. Luke 16:9; 12:33,34; Matt 19:21.
15. Donald B. Kraybill, Op. Cit., p. 216; Matt 6:33; Matt 4:4.
16. Matt 10:1; Luke 10:19; 2 Cor 10:8; 2:15; Titus 2:15.
17. Rom 8:28, 35 ff; 1 Cor15:54-58.
18. Phil 2:11.
19. Luke 15:20; 19:10.
20. Luke 19:10; Luke 15; Luke 5:10; Luke 9:2; Acts 8:12; Acts 28:31.
21. Matt 28:19-20.

CHAPTER SIX

1. Matt 12:26-29; Eph 2:1-2.
2. Gal 3:22.
3. 1 John 5:19; 2 Tim 2:25-26.

4. Gen 1:26-28.

5. Eph 4:19 ff.

6. Michael Green, *I Believe in Satan's Downfall* (London: Hodder and Stoughton, 1981), p. 23.

7. John 10:10.

8. 2 Cor 4:4; Rom 1:16 ff.

9. Isa 14; Ezek 28.

10. 1 John 4:4

11. Matt 4:17, 23; 9:35; 13; Luke 4:43; 8:1.

12. 1 John 3:8.

13. Eph 5:5; Rev 11:15; Col 1:13.

14. Luke 17:20-21.

15. A.M. Hunter, *Christ and the Kingdom* (Edinburgh: St. Andrew Press, 1980), p. 6.

16. Eph. 1:18-19.

17. Mark 10:45.

18. 1 Cor 1:23.

19. John Bright, *The Kingdom of God* (Nashville: Abingdon Press, 1953), p. 210; Matt 20:26; Mark 9:48; John 13:14-17.

20. Mark 3:27.

21. David Watson, *I Believe in the Church* (Grand Rapids: Wm. B. Eerdmans, 1978), p. 81.

22. Eddie Gibbs, *I Believe in Church Growth* (London: Hodder and Stoughton, 1981), p. 80.

23. George W. Peters, *A Theology of Church Growth* (Grand Rapids: Zondervan, 1981), p. 37.

24. A.M. Hunter, Op. Cit., p. 6;1 Cor 11:25; Mark 14:24.

25. Acts 2:38-39.

26. John Bright, Op. Cit., p. 10. While it is difficult to condense all that the Bible has to say under a single catchword, the kingdom of God is a major unifying theme in the Bible. The kingdom of God is of central importance and includes the themes of redemption and salvation, as well as those concepts which revolve around the idea of a people of God who are called to live under God's rule. Other major biblical themes such as peace or shalom, land, house, city, justice, Sabbath and Jubilee can be related to the concept of the kingdom of God.

27. John Stott, ed., *Evangelism and Social Responsibility*, Lausanne Occasional Papers No. 21, Grand Rapids Report (Grand Rapids: Lausanne Committee for World Evangelism and World Evangelical Fellowship, 1982), p. 20.

28. Howard A. Snyder, *The Community of the King* (Downers Grove: InterVarsity Press, 1977), p. 18.

29. Mark 3: 27.

CHAPTER SEVEN

1. Dan Wooding, "Memories of the Jesus Movement" in *Charisma and Christian Life* (Lake Mary, Fl.: Strang Communication Co., September, 1993, Volume 19,

Number 2), p. 18.

2. Dean S. Gilliland defines contextualized theology as a dynamic reflection carried out by a particular church upon its own life in light of the Word of God and historic Christian truth. Guided by the Holy Spirit, the church continually challenges, incorporates and transforms elements of the cultural milieu, bringing these under the lordship of Christ. As members of the body of Christ interpret the Word, using their own thoughts and employing their own cultural gifts, they are better able to understand the gospel as incarnation. Quoted from *The Word Among Us: Contextualizing Theology for Mission Today* (Dallas: Word, 1989), pp. 12-13.

3. Donald W. Hohensee, The Need for Contextualization" from *The Word Became Flesh: A Reader in Contextualization*, edited by Dean S. Gilliland and Evertt W. Huffard (Pasadena: Fuller Theological Seminary, n.d.), p. 8.

4. Acts 2:22 ff; 3:11-24; 4:8-12, 23-37; 5:1-16; 4:32 (with John 17:22-23); Acts 2:38-41; Acts 4:33.

5. Acts 2:46; 3:1-2.

6. Acts 11:19,20.

7. 1 Cor 9:20-24.

8. *The Macintosh Church Growth Net.*, Dec. 1990, Vol. 2 #12.

9. Win Arn, *The Pastor's Manual for Effective Ministry* (Monrovia: Church Growth, 1988), p. 41.

CHAPTER EIGHT

1. Doug Murren, *The Baby Boomerang* (Ventura: Regal Books, 1990).

2. Interview with John Decker, Seattle, Washington, August, 1991.

3. Ibid.

4. John 15:4,7,9; 14:27.

5. Luke 5:5-7.

6. Matt 13:8,31-48.

7. Luke 14:21-24; 19:16-19; 13:6-9.

8. Mark 14:9; John 12:24.

9. Luke 5:1-11; Mark 3:13 ff; Luke 10:1 ff; Acts 1:15; 2:41.

10. Acts 2:47; 5:14; 6:7.

11. Acts 8-12; 13:16:9; 16:9 ff.

12. 1 Thes 1:8.

13. Rom 1:5,8; 16:26; 1 Thes 1:8; Col 1:6.

14. Charles Van Engen, *The Missionary Nature of the Church: A New Paradigm* (Pasadena: Fuller Theological Seminary Course Syllabus, Spring, 1989).

15. Ibid., p. 74.

16. Acts 1:8.

17. Ibid.

18. The emerging dynamic sees both the gift and task, the present and the future, the essence and action and the faith and reality of the church at one and the same time. From Augustine's day the church moved from categories of self-congratulations and static definition, culminating in the "triumphalism" of

the Council of Trent where there was a near identification of the Roman church with the kingdom of God and a celebration of the fact that the few attributes (one, holy, catholic and apostolic) were descriptions of the Roman church itself.

Meanwhile, Orthodox Christianity had moved into a mystical perspective of the church. The church of the Reformation brought into focus the "marks" of the church: pure doctrine preached, pure administration of the sacraments, church discipline in punishing sin. The presence or absence of these "marks" supposedly would point out the limits beyond which the church ceased to be the church. The Roman church, Orthodox churches, Reformers and Anabaptists all defined the church by certain logical, ordered, systematic definitions derived sometimes from scripture, and often from logical constituents (Van Engen, p. 18).

Toward the turn of the 20th century the question of the church began to take on new meaning in relation to "new, searching and urgent questions regarding the mission of the church." The capitulation of the church to the political government of World War II, the "globalization" of the world and the call for the church to relate to global issues and be a world Christian community, the rise of the global Christian missionary movement and the need for understanding the church's nature in mission, the world-wide spread of the church, the rise of national and international Christian councils, the development of missions and younger Third World churches, and post Vatican II's re-examination of its ecclesiology have all contributed to this need for a fresh understanding of the church (Van Engen, pp. 18-21).

Emerging from this has been an emphasis on the dual nature of the church as both a sociological reality and a spiritual organism (cf Dulles, Getz, Snyder). Charles Van Engen describes this dual nature as viewed "from above" and "from below" (see Van Engen diagram, p. 24).

Historically a wedge has been driven between the two perspectives creating an unnecessary dilemma. They both refer to the same reality, the church of Jesus Christ. Van Engen's "emerging" church unites the two definitions around a single nature of the church. This involves the idea of the church as an 'emerging' reality which, as it is built up in the world, becomes in fact what it is in faith. It is like a coin with two sides (Van Engen, p. 25).

19. North River Community Church promotional material (Duluth, Georgia, n.d.).
20. Ibid., p. 30.
21. Col 2:19.
22. Col 3:15-16.
23. Paul S. Minear, *Images of the Church in the New Testament* (Philadelphia: Westminster Press, 1960), pp. 212-213; Col 3:18-4:1.
24. Van Engen, Op. Cit., p. 28. Van Engen proposes a diagram of the dynamic relationship between the church "from above" and "from below" (p. 27). This diagram combines both perspectives and involves a continuous movement from the "above" side to the "below" side. This dynamic emerging view of the church means that after understanding and articulating the church's nature

in relation to the church's purpose and role in the world, these conclusions can be translated into action in the real "below" world through goal setting.

Once the "from below" goals, strategies, marks of the church and plans have been implemented by and through its membership, leadership and administrative programs, it is time to check with and evaluate from the perspective of "from above."

CHAPTER NINE

1. Herbert J. Betz, "Evangelism and Advertising — The Role of Advertising and Church Growth" in an "Inter-disciplinary Study" for the Betriebswirtschaftliches Institut, p. 137.

2. Howard Hendricks, Quoted from *The Arn Growth Report*, No. 18 (Pasadena: The Institute for American Church Growth, n.d.).

3. Col 1:27-28.

4. John Stott, from taped lecture "Acts 2:42-47," n.d.

5. William Temple, *Readings in St. John's Gospel* (New York: McMillan, 1939), p. 68.

6. Rom 8:15; Gal 4:5-6.

7. Psalms 47, 134, 95, 100, 149.

8. 2 Pet 1:4; 2 Cor 13:14; 1 John 1:3.

9. C. Peter Wagner, *Church Growth and the Whole Gospel: A Biblical Mandate* (San Francisco: Harper and Row, 1981), p. 56.

10. Charles Van Engen, *The Missionary Nature of the Church: A New Paradigm* (Pasadena: Fuller Theological Seminary, Spring 1989), p. 73.

11. Bob Biehl, "The Masterplanning Arrow" (Laguna Nigel, Ca.: The Masterplanning Associates, 1981). Masterplanning Associates has a number of helpful tools to aid vision development, planning and goal setting. Peter Brierley's *Vision Building* (London: Hodder and Stougton, 1989) and George Barna's *The Power of Vision* (Ventura: Regal Books, 1992) are also useful resources on the subject of vision.

12. George Barna, *The Power of Vision*, p. 28.

13. The *mission* of Christian Associates International is to fulfill the Great Commission. The *purpose* of CAI is to reach and disciple secular, unchurched, urban people for Christ. The *vision* of CAI is to carry out this purpose by establishing "high-impact" churches in 40 targeted cities in Europe.

14. Barney Hamady, "The Shepherd's Voice," from *The Shepherd's Staff* (Sierra Madre: October/November, 1991), p. 1. Hamady elaborates this vision statement in the above mentioned article, p. 2:

> First of all, notice that we are a "called" people. This means that God initiated our purpose and our vision: He's the Headwaters out of which our Church's existence flows. Then, notice the phrase "culturally relevant." God's desire is that we minister His unchanging truth to those around us in an ever-changing world. Our California culture is a diverse conglomeration of patterns and lifestyles that almost defies definition. But we must ever seek to speak and express God's

truth in such a way that it makes sense to the culture around us. This doesn't mean that we compromise the Truth, just that we use contemporary and relevant "means and ways" to meet the needs of the world around us. The third aspect of this vision relates to the people we're trying to reach: "secular, unchurched"...and unreached. What a great and exciting challenge! At one time, those three words described me, your Pastor. And I have a tremendous burden to see the lost, broken people of our culture won to Christ.

And I know that many of you feel that same burden. But it's not enough just to win them, we've also got to grow them. This is what it means to "disciple" the saints. We grow disciples by instructing them in God's Word, by encouraging them to worship and prayer and by helping them to find a place to serve the Body of Christ. Lastly, our ultimate goal is to send these mature disciples back into the world around us, both locally and globally, to lead others to Christ and to disciple them towards maturity in Christ.

CHAPTER TEN

1. Linus J. Morris, "Report on Need and Opportunity for Christian Associates' Church Planting and Church Renewal in Amsterdam" (Amsterdam, August 22, 1986).
2. David Shaw, "Amid L.A.'s Ethnic Mix, the Times Plays Catch-up" (*Los Angeles Times*, March 15, 1989).
3. Matt 28:19.
4. Dean S. Gilliland, *The Word Among Us: Contextualizing Theology for Mission Today* (Dallas: Word, 1989), p. 17.
5. Eddie Gibbs, "Contextual Considerations in Responding to Nominality" in *The Word Among Us: Contextualizing Theology for Mission Today*, edited by Dean S. Gilliland (Dallas, Tx.: Word, 1989), p. 249.
6. Ibid., p. 250.
7. C. Peter Wagner, *Church Planting for a Greater Harvest* (Ventura: Regal Books, 1990), p. 80.
8. Eddie Gibbs., Op. Cit, p. 249.
9. C. Peter Wagner, Op. Cit., pp. 88-89. Church Information and Development Services (CIDS) address is 3001 Redhill Avenue, Suite 2-220, Costa Mesa, CA, 92626-9664. Telephone number: (800) 442-6227.
10. Ibid., p. 43.
11. Raymond Bakke, *The Urban Christian*, p. 42.
12. Acts 16:1 ff.
13. Ralph W. Neighbour, Jr., *Where Do We Go From Here: A Guidebook for Cell Group Churches* (Houston, Texas: Touch Publications, 1990), p. 243.
14. Ibid., p. 248.
15. The following steps are recommended in starting a felt need ministry:
    1. Pray and set your plan.

   a. Determine who you are trying to reach (hurting or healthy).

   b. Establish a plan that targets meeting needs.

2. Recruit a ministry partner and/or team.

   a. Impart your vision and ask them to pray about joining you.

   b. Set measurable job descriptions based on gifts and strengths.

3. Gather a core of people from the target group.

   a. Have a friendship building introductory event.

   b. Invite to meet for a set period of time around a felt need topic.

4. Continue meeting in a cell group format with those who respond.

5. Start a weekly or monthly special event (congregation).

   a. Provide larger group atmosphere when there are sufficient numbers.

   b. Orient the event toward a felt need.

16. Robert Fishman, *Bourgeois Utopias: The Rise and Fall of Suburbia* (New York: Basic Books, 1987), p. 16.

17. Mike Breen, *Growing the Smaller Church* (London: Marshall Pickering, 1992), pp. 24-28.

18. C. Peter Wagner, "A Vision for Evangelizing the Real America," address given at the National Convocation on Evangelizing Ethnic America, Houston, Texas, April 15-18, 1985. Leith Anderson notes that new churches are "flexible, open to newcomers, entrepreneurial, outreaching and not burdened with servicing old internal relationships and demands." Leith Anderson, *A Church for the 21st Century* (Minneapolis: Bethany, 1992), p. 60.

CHAPTER ELEVEN

1. Win Arn and Charles Arn, *The Masters Plan for Making Disciples* (Pasadena: Church Growth Press, 1982), p. 43.

2. Lloyd Ogilvie, "People Ministry: The Birth of a New Evangelism," taken from 1977 tape given at Hollywood Presbyterian Church, Hollywood, California.

3. Dr. Paul Yonggi Cho with Harold Hostetler, *Successful Home Cell Groups* (Plainfield: Logos International, 1981), p. 59.

4. Joseph C. Aldridge, *Life-Style Evangelism* (Portland: Multnomah Press, 1981), p. 94. Maslov's hierarchy of needs is pyramidal with the most basic needs on the bottom ascending upward as each level of need is met. Maslov's hierarchy is as follows:

      Self Actualization Needs

      Esteem Needs

      Love and Affection Needs

      Safety and Security Needs

      Physiological Needs

5. Win Arn and Charles Arn, *The Masters Plan for Making Disciples*, Op. Cit., pp. 90-91. Pages 16 and 17 give a Receptivity-Rating Scale for life transitions.

6. James Engel, *What's Gone Wrong With the Harvest: A Communication Strategy for the Church and World Evangelism* (Grand Rapids: Zondervan, 1975), p. 45.

7. Eph 4:11-12; 2 Tim. 4:5.

8. D. James Kennedy, *Evangelism Explosion* (Wheaton: Tyndale House Publish-

ers, 1975).

9. Ralph W. Neighbour, Jr., *Knocking on Doors, Opening Hearts* (Houston: Touch Outreach, 1990).

10. John 3:3-6.

11. David Watson, *I Believe in the Church* (Grand Rapids: Wm. B. Eerdmans, 1978), p. 171.

12. Bill Thomas (Strasbourg, France, May, 12, 1987). For further information on "power evangelism" see John Wimber with Kevin Springer, *Power Evangelism: Signs and Wonders Today,* (London: Hodder and Stoughton, 1985).

CHAPTER TWELVE

1. Dale Galloway, *20-20 Vision: How to Create a Successful Church* (Portland, Ore.: Scott Publishing, 1986), p. 11. According to "Churchmen say people go west, shed religion" (Portland: *The Oregonian,* April 13, 1991), 17% of Oregonians claim no religious affiliation — more than double the national average of 8% (13% said they had no religion in California, 14% in Washington). These statistics are based on a City University of New York study which concludes that Oregon is the state with the highest proportion of people who do not claim a religious affiliation.

2. Ibid., p. 28.

3. Dr. Paul Yonggi Cho with Harold Hostetler, *Successful Home Cell Groups* (Plainfield, N.J.: Logos International, 1981), p. 58.

4. Ibid., p. 59.

5. Matt 10:1-14; Mark 6:7-12; Luke 9:1-9; 10:1-12.

6. Acts 16:15; 31-34; 40; 17:5; 20:20.

7. George Peters, *A Theology of Church Growth* (Grand Rapids: Zondervan, 1981), p. 58.

8. 1 John 1:3.

9. Ralph W. Neighbour, Jr., *Where Do We Go From Here: A Guidebook to the Cell Group Church* (Houston: Touch Publications, 1990), p. 198.

10. Gal 5:16 ff; Rom 1:14-16.

11. 1 Cor 12:6; Gal 6:2.

12. Jas 4:8.

13. Dale Galloway, *20-20 Vision,* Op.Cit., p. 30. Taken from Rosiland Rinker. The four steps of conversational prayer are:
    1. JESUS IS HERE
       Visualize his presence. Begin with silence before him. Be aware of his love for you and those in the group (Matt 18:19,20).
    2. THANK YOU, LORD
       Let gratitude fill your heart. Vocalize your thanks to God in the group. Be brief and specific. Don't pray more than two or three short sentences at a time. Then pause so that someone else can add their thanks (Phil 4:4-7).
    3. FORGIVE ME LORD
       Confession is a part of worship. Be honest. Pray for yourself, then others will pray for you (Jas 5:13-16).

4. I PRAY FOR MY BROTHER/SISTER
Use first names and pray with love and thanksgiving. Give thanks when someone prays for you. This is agreeing in prayer. Remember, the Holy Spirit will give you words when you pray (Mark 11:22-25).

CHAPTER THIRTEEN

1. Carl George, from "Meta Church, the Church of the Future" (Pasadena, Ca.: Charles E. Fuller Institute for Evangelism and Church Growth) cassette tape U016 of "The Pastor's Update."
2. Catholic hierarchical structure is the result of Catholic theology, while Protestant hierarchical structure (including more recent evangelical and Pentecostal expressions) has resulted from tradition and is more functional. Both have their roots in the medieval church.
3. Eph 4:11-12.
4. For further study in the area of assimilation, see *Assimilating New Members* by Lyle E. Schaller (Nashville: Abingdon Press, 1978) and *Assimilation: Incorporating New People Into the Life of your Church* (Pasadena: Charles E. Fuller Institute of Evangelism and Church Growth, 1989).
5. Charles Shaver, "The Morning After," in *How to Effectively Incorporate New Members* (Pasadena: Institute for American Church Growth, n.d.), p. 56.
6. Ralph W. Neighbour, Jr., *Cover the Bible* (Houston: Touch Outreach Ministries, 1991). Neighbour has designed a cell-based training of three levels of maturity found in 1 John 2:12-14. New believers start with a Spiritual Formation Weekend where they receive a clear vision for the church, an explanation for a shepherd group and an introduction to spiritual gifts. At this point, the new believer is considered a "Child" in the faith and begins to experience new cell life which includes a study of Dr. Neighbour's *Arrival Kit for New Believers, Journey Guide* and *Cover the Bible* (Houston: Touch Publication).
   The believer enters what is called the "Young Man" stage. This commences with a "Spiritual Warfare Weekend" where further instruction is given on spiritual gifts and healing and warfare prayer. The "Young Man" continues in a shepherd group, disciples someone in the "Children" stage and studies Dr. Neighbour's *Knocking on Doors, Opening Hearts* (Touch Publication).
   The "Father Stage" is commenced with a "Ministry Outreach Weekend" which covers "Share Group" and is responsible to disciple a "Young Man." This is followed by a "Shepherd Intern Formation Weekend" which focuses on the *Shepherd's Guidebook*. The "Father" is then considered a "Shepherd" who helps cell members discover spiritual gifts and minister to unbelievers. The next level of training is a "Zone Shepherd Formation Weekend" which covers the necessary ingredients of being a Zone Shepherd.
7. Holy Trinity Brompton, Brompton Road, London, SE7 1JA, England.
8. *The Networking Seminar* by Bruce Bugby, (Pasadena: Charles E. Fuller Institute of Evangelism and Church Growth), used by Willow Creek Community Church, combines formal instruction, testing and gift guidance counseling.

The tests determine the individual's passion, temperament, gifts, talents and maturity to lead in the overall ministry of the church.
Using Your Spiritual Gifts by C. Peter Wagner (Ventura: Regal Press, 1980) and *Wagner-Modified Houts Questionnaire* by C. Peter Wagner, editor, (Pasadena: Charles E. Fuller Institute, 1978) are useful for gift discovery.

9.   Ralph W. Neighbour, Jr., *Where Do We Go From Here? A Guidebook to the Cell Group Church*, Op. Cit., p. 365.

CHAPTER FOURTEEN

1.   Exodus 18:21.
2.   Longman, *Dictionary of Contemporary English* (Harlow, Essex, England: Longman Group Ltd., 1987).
3.   Ralph W. Neighbour, Jr., *Zone Supervisors Manual* (Singapore: Faith Community Baptist Church, 1991), p. 3.
4.   Ralph W. Neighbour, Jr., *Where Do We Go From Here?*, Op. Cit., p. 372.

CHAPTER FIFTEEN

1.   Gal 5:22; 1 Cor 12-14.
2.   John 17:1 ff.; 1 Thes 1:4-7.
3.   Joseph C. Aldridge, *Life-Style Evangelism: Crossing Traditional Boundaries to Reach the Unbelieving World* (Portland, Oregon: Multnomah Press, 1981), p. 29.
4.   Acts 5:12-14.
5.   Acts 16:15, 31.
6.   Acts 2:42-47; 20:20.
7.   David Watson, *I Believe in the Church*, p. 137.
8.   Rom 5:20; 7:5; Gal 3:10-14, 21-25; Jas 2:10.
9.   Gal 3:25-26; Rom 8:1-4.
10. Eph 2:8-9; 5:18-20; Gal 2:20-21.
11. Eph 1:18-20; 3:16-21; Phil 3:8-11; Col 1:29.
12. Matt 9:9-13; Luke 19:1-7; John 4:1 ff.
13. John 13:34-35.
14. 1 Jn 4:4.
15. 1 Thes 1:4 ff.
16. 1 Cor 10:31.
17. Lyle E. Schaller, *The Small Church is Different* (Nashville, Tenn.: Abingdon Press, 1982), p. 55.

CHAPTER SIXTEEN

1.   "Willow Creek Community Church Overview " (Barrington, Ill.: Willow Creek Community Church, 1991).
2.   Willow Creek Community Church, Conference Syllabus Overview (Barrington, Ill.: Willow Creek Community Church, 1991), pp. 1.3-10.
3.   Interview with Fred Heumann, director of Creative Ministries of Youth for

Christ in Brittain (Thousand Oaks, Ca.: August 20, 1993). The Church of Christ the King was formerly Clarendon Church and is part of New Frontiers led by Terry Virgo, and is one of the streams rising out of the house church movement in the UK.

4. Willow Creek holds a "New Community" worship service each Wednesday night for believers. Until recently, the only small group ministry Willow Creek was their two year discipleship groups. More recently the church has been transitioning to the Meta Church model which emphasizes the multiplication of cell groups. For insight into the Meta Model, see Carl George's *Prepare Your Church for the Future* (Ventura: Regal, 1992). Martin Robinson's *A World Apart: Creating a Church for the Unchurched* gives an in-depth insight into the philosophy of Willow Creek Community Church (Tunbridge Wells, England: Monarch, 1992).

    Fellowship Bible Church of Park Cities complements its Sunday morning "seeker-sensitive" services with in-depth Bible teaching on Wednesday nights, a Sunday morning adult education program, monthly leadership training, an every other month concert of praise and home fellowship groups.

5. Russell Chandler, *Racing toward 2001* (Grand Rapids: Zondervan, 1992), p. 41. On page 299, Chandler quotes Doug Murren of Eastside Foursquare Church in Kirkland, Washington who says, "you will find that the music of the baby boomer generation (predominately rock 'n' roll) is likely to dominate the culture of our society well into the next century. Even our children."

6. Rick Warren, from cassette tape, "Preaching that Produces Growth" (Mission Viejo, Ca.: The Encouraging Word, n.d.).

7. Paul G. Hiebert, *Anthropological Insights for Missionaries*. (Grand Rapids: Baker Book House, 1985).

8. R. Daniel Reeves, "Societal Shifts Affecting the 21st Century Church from *Ministry Advantage*, Vol. 4, No. 5, May/June 1993, p. 1.

CHAPTER SEVENTEEN

1. Bill Hybels, "Speaking to the Secular Mind," from a reprint of *Leadership/88*, a publication of Christianity Today, Inc., Summer Quarter, p. 28.

2. Leith Anderson, *A Church for the 21st Century* (Minneapolis: Bethany, 1992). pp. 209-210.

3. Dave Chadwick, "The Mission and Vision of Forest Hills Church" (unpublished document, nd.).

4. Leith Anderson, Op. Cit., p. 44.

5. Rick Warren, from "Encouraging Preaching" (Mission Viejo, Saddleback Church Growth Conference, 1991).

6. Russell Chandler, Racing Toward 2001 (Grand Rapids: Zondervan, 1992), p. 251.

7. Bill Hybels, "Preaching for Total Commitment," from a reprint of *Leadership/* 89, a publication of *Christianity Today*, Inc., Summer Quarter.

8. Leith Anderson, Op. Cit., p. 201.

9. Carl George, *How to Break Growth Barriers* (Grand Rapids: Baker, 1993), p. 80.

10. Leith Anderson, Op. Cit., p. 209.
11. Ibid., p. 210.

CHAPTER EIGHTEEN

1. Interview with George Winston of the Faculté Libré Theologe Evangélique, Vaux-Sur-Seine, France, July, 1986.
2. Peter Brierley, *Towards 2000, MARC Monograph Number 1* (Bromley, Kent: MARC Europe, May, 1984), p. 13.
3. Mike Breen, *Growing the Smaller Church* (London: Marshall Pickering, 1992), p. 5. Earlier research by Peter Brierley indicated that 61% of churches in England have a congregation of 50 or fewer on a Sunday, including morning and evening services where both are held. A further 31% have congregations of between 51 and 150 attenders, and only the remaining 8% of churches have congregations with more than 150 people. Source: Peter Brierley, *Where is the Church Going? MARC Monograph Number 5* (Bromley, Kent: MARC Europe, January, 1986), p. 14.
4. Lyle Schaller, *The Small Church is Different* (Nashville: Abingdon Press, 1982), p. 1.
5. Win Arn, "Is Your Church in a Mid-Life Crisis?" in *The Win Arn Growth Report*, Number 7 (Pasadena: the Institute for American Church Growth), p. 1.
6. Mike Breen, Op. Cit., pp. 10-11.
7. Carl Dudley, *Making the Small Church Effective* (Nashville: Abingdon, 1988), pp. 13, 21.
8. Lyle Schaller, Op. Cit., p. 12.
9. Lyle Schaller, *44 Steps Up Off the Plateau* (Nashville: Abingdon, 1992), p. 121.
10. Carl Dudley, Op. Cit., p. 23.
11. I am contrasting a regional church not only with a small neighborhood church but also with a parish church which claims a large membership, but is in actuality poorly attended and does not promote evangelical belief and outreach or active participation of its members in ministry using spiritual gifts.
12. MARC Europe is now called Christian Research Association.
13. Peter Brierley, *Where is the Church Going? MARC Monograph Number 5* (Bromley, Kent: MARC Europe, January, 1986), p. 14. This means that for the 47% of church-goers their "model" of a church is a one-minister, one-church model.
14. Carl Dudley, Op. Cit., pp. 19-20.
15. John N. Vaughan, *The Large Church* (Grand Rapids: Baker Book House, 1985), p. 15.
16. Donald A. McGavran, with Win Arn, *How to Grow a Church* (Glendale, Calif.: Regal, 1973), p. 72.
17. Ralph W. Neighbour, Jr., *Where Do We Go From Here: A Guidebook for the Cell Group Church* (Houston, Tx.: Touch Publication, 1990), p. 203.
18. Win Arn, Op. Cit., p. 4.
19. Carl George, "Meta Church Cluster Consultation" (Pasadena, Ca.: Charles E. Fuller Institute of Evangelism and Church Growth, 1990) p. 4.

20. Carl George, *How to Break Growth Barriers* (Grand Rapids: Baker Book House, 1993), p. 130.
21. Peter Brierley, *Where the Church is Going, MARC Monograph 5*, Op. Cit., p. 14.
22. C. Peter Wagner, *Leading Your Church to Growth* (Ventura: Regal Books, 1984), pp. 17-18.
23. Win Arn, Op. Cit., p. 4.
24. Carl George, Op. Cit., p. 1.
25. Ibid., p. 4.
26. Ibid.
27. Win Arn, Op. Cit.
28. Carl George, "Meta-Church, the Church of the Future" from "The Pastor's Update" (Pasadena, Ca.: Charles E. Fuller Institute of Evangelism and Church Growth, 1990).
29. Carl George, "Meta Church Cluster Consultation," Op. Cit.

CHAPTER NINETEEN

1. C. Peter Wagner, *Your Church Can Grow* (Ventura: Regal Books, 1976), p. 63.
2. John Wimber, "Helping the Small Church to Grow" from the syllabus for "Church Growth II" (Pasadena: Fuller Theological Seminary, 1985), p. 3.
3. Ibid.
4. Lyle Schaller, *44 Steps Up Off the Plateau* (Nashville: Abingdon, 1992), p. 73.
5. Ibid., p. 74.
6. Ibid., pp. 71-72.
7. Ibid., pp. 70-71.
8. Ibid., p. 52.
9. C. Peter Wagner, *Leading Your Church to Growth*, Op. Cit., p. 134.
10. Bruce Patrick, *Breaking the 200 Barrier* (Auckland, New Zealand: Baptist Home Mission, 1989).
11. Carl George gives additional information on property and facilities in his chapter on "How to Break the 200 Barrier" in his book *How to Break Growth Barriers* (Grand Rapids: Baker, 1993), pp. 137-142.
12. Carl George's "How to Break the 400 Barrier" in *How to Break Growth Barriers* (pp. 145-159) presents additional information on working with church governing boards, staff selection and delegation, all critical factors at this stage of development.
13. Carl George, from seminar syllabus, *Beyond 800* (Pasadena, Ca.: Charles E. Fuller Institute of Evangelism and Church Growth, 1989), pp. 4-5.
14. Ibid., p. 42.
15. John McClure, "Managing your Five Year Plan" from the syllabus, *Managing your Church toward 500* (Newport, Ca.: Vineyard Christian Fellowship, 1987), p. 4.
16. For further insight see Carl George's "How to Break the 800 Barrier" in *How to Break Growth Barriers*.
17. Ibid.
18. C. Peter Wagner, "Breaking the 200 Barrier" from *How to Break the 200 Barrier*

Seminar (Pasadena: Charles E. Fuller Institute of Evangelism and Church Growth, 1987). pp. 17-18. The common characteristics that Wagner observed in each church were:

a. An evangelical theology with a high view of biblical authority. Because of their high view of Jesus, they engaged in a lot of evangelism.
b. Strong pastoral leadership. The larger the church the more crucial this became. His authority was prominent and there was a commitment to a long term tenure. The leader was optimistic about the future and modeled radical obedience.
c. Participatory worship and music written within the past ten years. There was a freedom of expression and often long periods of worship.
d. Participatory powerful prayer.
e. The Holy Spirit was acknowledged as a person and a prominent member of the Trinity. The church was open to the Spirit's leading and supernatural intervention.
f. Lay ministry where each member was expected to minister using spiritual gifts.
g. Practical Bible teaching, centered more on the needs of people than on the content of the Bible.
h. A direct missions involvement with the church recruiting, training and sending their own people.
i. Abundant finances.
j. A positive self image.

CHAPTER TWENTY

1. Leith Anderson, *A Church for the 21st Century* (Minneapolis: Bethany, 1992), p. 51.
2. Joe S. Ellis, *The Church on Purpose: Keys to Effective Church Leadership* (Cincinnati: Standard Publishing, 1982). p. 129.
3. Dale E. Galloway, *20-20 Vision: How to Create a Successful Church* (Portland, Ore.: Scott Publishing, 1986), p. 27.
4. Lyle Schaller, *44 Steps Up Off the Plateau* (Nashville: Abingdon, 1992), p. 62.
5. C. Peter Wagner, *Your Church Can Grow* (Ventura: Regal Books, 1976), p. 63.
6. Carl George, "Meta Church Cluster Consultation" Syllabus (Pasadena: Charles E. Fuller Institute for Evangelism and Church Growth, 1990), pp. 7-16.
7. John Wimber, "The Change Agent" from the syllabus for "Church Growth II" (Pasadena: Fuller Theological Seminary, 1985), p. 7.
8. Paul Beasley-Murray, *Dynamic Leadership* (Eastbourne, E. Sussex: MARC-Europe, Monarch Publications, 1990), p. 15.
9. C. Peter Wagner, *Leading Your Church to Growth* (Ventura: Regal Books, 1984), p. 88.
10. Ibid.
11. C. Peter Wagner, editor, "Wagner-Modified Houts Questionnaire: For Discovering Your Spiritual Gifts" (Pasadena: Fuller Evangelistic Association, 1985), pp. 14-15.

12. Ibid.
13. Eddie Gibbs, *Followed or Pushed: Understanding and Leading Your Church* (Bromley, Kent, UK: MARC Europe, 1987), p. 50-60.
14. Europe provides a different scene with its historic protectionism of state or folk churches and its parochial system.
15. Peter F. Drucker, *The Effective Executive* (New York: Harper and Row, 1966), pp. 23-24.
16. Carl George contrasts sheepherders and ranchers in his book *How to Break Growth Barriers* (Grand Rapids: Baker, 1993), pp. 88-97. He observes that 90-95% of pastors begin their ministry as sheepherders. The most common characteristics of sheepherders and ranchers are:

Sheepherders	Ranchers
1. Primary caregiving.	1. Emphasis on the big picture.
2. Overestimated significance.	2. Take charge competence.
3. Expectation drivenness.	3. One-another ministry expectation.
4. Availability.	4. Group focus.
5. Performance.	5. Flexible supervision.
6. Role comfort.	6. Outcome objectives.
7. Poor delegating ability.	7. Large-picture focus.
8. Poor planning.	8. Role creation.
9. Individualism.	9. Nondependency.
10. Managerial skills.	10. Ignorance of trends.

17. 1 Cor 1-7.
18. Bob Biehl of Masterplanning Group International (Laguna Niguel, California) describes the servant leader as a powerful servant.
19. cf Matt 16:22-28; John 11:7-16.
20. The pathway to leadership development occurs in phases. In his book, *The Making of a Leader*, (Colorado Springs: NavPress, 1988). J. Robert Clinton formulates a time line for the development of a leader which includes five stages. At first, God works providentially to build foundational items into the life of the leader-to-be. This is where character traits are deeply embedded. These traits will mature and be used by God.

   In the second stage, an emerging leader usually receives formal or informal training (imitation modeling, informal apprenticeships or mentoring). While it may appear that ministry training is the focus of this phase, the real training and testing occur in the heart of the person.

   During the third phase, ministry becomes the prime focus of the emerging leader's life. Further training is obtained through self-study growth projects or functionally oriented workshops. In the fourth phase, the leader has identified his gift mix and begins to use them maturely and fruitfully.

   The fifth and last stage, according to Clinton, is convergence. Here, the leader has moved to a role that matches his gift-mix. The leader is removed from ministry for which he is not gifted and the leader uses the best he has to offer.

Because leadership development is a process, weaknesses, inadequacies and limitations need not be the final word. Each situation, including failure, is an opportunity to learn from God. God uses circumstances, failures and weaknesses to teach and train and each of these can be overcome with God's help.

21. The Charles E. Fuller Institute for Evangelism and Church Growth and the American Institute for Church Growth, both located in Pasadena, California are excellent sources for tapes, books and seminars. Saddleback Community Church of Mission Viejo and Willow Creek Community Church of Barrington, Illinois offer excellent seminars and a growing number of seminaries are offering practical courses or practically oriented Doctor of Ministry programs.

CHAPTER TWENTY-ONE

1. 1 Cor 12.
2. Carl George, "Meta-Church Cluster Consultation Syllabus" (Pasadena: Charles E. Fuller Institute, 1990).
3. David Cormack, *Seconds Away: Fifteen Rounds in the Fight for Effective Use of Time* (Bromley, Kent: MARC Europe, 1986), p. 40.
4. Ibid.
5. Don Cousins, Leith Anderson and Arthur DeKruyter, *Mastering Church Management* (Portland: Multnomah Press, 1990), p. 17.

CHAPTER TWENTY-TWO

1. Jim Montgomery, *DAWN 2000: 7 Million Churches to Go* (Pasadena: William Carey Library, 1989). DAWN is an anacronym for Disciple A Whole Nation.